Rick Steves'
ROME
2002

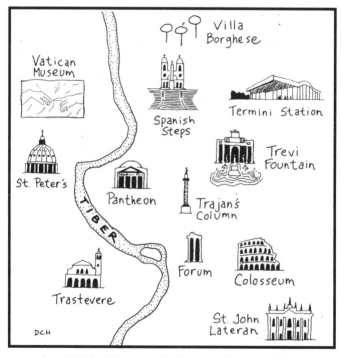

Villa Borghese

Vatican Museum

Spanish Steps

Termini Station

St. Peter's

Pantheon

Trevi Fountain

TIBER

Trajan's Column

Trastevere

Forum

Colosseum

St. John Lateran

DCH

by Rick Steves & Gene Openshaw

AVALON
TRAVEL

Other ATP travel guidebooks by Rick Steves
Rick Steves' Best of Europe
Rick Steves' Europe 101: History and Art for the Traveler (with Gene Openshaw)
Rick Steves' Europe Through the Back Door
Rick Steves' Mona Winks (with Gene Openshaw)
Rick Steves' Postcards from Europe
Rick Steves' France, Belgium & the Netherlands (with Steve Smith)
Rick Steves' Germany, Austria & Switzerland
Rick Steves' Great Britain
Rick Steves' Ireland (with Pat O'Connor)
Rick Steves' Italy
Rick Steves' Scandinavia
Rick Steves' Spain & Portugal
Rick Steves' Florence (with Gene Openshaw)
Rick Steves' London (with Gene Openshaw)
Rick Steves' Paris (with Steve Smith and Gene Openshaw)
Rick Steves' Venice (with Gene Openshaw)
Rick Steves' Phrase Books: German, Italian, French, Spanish/Portuguese, and
  French/Italian/German

Avalon Travel Publishing, 5855 Beaudry Street, Emeryville, CA 94608

Text copyright © 2002, 2001, 2000, 1999 by Rick Steves
Cover copyright © 2002, 2001 by Avalon Travel Publishing, Inc. All rights reserved.
Maps copyright © 2002 by Europe Through the Back Door

Printed in the United States of America by R.R. Donnelley
Second printing March 2002
Distributed to the book trade by Publishers Group West, Berkeley, California

Portions of this book were originally published in *Rick Steves' Mona Winks* © 2001,
1998, 1996, 1993, 1988 by Rick Steves and Gene Openshaw, and in *Rick Steves' Italy*
© 2002, 2001, 2000, 1999, 1998, 1997, 1996, 1995 by Rick Steves.

ISBN 1-56691-359-4
ISSN 1527-4780

For the latest on Rick's lectures, guidebooks, tours, and public television
series, contact Europe Through the Back Door, Box 2009, Edmonds,
WA 98020, tel. 425/771-8303, fax 425/771-0833, www.ricksteves.com, or
e-mail: rick@ricksteves.com.

Europe Through the Back Door Editors: Risa Laib, Lauren Mills
Avalon Travel Publishing Editor: Kate Willis
Research Assistance: Tom Rankin, Risa Laib
Copy editor: Chris Hayhurst
Production & Typesetting: Kathleen Sparkes, White Hart Design
Cover and Interior Design: Janine Lehmann
Maps: David C. Hoerlein
Photography: p. 61: Dominic Arizona Bonuccelli; p. 114, 116, 117 &118:
  Risa Laib; all others: Rick Steves and Gene Openshaw
Front cover photo: Colosseum, Rome, Italy; copyright © Blaine Harrington III

CONTENTS

rome

INTRODUCTION 1
Welcome to Our Rome City Guide 2 • Trip Costs 3 • Exchange Rate 4 • Prices, Times, and Discounts 4 • When to Go 4 • Red Tape, Business Hours, and Banking 5 • Travel Smart 6 • Tourist Information 6 • Recommended Guidebooks 7 • Rick Steves' Books and Videos 7 • Maps 9 • Tours of Rome and Italy 9 • Transportation 9 • Telephones, Mail, and E-mail 9 • Sleeping 12 • Eating 15 • Culture Shock 20 • Send Us a Postcard, Drop Us a Line 21 • Back Door Travel Philosophy 22

ORIENTATION 23
Planning Your Time 23 • Rome in a Day 24 • Rome in Two to Three Days 24 • Rome in Seven Days 25 • Arrival in Rome 26 • Tourist Information 26 • Dealing with Problems 27 • Getting around Rome 28 • Tours of Rome 30

SIGHTS 32

TOURS
Night Walk Across Rome 54
Ancient Rome
Colosseum Tour 59 • Roman Forum Tour 64 • Palatine Hill Tour 75 • Trajan's Column, Forum, and Market 83 • Pantheon Tour 87 • Baths of Diocletian Tour 95
Museums
National Museum of Rome Tour 101 • Capitol Hill Museum Tour 114 • Borghese Gallery Tour 120 • Vatican Museum Tour 129
Churches
St. Peter's Basilica Tour 155 • Pilgrim's Rome 171

DAYTRIPS 182
Tivoli 182 • Ostia Antica 183 • Naples and Pompeii 184

SLEEPING IN ROME 202

EATING IN ROME 214

ROME WITH CHILDREN 221

SHOPPING IN ROME 223

NIGHTLIFE IN ROME 225

TRANSPORTATION CONNECTIONS 228

APPENDIX 232

INDEX 242

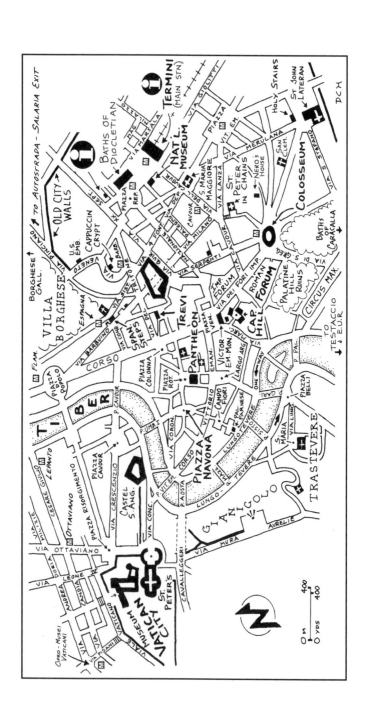

INTRODUCTION

rome

Rome is magnificent and brutal at the same time. Your ears will ring; if you're careless, you'll be run down or pickpocketed; you'll be frustrated by the kind of chaos that only an Italian can understand. You may even come to believe Mussolini was a necessary evil. But Rome is required, and still aglow after the improvements made for Jubilee 2000, it's more exciting and easier than ever.

If your hotel provides a comfortable refuge; if you pace yourself; if you accept, and even partake in, the siesta plan; if you're well-organized for sightseeing; and if you protect yourself and your valuables with extra caution and discretion, you'll do fine.

Two thousand years ago, the word Rome meant civilization itself. Everything was either civilized (part of the Roman Empire, Latin- or Greek-speaking) or barbarian. Today, Rome is Italy's political capital, the capital of Catholicism, and a splendid "junk pile" (OK, that's not quite the right term) of Western civilization. As you peel through its fascinating and jumbled layers, you'll find Rome's buildings, cats, laundry, traffic, and 2.6 million people endlessly entertaining. And then, of course, there are its magnificent sights.

Tour St. Peter's, the greatest church on earth, and scale Michelangelo's 100-meter-tall dome, the world's largest. Learn something about eternity by touring the huge Vatican Museum. You'll find the story of creation—bright as the day it was painted—in the restored Sistine Chapel. Do the "Caesar Shuffle" through ancient Rome's Forum and Colosseum. Savor Europe's most sumptuous building, the Borghese Gallery, and take an early evening "Dolce Vita Stroll" down the Via del Corso with Rome's beautiful people. Enjoy an after-dark walk from Campo de' Fiori to the Spanish Steps, lacing together Rome's Baroque and bubbly night spots.

This Information Is Accurate and Up-to-Date

This book is updated every year. Most publishers of guidebooks can afford an update only every two or three years (and even then, it's often by letter). Since this book is selective, we can personally update it annually. Even so, things change. But if you're traveling with the current edition of this book, we guarantee you're using the most up-to-date information available (for the very latest, visit www.ricksteves.com/update). This book will help you have an inexpensive, hassle-free trip. Your trip costs about $10 per waking hour. Your time is valuable. This guidebook saves lots of time.

Welcome to Our Rome City Guide

This book is organized this way:

Orientation includes tourist information and public transportation. The "Planning Your Time" section offers a suggested schedule with thoughts on how to best use your limited time.

Sights provides a succinct overview of Rome's most important sights, arranged by neighborhood, with ratings: ▲▲▲—Don't miss; ▲▲—Try hard to see; ▲—Worthwhile if you can make it; No rating—Worth knowing about.

The **Night Walk Across Rome** connects Rome's great monuments and atmospheric squares.

The **Self-Guided Tours** lead you through Ancient Rome, with tours of the Colosseum, Roman Forum, Palatine Hill, Trajan's Column, the Pantheon, and the Baths of Diocletian. You'll tour the pilgrimage churches, including the grandest of all: St. Peter's. And you'll see the great museums: the Vatican Museum, the National Museum of Rome, the Capitol Hill Museum, and the exciting Borghese Gallery.

Daytrips covers nearby sights: Tivoli, Ostia Antica, Naples, and Pompeii.

Sleeping is a guide to my favorite budget hotels, mainly in several convenient (and for Rome, relatively quiet) neighborhoods near the sights.

Eating offers restaurants ranging from inexpensive eateries to splurges, with an emphasis on good value.

Rome with Children contains tips on visiting Rome with kids, **Shopping in Rome** has advice on shopping, and **Nightlife in Rome** is a guide to Rome's best evening activities.

Transportation Connections covers connections by train and by plane (with information on Rome's airports), laying the groundwork for your smooth arrival and departure.

The **appendix** includes history, a climate chart, and a handy list of Italian survival phrases.

Throughout this book, when you see a ✪ in a listing, it

means that the sight is covered in much more detail in one of my tours—a page number will tell you just where to look to find more information.

Browse through this book and choose your favorite sights. Then have a great trip! You'll become your own guide with our tours. Traveling like a temporary local, you'll get the absolute most out of every mile, minute, and dollar. You won't waste time on mediocre sights because, unlike other guidebooks, this one covers only the best. Since your major financial pitfall is lousy, expensive hotels, We've worked hard to assemble the best accommodations values.

Trip Costs

Six components make up your trip costs: airfare, surface transportation, room and board, sightseeing/entertainment, shopping/miscellany, and gelato.

Airfare: Don't try to sort through the mess. Find and use a good travel agent. A basic, round-trip United States–to–Rome (or even cheaper, Milan) flight should cost $700 to $1,000, depending on where you fly from and when. Always consider saving time and money in Europe by flying "open jaw" (flying into one city and out of another).

Surface Transportation: For a typical one-week visit, allow $60 to $100 for taxis (which can be shared by up to 4 people); if you opt for buses and the Metro, figure about $20 per person. The cost of round-trip transportation to daytrip destinations ranges from minimal ($6–10 for Tivoli, about $6 for Ostia Antica) to affordable ($60 for Naples and Pompeii). For a one-way trip between Rome's major airport and the city center, allow $8 per person by train or about $35 by taxi (can be shared).

Room and Board: You can thrive in Rome on $80 a day per person for room and board. This allows $10 for lunch, $20 for dinner, and $50 for lodging (based on 2 people splitting the cost of a $100 double room that includes breakfast). If you've got more money, I've listed great ways to spend it. Students and tightwads can enjoy Rome for as little as $40 a day ($20 for a bed, $20 for meals and snacks). But budget sleeping and eating require the skills covered later in this chapter (and in greater detail in *Rick Steves' Europe Through the Back Door*).

Sightseeing and Entertainment: Figure about $6 per major sight (Colosseum, museums), $2 for smaller ones (church treasuries), and $25 for splurge experiences (like tours). An overall average of $15 per day works for most. Don't skimp here. After all, this category directly powers most of the experiences all the other expenses are designed to make possible.

Shopping and Miscellany: Figure $1 per postcard, coffee, and soft drink and $2 per gelato. Shopping can vary in cost from nearly nothing to a small fortune. Good budget travelers find that this category has little to do with assembling a trip full of lifelong and wonderful memories.

Exchange Rate

I've priced things throughout this book in euros. Italy, along with 11 other member countries of the European Union, has adopted the euro currency.

---

1 euro (€) = about 90 cents; €1.10 = about $1.

One euro is broken down into 100 cents. You'll find coins ranging from 1 cent to 2 euros, and bills from 5 euros to 500 euros. To convert prices in euros to dollars, take 10 percent off the price in euros: €25 = about $22, and €140 = about $125. For information on the euro, see the European Central Bank's Web site: www.euro.ecb.int.

Prices, Times, and Discounts

The opening hours and telephone numbers listed in this book are accurate as of mid-2001—but once you pin Rome down, it wiggles. Especially in Rome, the opening hours of sights can change from month to month. Always get the latest listing of sights (including hours and entry fees) at a local tourist information office. Any guidebook on Italy starts to yellow even before it's printed—especially in this transition year of the euro, when many businesses may adjust their prices at the beginning of the year, depending on the latest exchange rate. Because of that, prices in this book are approximate.

In Rome—and in this book—you'll use the 24-hour clock. It's the same through 12:00 noon, then keep going—13:00, 14:00 . . . . For anything over 12, subtract 12 and add p.m. (14:00 is 2:00 p.m.)

Discounts for sights are not listed in this book because they are generally limited to European residents and countries which offer reciprocal deals (the U.S. doesn't).

When to Go

Rome's best travel months (also busiest and most expensive) are May, June, September, and October. Between November and April you can usually expect pleasant weather and generally none of the sweat and stress of the tourist season. The most grueling thing about travel in Rome is the summer heat in July and August. We like Rome in the winter.

In Rome, temperatures hit the high 80s and 90s in summer and drop to the 40s and 50s in winter. Spring and fall can be chilly, and many hotels do not turn on their heat. Air-conditioning, when available, usually only operates from June through September. Most mid-range hotels come with air-conditioning—a worthwhile splurge in the summer. (See climate chart in the appendix.)

Red Tape, Business Hours, and Banking

You need a passport but no visa or shots to travel in Italy.

Business Hours: Traditionally, Italy uses the siesta plan. People work from about 08:00 to 13:00 and from 15:30 to 19:00, Monday through Saturday. Many businesses have adopted the government's new recommended 08:00 to 14:00 workday. In tourist areas, shops are open longer.

If you're buying more than $200 worth of souvenirs, ask in the shops about getting the 10 to 19 percent VAT tax back at the airport upon departure.

Banking: You'll want to spend local hard cash. The fastest way to get it is by using plastic: your ATM, credit, or debit card at a cash machine (Bancomat). Bring some traveler's checks only as a backup.

To get a cash advance from a bank machine, you'll need a four-digit PIN (numbers only, no letters, 7-digit PIN won't work) with your bank card. Before you go, verify with your bank that your card will work.

Visa and MasterCard are more commonly accepted than American Express. Bring two cards in case one is demagnetized, eaten by a machine, or rejected by a temperamental cash machine. (If your card is rejected, try again and request a smaller amount; some cash machines won't let you take out more than about €150— don't take it personally). Just like at home, credit or debit cards work easily at larger hotels, restaurants, and shops, but smaller businesses prefer payment in hard cash.

Regular banks have the best rates for cashing traveler's checks. For a large exchange, it pays to compare rates and fees. Bank of Sicily consistently has good rates. Banking hours are generally 08:30 to 13:30 and 15:30 to 16:30 Monday through Friday, but they can vary wildly. Banks are slow; simple transactions can take 15 to 30 minutes. Post offices and train stations usually change money if you can't get to a bank.

Use a money belt. Thieves target tourists. A money belt (call 425/771-8303 for our free newsletter/catalog) provides peace of mind and allows you to carry lots of cash safely.

Don't be petty about changing money. The greatest avoidable money-changing expense is wasting time every few days to return to a bank. Change a week's worth of money, get big bills, stuff them in your money belt, and travel!

Travel Smart

Many people travel through Rome thinking it's a chaotic mess. They feel any attempt at efficient travel is futile. This is dead wrong—and expensive. Rome, which seems as orderly as spilled spaghetti, actually functions well. Only those who understand this and travel smart can enjoy Rome on a budget.

Buy a phone card and use it for reservations and double-checking hours of sights. (I've included phone numbers for this purpose.) Enjoy the friendliness of the local people. Ask questions. Most locals are eager to point you in their idea of the right direction. Pack along a pocket-size notebook to organize your thoughts. Those who expect to travel smart, do.

Museums and sights, especially large ones, usually stop admitting people 30 to 60 minutes before closing time.

Sundays have the same pros and cons as they do for travelers in the United States: Sightseeing attractions are generally open; shops and banks are closed. City traffic is light. Rowdy evenings are rare on Sundays. Saturdays are virtually weekdays with earlier closing hours.

Hotels are often booked up on Easter, April 25, May 1, in August, and on Fridays and Saturdays. Religious holidays and train strikes can catch you by surprise anywhere in Italy.

Really, this book can save you lots of time and money. But to have an "A" trip, you need to be an "A" student. Read it all before your trip; note the days when museums are closed and whether reservations are mandatory. For instance, if you want to see the Borghese Gallery or Nero's Golden House, you must reserve ahead. If you go to the Vatican Museum on a Sunday, you'll run smack into closed doors, or—if it's the last Sunday of the month—huge crowds. You can wait an hour to get into the Colosseum, or buy your ticket at another kiosk and walk right in. Daytripping to Ostia Antica on Monday is bad news. A smart trip is a puzzle—a fun, doable, and worthwhile challenge.

Tourist Information

Rome has a number of tourist information offices (abbreviated TI in this book); for a list, see page 26.

Before your trip, contact the nearest Italian TI in the United States and briefly describe your trip and request information. You'll get the general packet and, if you ask for specifics (city map, calendar of festivals, etc.), an impressive amount of help. If you have a specific problem, they're a good source of sympathy.

Contact the office nearest you...

In **New York:** 630 5th Avenue #1565, New York, NY 10111, brochure hotline tel. 212/245-4822, tel. 212/245-5618, fax 212/586-9249, e-mail: enitny@italiantourism.com.

In **Illinois:** 500 N. Michigan Avenue #2240, Chicago, IL 60611, brochure hotline tel. 312/644-0990, tel. 312/644-0996, fax 312/644-3019, e-mail: enitch@italiantourism.com.

In **California:** 12400 Wilshire Boulevard #550, Los Angeles, CA 90025, brochure hotline tel. 310/820-0098, tel. 310/820-1898, fax 310/820-6357, e-mail: enitla@earthlink.net.

Web sites on Italy: www.italiantourism.com (Italian Tourist Board in the United States), www.museionline.it (museums in Italy, in English), and www.fs-on-line.com (train info and schedules).

Web sites on Rome: www.romaturismo.com (music, exhibitions, events, kid stuff, in English), www.wantedinrome.com (job openings and real estate, but also festivals and exhibitions, in English), and www.vatican.va (the pope's Web site, in English).

Recommended Guidebooks

For most travelers, this book is all you need. The tall, green Michelin guide to Rome has solid, encyclopedic coverage of sights, customs, and culture, though very little on room and board (sold in English in Italy).

The well-researched Access and the colorful Eyewitness guides to Rome are very popular with travelers. Eyewitness is fun for its great, easy-to-grasp graphics and photos, and it's just right for people who want only factoids. But the Eyewitness books are relatively skimpy on content and they weigh a ton. We buy them in Rome (no more expensive than in the U.S.) or simply borrow them for a minute from other travelers at certain sights to make sure we're aware of that place's highlights. *Let's Go Rome* is youth-oriented, with good coverage of nightlife, hosteling, and cheap transportation deals. If you'll be traveling elsewhere in Italy, consider *Rick Steves' Italy 2002*.

In Rome, the American Bookstore sells all the major guidebooks (Via Torino 136, Metro: Repubblica, tel. 06-474-6877).

Rick Steves' Books and Videos

Rick Steves' Europe Through the Back Door 2002 gives you budget travel skills on minimizing jet lag, packing lightly, planning your itinerary, traveling by car or train, finding budget beds without reservations, changing money, avoiding rip-offs, outsmarting thieves, hurdling the language barrier, staying healthy, taking great photographs, using your bidet, and much more. The book also includes chapters on 35 of Rick's favorite "Back Doors," six of which are in Italy.

Rick Steves' Country Guides are a series of eight guide-books that cover: Italy; Britain; Ireland; France/Belgium/Netherlands; Spain/Portugal; Germany/Austria/Switzerland (with Prague); Scandinavia; and the Best of Europe. All are updated annually and come out each December and January.

Rick Steves' City Guides include this book, *Paris*, and *London* (all available in January), and—new for 2002—*Venice and Florence* (available in March). For thorough coverage of Europe's greatest cities, complete with extensive self-guided tours through the greatest museums, consider these handy, easy-to-pack guidebooks.

Rick Steves' Europe 101: History and Art for the Traveler (with Gene Openshaw, 2000), which gives you the story of Europe's people, history, and art, is heavy on Italy's ancient, Renaissance, and modern history. Written for smart people who were sleeping in their history and art classes before they knew they were going to Europe, *101* helps resurrect the rubble.

Rick Steves' Mona Winks: Self-Guided Tours of Europe's Top Museums (with Gene Openshaw, 2001) gives you fun, easy-to-follow self-guided tours of Europe's 25 most exhausting, important muse-ums and cultural sites. All of the *Mona Winks* chapters on Rome are included in this Rome guidebook. But if you'd like similar coverage for the great museums in London, Amsterdam, Paris, Madrid, Venice (St. Mark's, Doge's Palace, and Accademia Gallery), and Florence (Uffizi Gallery, Bargello, and Michelangelo's *David*), *Mona*'s for you.

In Italy, a phrase book is as fun as it is necessary. My *Rick Steves' Italian Phrase Book* (1999) will help you meet the people and stretch your budget. It's written by a monoglot who, for 25 years, has fumbled through Italy struggling with all the other phrase books. Use this fun and practical communication aid to make accurate hotel reservations over the telephone, ask for a free taste of cantaloupe-flavored gelato at the *gelateria*, have the man in the deli make you a sandwich, and tell your cabbie that if he doesn't slow down, you'll throw up.

Rick's current public-television series, *Rick Steves' Europe*, airs 16 episodes, including two on Rome. Thirteen new episodes—with five on Italy—will debut in late 2002. The earlier *Travels in Europe* series, with 52 episodes, includes six half-hour shows on Italy. These air throughout the United States on public television stations and the Travel Channel. Each episode is also available on an information-packed home video, as is Rick's two-hour slide-show lecture on Italy (call us at 425/771-8303 for our free newsletter/catalog or check www.ricksteves.com).

Rick Steves' Postcards from Europe (1999), an autobiographical book, packs 25 years of travel anecdotes and insights into the ultimate 3,000-mile European adventure. Through his guidebooks, Rick shares his favorite European discoveries with you. In *Postcards*, he introduces you to his favorite European friends. Half of the book is set in Italy: Rome, Venice, Florence, and the Cinque Terre.

All of Rick Steves' books are published by Avalon Travel Publishing (www.travelmatters.com).

Maps
The maps in this book, designed and drawn by Dave Hoerlein, are concise and simple. Dave is well-traveled in Rome and Italy and has designed the maps to help you orient quickly and get to where you want to go painlessly. In Rome, your hotel or the tourist office have helpful free maps, but the €2.75 map sold at kiosks listing all the streets is much better.

Tours of Rome and Italy
Travel agents will tell you about normal tours of Italy, but they won't tell you about ours. At Europe Through the Back Door, we offer one-week winter and spring getaways to **Rome** (departures Oct–April, 20 people maximum). Our 20-day **Best of Italy** tour, featuring all of the biggies and a few of our favorite "back doors" (April–Oct, 24 people), and our new 15-day **Village Italy** adventure, which laces together intimate towns (April, Sept, and Oct, 20 people), come with two great guides and a big roomy bus. For more information call 425/771-8303 or visit www.ricksteves.com.

Transportation
Transportation concerns within Rome are limited to the Metro, buses, and taxis, all covered in the Orientation chapter. If you have a car, stow it. You don't want to drive in Rome. Transportation to daytrip destinations is covered in the Daytrips chapter. For specifics on transportation throughout Italy by train or car, see *Rick Steves' Italy 2002*.

In Rome, get train tickets and railpass-related reservations and supplements at travel agencies, rather than dealing with the congested train station. The cost is either the same or there's a minimal charge. Your hotel can direct you to the nearest travel agency. Quo Vadis, near the Pantheon, is handy (Via dei Cestari 21, tel. 06-413-1831).

Telephones, Mail, and E-mail
Smart travelers use the telephone every day—especially in Rome—to confirm hotel reservations, check opening hours, and phone home.

Phone cards: Italy's phone cards are cards you insert in the phone instead of coins. They're sold in varying denominations at tobacco shops, post offices, and machines near phone booths (many phone booths indicate where the nearest phone-card sales outlet is located). Rip off the perforated corner to "activate" the card before you insert it into the phone.

The orange SIP public telephones are everywhere and take cards or coins. About a quarter of the phones are broken (which could explain why so many Italians carry cell phones). The rest of the phones work reluctantly. Dial slowly and deliberately, as if the phone doesn't understand numbers very well. Often a recorded message in Italian will break in, brusquely informing you that the phone number does not exist (*non-esistente*), even if you're dialing your own home phone number. Dial again with an increasing show of confidence, in an attempt to convince the phone of your number's existence. If you fail, try a different phone. Repeat as needed.

Italian phone numbers vary in length; a hotel can have, say, a 10-digit phone number and 11-digit fax number. When spelling out your name on the phone, you'll find *a* (pronounced "ah" in Italian), *i* ("ee"), and *e* ("ay") are confusing. Say "*a*, Aosta," "*e*, Empoli," and "*i*, Italia" to clear up that problem. If you plan to access your voicemail from Italy, be advised that you can't always dial extensions or secret codes once you connect (you're on vacation—relax).

Dialing within Italy: Italy has a direct-dial phone system (no area codes). To call anywhere within Italy, just dial the number. For example, the number of one of my recommended Rome hotels is 06-482-4696. To call it from the Rome train station, dial 06-482-4696. If you call it from Venice, it's the same: 06-482-4696. (All normal Rome telephone numbers—not including toll-free or cell-phone numbers—start with 06.)

Italian phone numbers vary in length; a hotel can have, say, a 10-digit phone number and an 11-digit fax number.

Italy has toll-free numbers that start with 800 (like 800 numbers in the U.S., though in Italy you don't dial a "1" first). In Italy, you can dial these 800 numbers—called *freephone* or *numero verde* (green number)—free from any phone without using a phone card or coins.

In 2001, the phone system dropped the initial zero from Italy's cellular phone numbers; if, during your travels, you come across old information that lists cell-phone numbers starting with zero, drop the zero and try the number.

Dialing International Calls: When calling internationally, dial the international access code (00 if you're calling from Europe, 011 from the U.S. or Canada), the country code (of the country you're calling; see appendix for list), and the local number. To call a Rome hotel from the United States, dial 011 (the U.S. international access code), 39 (Italy's country code), then 06-482-4696.

To call our office from Italy, we dial 00 (Europe's international access code), 1 (the U.S. country code), 425 (Edmonds' area code), and 771-8303. European time is six/nine hours ahead of the east/west coasts of the United States.

Hotel-room phones are reasonable for calls within Italy (the faint beeps stand for €0.10 phone units), but a terrible rip-off for calls to the United States (unless you use a PIN card or your hotel allows toll-free access to your USA Direct service—see below).

PIN Cards: Calling the United States from Italy is now cheapest with the new PIN cards sold at newsstands and hole-in-the-wall long-distance phone shops. Because there are so many brand names, just ask for an international telephone card (specify that you want a card for making calls to the U.S. or Canada to avoid getting the PIN cards that are only good within particular regions in Italy). After you buy a card, scratch off and reveal your Personal Identification Number, dial the toll-free access number, punch in your PIN, and talk. You'll get about three minutes per dollar. Because you don't insert these cards into a phone, you can use them at most phones, including your hotel room (unless it's an older phone). If the PIN doesn't work on one phone, try another phone. Get a lower denomination in case the card is a dud. On our last trip, we had difficulty using PIN cards to make local calls, so we used Italian phone cards, coins, or hotel-room phones for local calls, and saved the PIN card for international calls.

USA Direct Services: While still convenient, these services, such as AT&T, MCI, and Sprint, are no longer a good value. It's much cheaper to call the United States using a PIN card or Italian phone card, but some people prefer to use their easier, pricier calling cards. Each card company has a toll-free number in each European country (for Italy: AT&T—tel. 172-1011, MCI—tel. 172-1022, Sprint—tel. 172-1877), which puts you in touch with an English-speaking operator. The operator takes your card number and the number you want to call, puts you through, and bills your home phone number for the call. Oddly, you need to use a small-value coin or Italian phone card to dial the toll-free number. Sprint is the priciest, costing $3 for the first minute with a $4.50 connection fee; if you get an answering machine, it'll cost you $7.50 to say "Sorry I missed you." For less than 25 cents, call first with a coin or European phone card to see if the answering machine is off or if the right person's at home. It's outrageously expensive to use USA Direct for calls between European countries; it's much cheaper to call direct using an Italian phone card.

Cell Phones: Affluent travelers like to buy cell phones ($60 and up) in Europe to use for making local and international calls. The cheaper phones generally work only if you're making calls from the country where you purchased it (e.g., a phone bought in Italy won't work in France). Pricier phones allow you to call from any country, but it'll cost you about $40 to outfit the phone per country with the necessary chip and prepaid phone time. If you're interested, stop by any European shop that sells cell phones (you'll see an array of phones prominently displayed in the store window). Depending on your trip and budget, ask for a phone that works only in that country or one that can be used throughout Europe. And if you're really on a budget, skip cell phones and use PIN cards instead.

Mail: Mail service is miserable throughout Italy. Postcards get last priority. If you must have mail stops, consider a few pre-reserved hotels along your route or use American Express offices. Most American Express offices in Italy will hold mail for one month. This service is free to anyone using an AmEx card or AmEx traveler's checks (and available for a small fee to others). Allow 14 days for U.S.-to-Italy mail delivery, but don't count on it. Federal Express makes pricey two-day deliveries. Phoning is so easy that we've completely dispensed with mail stops. If possible, mail nothing precious from Italy. But, if you must, use the mail service at the Vatican City (they have 2 post offices, one next to St. Peter's Basilica, the other within the Vatican Museum).

E-mail: E-mail use among Italian hoteliers is increasing. We've listed e-mail addresses when possible. Drab little cybercafés are popular in the bigger cities (even paired with laundrettes in Rome).

Sleeping

For hassle-free efficiency, we favor hotels and restaurants handy to your sightseeing activities. Rather than listing hotels scattered throughout Rome, we describe our favorite neighborhoods and recommend the best accommodations values in each, from $15 bunks to plush, with-all-the-comforts $200 doubles.

Sleeping in Rome is expensive. Cheap big-city hotels can be depressing. Tourist-information services cannot give opinions on quality. A major feature of this book is its extensive listing of good-value rooms. We like places that are clean, small, central, quiet at night, traditional, inexpensive, and friendly, with firm beds— and those not listed in other guidebooks. (In Rome, for us, 6 out of 9 attributes means its a keeper.)

Hotels

Double rooms listed in this book will range from about $50 (very simple, toilet and shower down the hall) to $200 (maximum plumbing and more), with most clustering around $120 (with private bathrooms). Three or four people economize by sharing

Sleep Code

To give maximum information in a minimum of space, I use this code to describe accommodations listed in this book. Prices listed are per room, not per person.

S	=	Single room (or price for 1 person in a double)
D	=	Double or Twin room. "Double beds" are often two twins sheeted together and are usually big enough for nonromantic couples.
T	=	Triple (generally a double bed with a single)
Q	=	Quad (usually 2 double beds)
b	=	Private bathroom with toilet and shower or tub
s	=	Private shower or tub only (the toilet is down the hall)
CC	=	Accepts credit cards (Visa and MasterCard, rarely American Express).
no CC	=	Doesn't accept credit cards; pay in local cash.
SE	=	Speaks English. This code is used only when it seems predictable that you'll encounter English-speaking staff.
NSE	=	Does not speak English. Used only when it's unlikely you'll encounter English-speaking staff.

According to this code, a couple staying at a "Db-€140, CC, SE" hotel would pay a total of €140 (about $125) for a double room with a private bathroom. The hotel accepts credit cards or Italian cash. The staff speaks English.

larger rooms. Solo travelers find that the cost of a *camera singola* is often only 25 percent less than a *camera doppia*. Most listed hotels have rooms for anywhere from one to five people. If there's room for an extra cot, they'll cram it in for you.

You normally get close to what you pay for. Prices are fairly standard. Shopping around earns you a better location and more character, but rarely a cheaper price.

However, prices at nearly any hotel can get soft if you do any of the following: arrive direct (without using a pricey middleman like the TI), offer to pay cash, stay at least three nights, or visit off-season. Breakfasts are legally optional (though some hotels insist they're not). Initial prices quoted often include breakfast and a private bathroom. Offer to skip breakfast for a better price.

You'll save $10 to $20 if you ask for a room without a shower and just use the shower down the hall. Generally rooms with a bath or shower also have a toilet and a bidet (which Italians use for quick sponge baths). Tubs usually come with a frustrating "telephone shower" (hand-held nozzle). If a shower has no curtain, the entire bathroom showers with you. The cord that dangles over the tub or shower is not a clothesline. You pull it when you've fallen and can't get up.

Double beds are called *matrimoniale*, even though hotels aren't interested in your marital status. Twins are *due letti singoli*.

Many hotel rooms have a TV and phone. Rooms in fancier hotels usually come with air-conditioning (sometimes you pay an extra per-day charge for this), a small safe, and a small stocked fridge called a *frigo bar* (FREE-goh).

When you check in, the receptionist will normally ask for your passport and keep it for a couple of hours. Hotels are legally required to register each guest with the local police. Relax. Americans are notorious for making this chore more difficult than it needs to be.

The hotel breakfast, while convenient, is often a bad value— €9 for a roll, jelly, and usually unlimited *caffè latte*. You can request cheese or salami (€3 extra). We enjoy taking breakfast at the corner café. It's OK to supplement what you order with a few picnic goodies.

Rooms are safe. Still, zip cameras and keep money out of sight. More pillows and blankets are usually in the closet or available on request. In Italy, towels and linen aren't always replaced every day. Hang your towel up to dry.

To avoid the time-wasting crowd at the reception desk in the morning, settle up your bill the evening before you leave.

Making Reservations

Reserve your Rome room with a phone call, fax, or e-mail as soon as you can commit to a date. It's possible to visit Rome without booking ahead, but given the high stakes and the quality of the gems we've found for this city guide, we would highly recommend making reservations.

To reserve from home, telephone first to confirm availability, then fax or e-mail your formal request. It's easy to reserve by phone. we've taken great pains to list telephone numbers with long-distance instructions (see "Telephones," above; also see the appendix). Most hotels listed are accustomed to English-only speakers. Fax costs are reasonable, e-mail's a steal, and simple English is usually fine. To fax, use the handy form in the appendix; for e-mailers, the form's online at www.ricksteves.com /reservation. If you don't get an answer to your fax request, consider that a "no." (Many little places get 20 faxes a day after they're full and can't afford to respond.)

A two-night stay in August would be "two nights, 16/8/02 to 18/8/02" (Europeans write the date day/month/year and hotel jargon uses your day of departure). You'll often receive a response back requesting one night's deposit. If your credit-card number is accepted as the deposit (which is usually the case), you can pay with your card or cash when you arrive; if you don't show up, you'll be billed for one night. Always reconfirm your reservations a day in advance by phone. (Don't needlessly reconfirm rooms through the tourist office; they'll take a commission.)

Honor (or cancel by phone) your reservations. Long distance is cheap and easy from public phone booths. Don't let these people down—we promised you'd call and cancel if for some reason you can't show up.

Eating

The Italians are masters of the art of fine living. That means eating...long and well. Lengthy, multicourse lunches and dinners and endless hours sitting in outdoor cafés are the norm. Americans eat on their way to an evening event and complain if the check is slow in coming. For Italians, the meal is an end in itself, and only rude waiters rush you. When you want the bill, mime-scribble on your raised palm or ask for it: "*Il conto?*"

Even those of us who liked dorm food will find that the local cafés, cuisine, and wines become a highlight of our Italian adventure. Trust us, this is sightseeing for your palate, and even if the rest of you is sleeping in cheap hotels, your taste buds will relish an occasional first-class splurge. You can eat well without going broke. But be careful; you're just as likely to blow a small fortune on a disappointing meal as you are to dine wonderfully for $20.

Roman Cuisine

In Rome, you'll enjoy risotto from the north and pasta from the south. And while you'll eat wonderful "Italian" while in Rome, you'll also find a few typically Roman dishes. Uniquely "Roman cuisine" originated as food for poor people—hearty servings of fresh local produce, simply prepared. Basic ingredients are tomatoes, garlic, cheese, and peppers. The meat is often the "fifth quarter"—organ meats. Try to venture away from the tourist-friendly pastas and grilled meats with potatoes. Here are some ideas:

Antipasto (appetizer): *Antipasto misto* (a mixed appetizer plate of cold sliced meats and cold cooked vegetables) is the popular standard here. Some restaurants display a grand buffet, and eaters are often welcome to assemble, "salad bar–style," their own plates of whatever looks good. Try *caprese* (tomato and fresh mozzarella topped with basil and drizzled with olive oil) and *bruschetta*

Eating with the Seasons

Italian cooks love to serve you fresh produce and seafood at its tastiest. If you must have porcini mushrooms outside of October and November, they'll be frozen. To get the freshest veggies at a fine restaurant, request *"Il piatto del la stagioni, per favore."* (A plate of what's seasonal, please).

Here are a few examples of what's fresh when:

April–May:	Calamari, squid, green beans, and zucchini flowers
April, May, Sept, Oct:	Black truffles
May–June:	Mussels, asparagus, zucchini, canteloupe, and strawberries
May–Aug:	Eggplant
Oct–Nov:	Mushrooms and white truffles
Fresh year-round:	Clams, meats, and cheese

(crunchy toasted garlic bread with olive oil—impossible to duplicate well outside of Italy).

Primo Piatto (first course): Among many pasta options, local specialties include *spaghetti alla carbonara* (with chopped bacon, cheese, and egg), *penne all' arrabbiata* (pasta tubes with a spicy tomato/garlic/parsley sauce, literally "angry pasta"), *pasta alla amatriciana* (with spicy tomato sauce and bacon bits), and *spaghetti alla puttanesca* (with peppers, black olives, tomato, and garlic—early fast food, literally "prostitute's spaghetti" . . . they could slurp it down between jobs). *Gnocchi alla Romana* is another good Roman standby (little oven-cooked potato dumplings with tomatoes or butter).

Secondo Piatto (main course): Typical main courses include *abbacchio* (milk-fed baby lamb, cooked various ways), *saltimbocca alla Romana* (veal with sage and ham cooked in butter and wine), and *fritto misto* (a mix of deep-fried meats and vegetables).

Contorni (vegetables): Along with *patate arrosto* (the standard roasted potatoes) and *spinaci* (spinach), be sure to try grilled vegetables (especially zucchini) and artichokes—*carciofi* (pressed flat and fried, served with oil and garlic) or *carciofi alla guidia* (served "Jewish style" with an anchovy-garlic sauce).

Vini (wines): The only distinctive local wine is Frascati (a light white), which is not good enough to merit ignoring other, better Italian wines.

Dolci (dessert): I'll see you at the *gelateria*.

Restaurants

When restaurant-hunting, choose places filled with locals, not the place with the big neon signs boasting, "We speak English and accept credit cards." Restaurants parked on famous squares generally serve bad food at high prices to tourists. Locals eat better at lower-rent locales. Family-run places operate without hired help and can offer cheaper meals. The word *osteria* (normally a simple, local-style restaurant) makes us salivate. For unexciting but basic values, look for a *menù turistico*, a three- or four-course, set-price menu. Galloping gourmets order à la carte with the help of a menu translator. (The *Marling Italian Menu Master* is excellent. *Rick Steves' Italian Phrase Book* has enough phrases for intermediate eaters.)

A full meal consists of an appetizer (*antipasto*, €3–6), a first course (*primo piatto*, pasta or soup, €4.50–7.50), and a second course (*secondo piatto*, expensive meat and fish dishes, €5.50–11). Vegetables (*contorni, verdure*) may come with the *secondo* or cost extra (€3.50) as a side dish. Restaurants normally pad the bill with a cover charge (*pane e coperto*—"bread and cover charge," around €1) and a service charge (*servizio*, 15 percent); these charges are listed on the menu. Italian waiters are paid well and tipping is not expected (though an extra €1 or €2 per person for good service is a nice touch).

The lire can add up in a hurry. Light and budget eaters get by with a *primo piatto* each and sharing an *antipasto*. Italians admit that the *secondo* is the least-interesting aspect of the local cuisine.

Delis, Cafeterias, Pizza Shops, and Tavola Calda (Hot Table) Bars

Rome offers many cheap alternatives to restaurants. Stop by a *rosticcería* for great cooked deli food; a self-service cafeteria (called "free flow" in Italian) that feeds you without the add-ons; a *tavola calda* bar for an assortment of veggies; or a Pizza Rustica shop for stand-up or take-out pizza.

Pizza is cheap and everywhere. Key pizza vocabulary: *capricciosa* (generally ham, mushrooms, olives, and artichokes), *funghi* (mushrooms), *marinara* (tomato sauce, oregano, garlic, no cheese), *quattro formaggi* (4 different cheeses), and *quattro stagioni* (different toppings on each of the 4 quarters for those who can't choose just 1 menu item). If you ask for *peperoni* on your pizza, you'll get green or red peppers, not sausage. Kids like *diavola* (closest thing in Italy to American "pepperoni") and *margherita* (tomato and cheese) pizzas. At Pizza Rustica take-out shops, slices are sold by weight (100 grams, or *un etto*, is a hot and cheap snack; 200 grams, or *due etti*, makes a light meal).

Ordering Food at Tavola Caldas

plate of mixed veggies	*piatto misto di verdure*	pee-AH-toh MEES-toh dee vehr-DOO-ray
"Heated, please."	*"Scaldare, per favore."*	skahl-DAH-ray, pehr fah-VOH-ray
"A taste, please."	*"Un assaggio, per favore"*	oon ah-SAH-joh, pehr fah-VOH-ray
artichoke	*carciofo*	kar-CHOH-foh
asparagus	*asparagi*	ah-spah-RAH-jee
beans	*fagioli*	fah-JOH-lee
green beans	*fagiolini*	fah-joh-LEE-nee
broccoli	*broccoli*	BROK-oh-lee
canteloupe	*melone*	May–LOH-nay
carrots	*carote*	kah-ROT-ay
ham	*prosciutto*	proh-SHOO-toh
mushrooms	*funghi*	FOONG-ghee
potatoes	*patate*	pah-TAH-tay
rice	*riso*	REE-zoh
spinach	*spinaci*	speen-AH-chee
tomatoes	*pomodori*	poh-moh-DOH-ree
zucchini	*zucchine*	zoo-KEE-nay
breadsticks	*grissini*	gree-SEE-nee

(Excerpted from *Rick Steves' Italian Phrase Book*)

For a fast, cheap, and healthy lunch, find a *tavola calda* bar with a buffet spread of meat and vegetables, and ask for a mixed plate of vegetables with a hunk of mozzarella (*piatto misto di verdure con mozzarella*). Don't be limited by what you can see. If you'd like a salad with a slice of cantaloupe and a hunk of cheese, they'll whip that up for you in a snap. Belly up to the bar and, with a pointing finger and key words in the chart in this chapter, you can get a fine mixed plate of vegetables. If something's a mystery, ask for *un assaggio* (a little taste).

Italian Bars/Cafés

Italian "bars" are not taverns but cafés. These local hangouts serve coffee, mini-pizzas, sandwiches, and cartons of milk from the cooler. Many dish up plates of fried cheese and vegetables from under the glass counter, ready to reheat. This is my budget choice, the Italian equivalent of English pub grub.

For quick meals, bars usually have trays of cheap, ready-made sandwiches (*panini* or *tramezzini*)—some kinds are delightful grilled. To save time for sightseeing and room for dinner, my favorite lunch is a ham and cheese *panini* at a bar (called *tost*, grilled twice to get really hot). To get food "to go," say, "*Da portar via*" (for the road). All bars have a WC (*toilette, bagno*) in the back, and the public is entitled to use it.

Bars serve great drinks—hot, cold, sweet, or alcoholic. Chilled bottled water (*natural* or *frizzante*) is sold cheap to go.

Coffee: If you ask for "*un caffè*," you'll get espresso. Cappuccino is served to locals before noon and tourists any time of day. (To an Italian, cappuccino is a breakfast drink and a travesty after anything with tomatoes.) Italians like it warm. To get it hot, request "*Molto caldo*" (very hot) or "*Più caldo, per favore*" (hotter, please; pron. pew KAHL-doh, pehr fah-VOH-ray).

Experiment with a few of the options:

- *caffè freddo*: sweet and iced espresso
- *cappuccino freddo*: iced cappuccino
- *caffè hag*: espresso decaf (decaf is easily available for any coffee drink)
- *macchiato*: with only a little milk
- *caffè latte*: coffee with lots of hot milk, no foam
- *caffè Americano*: espresso diluted with water
- *caffè corretto*: espresso with a shot of liqueur

Beer: Beer on tap is "*alla spina*." Get it *piccola* (33 cl), *media* (50 cl), or *grande* (a liter).

Wine: To order a glass (*bicchiere*; bee-kee-AY-ree) of red (*rosso*) or white (*bianco*) wine, say, "*Un bicchiere di vino rosso/bianco*." *Corposo* means full-bodied. House wine often comes in a quarter-liter carafe (*un quarto*). Trendy wines with small production (such as Brunello di Montalcino) are good but overpriced. There are better values on wines with greater production and less demand (such as Frescobaldi Montisodi).

Prices: You'll notice a two-tiered price system. Drinking a cup of coffee while standing at the bar is cheaper than drinking it at a table. If you're on a budget, don't sit without first checking out the financial consequences.

If the bar isn't busy, you'll often just order and then pay when you leave. Otherwise: 1) decide what you want; 2) find out the price by checking the price list on the wall, the prices posted near the food, or by asking the barman; 3) pay the cashier; and 4) give the receipt to the barman (whose clean fingers handle no dirty euros) and tell him what you want.

Picnics

In Rome, picnicking saves lots of euros and is a great way to sample local specialties. For a colorful experience, gather your ingredients in the morning at one of Rome's open-air produce markets (see page 220); you'll probably visit several small stores or market stalls to put together a complete meal. A local *alimentari* is your one-stop corner grocery store (most will slice and stuff your sandwich for you if you buy the ingredients there). A *supermercato* gives you more efficiency with less color for less cost.

Juice-lovers can get a liter of O.J. for the price of a Coke or coffee. Look for "100% *succo*" (juice) on the label. Hang onto the half-liter mineral-water bottles (sold everywhere for about €0.50). Buy juice in cheap liter boxes, then drink some and store the extra in your water bottle. (we drink tap water— *acqua del rubinetto*.)

Picnics can be an adventure in high cuisine. Be daring. Try the fresh mozzarella, *presto* pesto, shriveled olives, and any UFOs the locals are excited about. Shopkeepers are happy to sell small quantities of produce. But in a busy market, a merchant may not want to weigh and sell small, three-carrot-type quantities. In this case, estimate generously what you think it should cost, and hold out the coins in one hand and the produce in the other. Wear a smile that says, "If you take the money, I'll go." He'll grab the money. A typical picnic for two might be fresh rolls, 100 grams of cheese, 100 grams of meat (100 grams = about a quarter pound, called *un etto* in Italy), two tomatoes, three carrots, two apples, yogurt, and a liter box of juice. Total cost—about $10.

Culture Shock—Accepting Italy as a Package Deal

We travel all the way to Italy to enjoy differences—to become temporary locals. You'll experience frustrations. Certain truths that we find "God-given" or "self-evident," such as cold beer, ice in drinks, bottomless cups of coffee, hot showers, body odor smelling bad, and bigger being better, are suddenly not so true. One of the benefits of travel is the eye-opening realization that there are logical, civil, and even better alternatives. A willingness to go local ensures that you'll enjoy a full dose of Italian hospitality.

If there is a negative aspect to the image Italians have of Americans, it is that we are big, loud, aggressive, impolite, rich, and a bit naive. While Italians, flabbergasted by our Yankee excesses, say in disbelief, "*Mi sono cadute le braccia!*" ("I throw my arms down!"), they nearly always afford us individual travelers all the warmth we deserve.

Send Us a Postcard, Drop Us a Line

If you enjoy a successful trip with the help of this book and would like to share your discoveries, please fill out and send the survey at the end of this book to us at Europe Through the Back Door, Box 2009, Edmonds, WA 98020. We personally read and value all feedback. Thanks in advance—it helps a lot.

For our latest travel information on Italy, tap into our Web site at www.ricksteves.com. To check on any updates for this book, go to www.ricksteves.com/update. Rick's e-mail address is rick@ricksteves.com. Anyone is welcome to request a free issue of our *Back Door* quarterly newsletter.

Judging from all the happy postcards we receive from travelers who have used this book, it's safe to assume you'll enjoy a great, affordable vacation—with the finesse of an independent, experienced traveler. From this point, "we" (your coauthors) will shed our respective egos and become "I".

Thanks, and *buon viaggio*!

BACK DOOR TRAVEL PHILOSOPHY
As Taught in Rick Steves' Europe Through the Back Door

Travel is intensified living—maximum thrills per minute and one of the last great sources of legal adventure. Travel is freedom. It's recess, and we need it.

Experiencing the real Europe requires catching it by surprise, going casual... " Through the Back Door."

Affording travel is a matter of priorities. (Make do with the old car.) You can travel—simply, safely, and comfortably—anywhere in Europe for $80 a day plus transportation costs. In many ways, spending more money only builds a thicker wall between you and what you came to see. Europe is a cultural carnival and, time after time, you'll find that its best acts are free and the best seats are the cheap ones.

A tight budget forces you to travel close to the ground, meeting and communicating with the people, not relying on service with a purchased smile. Never sacrifice sleep, nutrition, safety, or cleanliness in the name of budget. Simply enjoy the local-style alternatives to expensive hotels and restaurants.

Extroverts have more fun. If your trip is low on magic moments, kick yourself and make things happen. If you don't enjoy a place, maybe you don't know enough about it. Seek the truth. Recognize tourist traps. Give a culture the benefit of your open mind. See things as different but not better or worse. Any culture has much to share.

Of course, travel, like the world, is a series of hills and valleys. Be fanatically positive and militantly optimistic. If something's not to your liking, change your liking. Travel is addictive. It can make you a happier American, as well as a citizen of the world. Our Earth is home to six billion equally important people. It's humbling to travel and find that people don't envy Americans. They like us, but with all due respect, they wouldn't trade passports.

Globetrotting destroys ethnocentricity. It helps you understand and appreciate different cultures. Travel changes people. It broadens perspectives and teaches new ways to measure quality of life. Many travelers toss aside their hometown blinders. Their prized souvenirs are the strands of different cultures they decide to knit into their own character. The world is a cultural yarn shop. And Back Door Travelers are weaving the ultimate tapestry. Come on, join in!

ORIENTATION

Sprawling Rome actually feels manageable once you get to know it. It's the old core—within the triangle formed by the train station, the Colosseum, and the Vatican. Consider it in these layers:

The ancient city had a million people. Tear it down to size by walking through just the core. The best of the classical sights stand in a line from the Colosseum to the Pantheon.

Medieval Rome was little more than a hobo camp of 50,000—thieves, mean dogs, and the pope, whose legitimacy required a Roman address. The medieval city, a colorful tangle of lanes, lies between the Pantheon and the river.

Window-shoppers' Rome twinkles with nightlife and ritzy shopping near Rome's main drag, Via del Corso—in the triangle formed by Piazza del Popolo, Piazza Venezia, and the Spanish Steps.

Vatican City is a compact world of its own with two great, huge sights: St. Peter's Basilica and the Vatican Museum.

Trastevere, the seedy, colorful, wrong-side-of-the-river neighborhood/village, is Rome at its crustiest—and perhaps most "Roman."

Baroque Rome is an overleaf that embellishes great squares throughout the town with fountains and church facades.

Since no one is allowed to build taller than St. Peter's dome, the city has no modern skyline. And the Tiber River is ignored. After the last floods (1870), the banks were built up very high and Rome turned its back on its naughty, unnavigable river.

Planning Your Time

After considering Rome's major tourist sights, I've covered just my favorites. You won't be able to see all of these, so don't try. You'll keep coming back to Rome. After several dozen visits, I still have a healthy list of excuses to return.

GREATER ROME

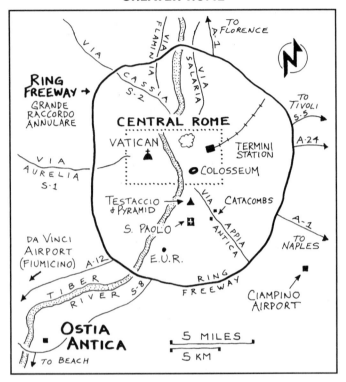

Rome in a Day

Some actually try to "do" Rome in a day. Crazy as that sounds, if all you have is a day, it's a great one. See the Vatican City (2 hrs in the Vatican Museum and Sistine Chapel, 1 hr in St. Peter's), taxi over the river to the Pantheon (picnic on its steps), then hike over Capitol Hill, through the Forum, and to the Colosseum. Have dinner on Campo de' Fiori and dessert on Piazza Navona.

Rome in Two to Three Days

On the first day, do the "Caesar Shuffle" from the Colosseum to the Forum, then over Capitol Hill to the Pantheon. After a siesta, join the locals strolling from Piazza del Popolo to the Spanish Steps (see my recommended Dolce Vita Stroll, page 226). Have dinner near your hotel. On the second day, see the Vatican City (St. Peter's, climb the dome, tour the Vatican Museum). Have dinner on the atmospheric Campo de' Fiori, then walk to the

Daily Reminder

Sunday: These sights are closed: Vatican Museum (except for the last Sunday of the month, when it's free) and the Catacombs of San Sebastian. The Pantheon and E.U.R.'s Museum of Roman Civilization close early in the afternoon. In the morning, the Porta Portese flea market hops, and the old center is delightfully quiet.

Monday: Many sights are closed: National Museum of Rome, Borghese Gallery, Capitol Hill Museum, Octagonal Hall and Museum of the Bath (both at Baths of Diocletian), Etruscan Museum, Castel Sant' Angelo, Trajan's Market, Protestant Cemetery, E.U.R.'s Museum of Roman Civilization, Ostia Antica, and Villa d'Este (at Tivoli). All of the ancient sites and the Vatican Museum, among others, *are* open. The Baths of Caracalla close early in the afternoon.

Tuesday: All sights are open in Rome except for Nero's Golden House. Not a good day to side-trip to Naples (its Archaeological Museum is closed).

Wednesday: All sights are open except for the Catacombs of San Callisto.

Thursday: All sights are open except for the Cappuccin Crypt.

Friday/Saturday: All sights are open in Rome.

Trevi Fountain and Spanish Steps (see my recommended Night Walk across Rome, page 54). With a third day, add the Borghese Gallery (reservations required) and the National Museum of Rome.

Rome in Seven Days

Rome's a great one-week getaway. Its sights can keep even the most fidgety traveler well-entertained for a week.

Day 1: City orientation tour (walking tour or bus tour), then the National Museum of Rome and the nearby Baths of Diocletian. Afternoon: Dolce Vita Stroll (page 226) and shopping.

Day 2: Do the "Caesar Shuffle" from Nero's Golden House (reservation required) to the Colosseum, Forum, Mammertine Prison, Trajan's Forum, Capitol Hill, and Pantheon.

Day 3: Vatican City: St. Peter's Basilica, climb the dome, Vatican Museum. (The museum is less crowded in the afternoon but last admission is early—either 12:30 or 15:30, depending on the day.)

Day 4: Side trip to Ostia Antica. Take recommended "Night Walk Across Rome" from Campo de' Fiori to the Spanish Steps.

Day 5: Borghese Gallery (reservation required) and Pilgrims'

Rome (the churches Santa Maria Maggiore, San Clemente, and San Giovanni in Laterano).

Day 6: Side trip to Naples and Pompeii.

Day 7: Personal choice—Hadrian's Villa, Appian Way with Catacombs, E.U.R., Castel Sant' Angelo, Testaccio sights, Baths of Caracalla, Cappuccin Crypt, more shopping, or more time at the Vatican.

Arrival in Rome

For a rundown on Rome's train station and airports, see "Transportation Connections," page 228.

Tourist Information

While Rome has three main tourist information offices, the dozen or so TI kiosks scattered around the town at major tourist centers are handy and just as helpful. If all you need is a map, forget the TI and get one at your hotel.

You'll find TIs at the airport (daily 08:15–19:00, tel. 06-6595-6074) and the train station (daily 08:00–21:00, off-season 09:00–20:00, near track 3, accessible from platforms or lobby, marked "Informazioni Turistiche/Tourist Info," crowded, combined with travel agency, tel. 06-4890-6300).

The central TI office, near Piazza della Repubblica's huge fountain, covers the city and the region. It's a five-minute walk out the front of the train station (Mon–Sat 08:15–19:00, next to car dealership, Via Parigi 5, free Internet access, www.romaturismo.com, tel. 06-488-991). It's air-conditioned, less crowded, and more helpful than the station TI, and it has seats and a study table.

At any TI, ask for a city map, a listing of sights and hours (in the free *Tesori di Roma* booklet), and *L'Evento*, the free bimonthly entertainment guide for evening events and fun. All hotels list an inflated rate to cover the hefty commission any TI room-finding service charges. Save money by booking direct.

Smaller TIs (daily 09:00–18:00) include kiosks near the Forum (on Piazza del Tempio della Pace), at Via del Corso (on Largo Goldoni), in Trastevere (on Piazza Sonnino), on Via Nazionale (at Palazzo delle Esposizioni), at Castel Sant' Angelo, Santa Maria Maggiore, and at San Giovanni in Laterano. For more information, call 06-3600-4399 (daily 09:00–19:00) or check out the Italian-language Web site, www.comune.roma.it.

Roma c'è is a cheap little weekly entertainment guide with a helpful English section (at the back) on musical events and the pope's schedule for the week (new edition every Thu, sold at newsstands for €1, www.romace.it). Fancy hotels carry a free English monthly, *Un Ospite a Roma* (*A Guest in Rome*).

Dealing with (and Avoiding) Problems

Theft Alert: With sweet-talking con artists meeting you at the station, well-dressed pickpockets on buses, and thieving gangs of children at the ancient sites, Rome is a gauntlet of rip-offs. There's no great physical risk, but green tourists will be scammed. Thieves strike when you're distracted. Don't trust kind strangers. Keep nothing important in your pockets. Assume you're being stalked. (Then relax and have fun.) Be most on guard while boarding and leaving buses and subways. Thieves crowd the door, then stop and turn while others crowd and push from behind. The sneakiest thieves are well-dressed businessmen (generally with something in their hands); lately many are posing as tourists with Tevas, fanny packs, and cameras. Scams abound: Don't give your wallet to self-proclaimed "police" who stop you on the street, warn you about counterfeit (or drug) money, and ask to see your wallet.

If you know what to look out for, the gangs of children picking the pockets and handbags of naive tourists are no threat but an interesting, albeit sad, spectacle. Gangs of city-stained children (sometimes as young as 8–10 years old), too young to be prosecuted but old enough to rip you off, troll through the tourist crowds around the Colosseum, Forum, Piazza Repubblica, and train and Metro stations. Watch them target tourists who are overloaded with bags or distracted with a video camera. The kids look like beggars and hold up newspapers or cardboard signs to confuse their victims. They scram like stray cats if you're onto them. A fast-fingered mother with a baby is often nearby. The terrace above the bus stop near the Colosseum Metro stop is a fine place to watch the action and maybe even pick up a few moves of your own.

Reporting Losses: To report lost or stolen passports and documents or to file an insurance claim, you must file a police report (with Polizia at track 1 or with Carabinieri at track 20, also at Piazza Venezia). To replace a passport, file the police report, then go to your embassy (see below). To report lost traveler's checks, call your bank (Visa tel. 800/874-155, Thomas Cook/Mastercard tel. 800/872-050, American Express tel. 800/872-000), then file a police report. To report stolen or lost credit cards, call the company (Visa tel. 800/-877-232, Mastercard tel. 800/870-866, American Express tel. 800/874-333), then file a police report. All of these toll-free 800 numbers are Italian (dialed free in Italy), not American.

Embassies: United States (Mon–Fri 08:30–13:00, 14:00–17:30, Via Veneto 119, tel. 06-46741) and Canada (Via Zara 30, tel. 06-445-981).

Emergency Numbers: Police tel. 113. Ambulance tel. 118.

Hit and Run: Walk with extreme caution. Scooters don't need to stop at red lights, and even cars exercise what drivers call the "logical option" of not stopping if they see no oncoming traffic. As Vespa scooters become electric, they'll get quieter (hooray) but more dangerous for pedestrians. Follow locals like a shadow when you cross a street (or spend a good part of your visit stranded on curbs).

Staying/Getting Healthy: The siesta is a key to survival in summertime Rome. Lie down and contemplate the extraordinary power of gravity in the eternal city. I drink lots of cold, refreshing water from Rome's many drinking fountains (the Forum has 3). There's a pharmacy (marked by a green cross) in every neighborhood, including a handy one in the train station (daily 07:30–22:00, located downstairs, at west end), and a 24-hour pharmacy on Piazza dei Cinquecento 51 (next to train station on Via Cavour, tel. 06-488-0019). Embassies can recommend English-speaking doctors. Consider MEDline, a 24-hour home medical service (tel. 06-808-0995, doctors speak English). Anyone is entitled to free emergency treatment at public hospitals. The hospital closest to the train station is Policlinico Umberto 1 (entrance for emergency treatment on Via Lancisi, translators available, Metro: Policlinico). The American Hospital is a private hospital on the edge of town accustomed to helping Yankees (tel. 06-225-571).

Getting around Rome

Sightsee on foot, by city bus, or by taxi. I've grouped your sight-seeing into walkable neighborhoods.

Public transportation is efficient, cheap, and part of your Roman experience. It starts running around 05:30 and stops around 23:30, sometimes earlier. After midnight, there are a few very crowded night buses, and taxis become more expensive and hard to get. Don't try to hail one—go to a taxi stand.

Buses and subways use the same ticket. You can buy tickets at newsstands, tobacco shops, or at major Metro stations or bus stops, but not on board (€0.80, good for 75 min—1 Metro ride and unlimited buses); all-day bus/Metro passes cost €3.25 (for more info, visit ww.atac.roma.it).

Buses (especially the touristic #64) and the subway are havens for thieves and pickpockets. Assume any commotion is a thief-created distraction.

By Metro: The Roman subway system (Metropolitana) is simple, with two clean, cheap, fast lines. While much of Rome is not served by its skimpy subway, these stops are helpful: Termini (train station, National Museum of Rome at Palazzo Massimo, recommended hotels), Repubblica (Baths of Diocletian/Octagonal Hall, main TI, recommended hotels), Barberini (Cappuccin Crypt,

ROME'S METRO

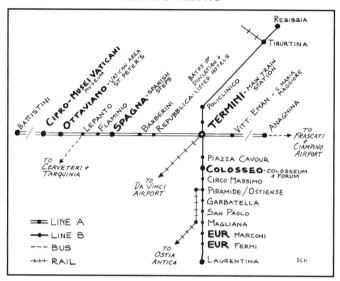

Trevi Fountain), Spagna (Spanish Steps, Villa Borghese, classy shopping area), Flaminio (Piazza del Popolo, start of recommended Dolce Vita Stroll down Via del Corso), Ottaviano (St. Peter's and Vatican City), Cipro-Musei Vaticani (Vatican Museum, recommended hotels), Colosseo (Colosseum, Roman Forum, recommended hotels), and E.U.R. (Mussolini's futuristic suburb).

By Bus: Bus routes are clearly listed at the stops. Punch your ticket in the orange stamping machine as you board (even if you've already stamped it for the Metro)—or you are cheating. Riding without a stamped ticket on the bus, while relatively safe, is stressful. Inspectors fine even innocent-looking tourists €52. If you hop a bus without a ticket, locals who use tickets rather than a monthly pass can sell you a ticket from their wallet bundle. Ideally, buy a bunch of tickets from a tobacco shop first thing so you can hop a bus without first having to search for a tobacco shop that's open.

Here are a few buses worth knowing about:

#64: Termini (train station), Piazza della Repubblica (sights), Via Nazionale (recommended hotels), Piazza Venezia (near Forum), Largo Argentina (near Pantheon), St. Peter's Basilica. Ride it for a city overview and to watch pickpockets in action (can get horribly crowded).

#8: This tram connects Largo Argentina with Trastevere (get off at Piazza Mastai).

#492: Stazione Tiburtina, Termini, Piazza Barberini, Piazza Venezia, Corso Rinascimento, Piazza Cavour (Castel Sant' Angelo), Piazza Risorgimento (near Vatican Museum).

#714: Termini, Santa Maria Maggiore, San Giovanni in Laterano, Terme di Caracalla (Baths of Caracalla).

Rome has cute "*electrico*" minibuses which wind through the narrow streets of old and interesting neighborhoods (daily except Sun). These are handy for sightseeing and fun for simply joyriding:

Electrico #116: Through the medieval core of Rome from Campo de' Fiori to Piazza Barberini via the Pantheon.

Electrico #117: San Giovanni in Laterano, Colosseo, Via dei Serpenti, Trevi Fountain, Piazza di Spagna, Piazza del Popolo.

"J" (for Jubilee) buses are bigger, come with a hostess, and provide more convenient access to some places farther out, such as St. Peters (Cavalleggeri stop) and the Catacombs. Purchase tickets (€1) on the bus (info: tel. 800-076-287).

By Taxi: Taxis start at about €2.75 (surcharges of €1 on Sun, €2.75 for night hrs of 22:00–7:00, €1 surcharge for luggage, €7.25 extra for airport, tip about 10 percent by rounding up to the nearest euro). Sample fares: Train station to Vatican-€9; train station to Colosseum-€6; Colosseum to Trastevere-€7. Three or four companions with more money than time should taxi almost everywhere. It's tough to wave down a taxi in Rome. Find the nearest taxi stand. (Ask a local or in a shop "*Dov'è* [DOH-vay] *una fermata dei tassi?*" Some are listed on my maps.) Unmarked, unmetered taxis at train stations and the airport are usually a rip-off. Taxis listing their telephone number on the door have fair meters— use them. To save time and energy, have your hotel call a taxi; the meter starts when the call is received. (To call a cab on your own, dial 06-3570, 06-4994, or 06-88177.)

Tours of Rome

Scala Reale—Tom Rankin (an American architect in love with Rome and his Roman wife) runs Scala Reale, a company committed to sorting out the rich layers of Rome for small groups with a longer-than-average attention span. Their excellent walking tours vary in length from two to four hours and start at €16 per person. Try to book in advance, since their groups are limited to six and fill up fast. Their fascinating "Rome Orientation" walks lace together lesser-known sights from antiquity to the present (tel. 06-474-5673, U.S. tel. 888/467-1986, www.scalareale.org, e-mail: info@scalereale.org).

Through Eternity—This company offers four walking tours, all led by native English speakers with relevant university degrees and with an emphasis on storytelling. The tours include St. Peter's and the Vatican Museum (€31, museum entry not included, 5.5 hrs, daily except Sun); the Colosseum and Roman Forum (€18, 2.5 hrs, daily); Rome at Twilight (€18, nightly); and a Wine Sampling Tour (€26, nightly, includes a glass at 4 or 5 wine bars). Call to get the schedule and to book in advance (max of 25 people, tel. 06-700-9336, cellular 347-336-5298, private tours possible, www.througheternity.com).

Walks of Rome—Students working for "Walks of Rome" give tours in fluent American or British English. They offer group tours (that individuals can join) and private tours (at a higher cost). Sample group tours include: Rome Through the Centuries (€34, 3 hrs, Mon, Wed, Fri at 10:00), Vatican City Walk (€52, includes admission to Vatican Museum, 4.5 hrs, Tue, Thu, Sat at 10:00), and the Colosseum (€19, includes admission, 1.5 hrs, offered daily). See their Web site for the latest (www.walksofeurope.com) and book in advance by e-mail (info@walksofeurope.com) or phone (tel. 06-484-853, cellular 347-795-5175). You'll need to give your hotel name and phone number. Your guide will call to let you know the meeting place. Their pub crawl tours meet at 20:00 at the Colosseum Metro stop (year-round) and finish at a disco six pubs later around midnight (€16, no need to reserve). I've never seen 50 young, drunk people having so much fun.

Hop-on Hop-off Bus Tour—The ATAC city bus tour offers your best budget orientation tour of Rome. In under two hours, you'll have 80 sights pointed out to you (by a live guide in English and maybe 1 other language) and have a chance to get out at nine different stops and catch a later bus. While the guide's spiel is limited to simple identification of the sights, this tour provides an efficient and economical orientation to Rome. The stops are: Piazza Barberini, Via Veneto, Villa Borghese, Piazza Cavour, St. Peter's Square, Corso Vittorio Emanuele (for Piazza Navona), Piazza Venezia, Colosseum, and Via Nazionale (€7.75, bus #110 departs every 30 min—at top and bottom of hour—from front of Termini train station, near platform C, buy tickets at info kiosk there—marked "i bus," runs March–Sept 09:00–20:00, Oct–Feb 10:00–18:00, tel. 06-4695-2252).

Archeobus—This handy new hop-on hop-off bus runs hourly from Piazza Venezia way out the Appian Way (buy €7.75 ticket on the bus, good from 09:00–17:00, 16-seat bus with hostess, pick up the guided-tour flier in English, tel. 06-4695-4695). They have cheap bike rentals at the appropriate Appian Way stop as well.

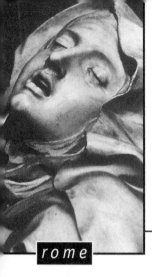

SIGHTS

rome

I've clustered Rome's sights into walkable neighborhoods, some quite close together. The Colosseum and the Forum are a few minutes' walk from Capitol Hill. Beyond that is the Pantheon, a 10-minute walk. I like to group these sights in one great day, starting at the Colosseum and ending at the Pantheon. (Note that the Pantheon closes at 13:00 on Sun.)

In this chapter, Rome's most important sights have the shortest listings and are marked with a ✪ (and page number). These sights are covered in much more detail in one of the tours included in this book.

To connect some of the sights by night, try my Night Walk Across Rome (page 54), which includes the Trevi Fountain and Spanish Steps. To join the parade of people strolling down Via del Corso every evening, take my recommended La Dolce Vita Stroll (see page 226).

Ancient Rome: The Colosseum and Forum Area

The core of the ancient city, where the grandest monuments were built, is between the Colosseum and Capitol Hill. Rome hopes to eventually close down its main drag, Via dei Fori Imperiali (a plan controversial for the traffic problems this would create), and turn this entire area into a vast archaeological park.

Beware of gangs of young thieves, particularly between the Colosseum and the Forum. They're harmless if you know what to look for (see "Theft Alert," page 27).

The following sights are listed in roughly geographical order from the Colosseum area to Capitol Hill. Except for the small St. Peter-in-Chains Church, the sights date from ancient Rome. St. Peter-in-Chains is included here because it's close to the Colosseum.

▲**St. Peter-in-Chains Church (San Pietro in Vincoli)**—Built in the fifth century to house the chains that held St. Peter, this church is most famous for its Michelangelo statue. Check out the much-venerated chains under the high altar, then focus on Moses (free, but pop in a coin to light the statue, Mon–Sat 07:00–12:30, 15:30–19:00, Sun 07:30–12:30, a short walk uphill from the Colosseum, modest dress required).

Pope Julius II commissioned Michelangelo to build a massive tomb, with 48 huge statues, crowned by a grand statue of this egomaniacal pope. The pope had planned to have his tomb placed in the center of St. Peter's Basilica. When Julius died, the work had barely been started, and no one had the money or necessary commitment to Julius to finish the project. Michelangelo finished one statue—Moses—and left a few unfinished statues: Leah and Rachel flanking Moses in this church, the "prisoners" now in Florence's Accademia, and the "slaves" now in Paris' Louvre.

This powerful statue of Moses—mature Michelangelo—is worth studying. The artist worked on it in fits and starts for 30 years. Moses has received the Ten Commandments. As he holds the stone tablets, his eyes show a man determined to stop his tribe from worshiping the golden calf and idols...a man determined to win salvation for the people of Israel. Why the horns? Centuries ago, the Hebrew word for "rays" was mistranslated as "horns."

▲**Nero's Golden House (Domus Aurea)**—The barren remains of Emperor Nero's "Golden House" were reopened to the public in 1999. The original entrance to the house was all the way over at the Arch of Titus in the Forum. This massive house once sprawled across the valley (where the Colosseum now stands) and up the hill—the part you tour today. Larger even than Bill Gates' place, it was a pain to vacuum. A colossal, 33-meter-tall (100 feet) bronze statue of Nero towered over everything. The house incorporated an artificial lake (where the Colosseum was later built) and a forest stocked with game. It was decorated with the best multicolored marble and the finest frescoes. No expense was too great for Nero—his mistress soaked daily in the milk of 500 wild asses kept for her bathing pleasure.

Nero (ruled A.D. 54–68) was Rome's most notorious emperor. He killed his own mother, kicked his pregnant wife to death, crucified St. Peter, and—most galling to his subjects—was a bad actor. When Rome burned in A.D. 64, Nero was accused of torching it to clear land for an even bigger house. The Romans rebelled and Nero stabbed himself in the neck, crying, "What an artist dies in me!"

While only hints of the splendid, colorful frescoes survive, the towering vaults and the basic immensity of the place are impressive. As you wander through rooms that are now underground, look up

Tips on Sightseeing in Rome

Museums: Plan ahead. The marvelous Borghese Gallery and Nero's Golden House both require reservations. For the Borghese Gallery, it's safest to make reservations well in advance of your trip (for specifics, see page 120). You can wait until you're in Rome to call for a reservation time at Nero's Golden House, but it's wise to book ahead (see page 33).

Audioguides are becoming increasingly common at museums. These small, portable devices give you information in English on what you're seeing. After you dial a number that appears next to a particular work of art, you listen to the spiel (cutting it short if you want). Though the information can be dry, it's usually worthwhile (about €3.60, sometimes 2 earphones are available at an extra cost).

A special **combo-ticket,** which costs €16, covers the National Museum of Rome, Colosseum, Palatine Hill, Baths of Caracalla, Crypt Balbi (medieval art), Museum of the Bath (Roman inscriptions), and Palazzo Altemps (so-so sculpture collection). The combo-ticket allows you to see seven sights for the price of three (purchase at participating sites, valid for 5 days). When you buy this, you can upgrade to a "Coupon Servizi" pass for an extra €5, giving you tours or audioguides at each site (normally about €3.60 each). The big plus of this ticket is that you avoid the long lines at the Colosseum (if you purchase it at a participating site other than the Colosseum).

Get a current listing of **museum hours** from one of Rome's TIs—ask for the booklet *Tesori di Roma* (Treasures of Rome). Some museums may stay open later in summer

at the holes in the ceiling. Imagine how much of old Rome still hides underground . . . and why the subway is limited to two lines.

Visits are allowed only with an escort (30 people every 15 min) and a reservation (€6.20, Wed–Mon 09:00–19:45, last entry at 18:45, closed Tue, tour lasts 45 min, escort speaks Italian only, audioguides-€1.60, but listen to the intro before entering or you'll be forever behind, 200 meters northeast of Colosseum, through a park gate, up a hill, and on the left). To reserve a place, call 06-3996-7700. If you just show up (particularly on a late afternoon on a weekday), you could luck out and get on a tour; if tours aren't booked up, the remaining seats are sold to drop-ins.

▲▲▲**Colosseum**—This 2,000-year-old building is *the* great example of Roman engineering (€7, covered by €16 combo-ticket, (usually on Sat). On holidays, expect shorter hours or closures. Hours listed anywhere can vary. Confirm sightseeing plans each morning with a quick 10-cent telephone call, asking, "Are you open today?" (*"Aperto oggi?"*; ah-PER-toh OH-jee) and "What time do you close?" (*"A che ora chiuso?"*; ah kay OH-rah kee-OO-zoh). I've included telephone numbers for this purpose.

Rooms can begin closing about 30 to 60 minutes before the overall closing time. If your heart is set on seeing a particular piece of art, don't save it for the finale.

In museums, art is dated with A.C. (for *Avanti Cristo*, or B.C.) and D.C. (for *Dopo Cristo*, or A.D.). O.K.?

WCs at museums are usually free and clean.

Churches: Churches offer some amazing art (usually free), a cool respite from the heat, and a welcome seat. They generally open early (around 07:00), close for lunch (roughly 12:00–15:00), and close late (around 19:00). Kamikaze tourists maximize their sightseeing hours by visiting churches before 09:00 and seeing the major sights that stay open during the siesta (St. Peter's, Colosseum, Forum, Capitol Hill Museum, National Museum of Rome) while Romans are taking it cool and easy.

Many churches have "modest dress" requirements, which means no bare shoulders, miniskirts, or shorts—for men, women, or children. This dress code is strictly enforced at St. Peter's (elsewhere, you'll see many tourists in shorts touring many churches).

A coin box near a piece of art often illuminates the art for a coin (and a better photo). Whenever possible, let there be light.

daily 09:00–19:00, tel. 06-3974-9907). ⊗ See Colosseum Tour on page 59.

To avoid the long lines here, buy your ticket at Palatine Hill entrances (inside Forum entry near Arch of Titus, and on Via di San Gregorio—facing Forum entry, go left) or get a €16 combo-ticket and walk right in (purchase at Palatine Hill entrances, National Museum of Rome, Baths of Caracalla, Museum of the Bath, or other participating sites).

▲**Arch of Constantine**—This well-preserved arch, which stands between the Colosseum and the Forum, commemorates a military coup and, more importantly, the acceptance of Christianity in the Roman Empire. When the ambitious Emperor Constantine (who'd had a vision he'd win under the sign of the cross) defeated his rival

Maxentius in A.D. 312, Constantine became sole emperor and legalized Christianity. ✪ See Colosseum Tour on page 59.

▲▲▲Roman Forum (Foro Romano)—This is ancient Rome's birthplace and civic center, and the common ground between Rome's famous seven hills (free, daily 09:00–19:15 or an hr before dark, Metro: Colosseo, tel. 06-3974-9907). ✪ See Forum Tour on page 64.

▲Palatine Hill—The hill overlooking the Forum was the home of the emperors and contains a museum, scant remains of imperial palaces, and a view of the Circus Maximus (€6.20, covered by €16 combo-ticket, daily 09:00–19:15 or an hour before dark, the ticket booths—which also sell Colosseum tickets, enabling smart sightseers to avoid that long line—are inside the Forum entry and on Via di San Gregorio). ✪ See Palatine Hill Tour on page 75.

▲Mammertine Prison—This 2,500-year-old, cistern-like prison, which once held Saints Peter and Paul, is worth a look (donation requested, daily 09:00–12:30, 14:30–18:30, at the foot of Capitol Hill, near Forum's Arch of Septimius Severus). When you step into the room, you'll hit a modern floor. Ignore that and look up at the hole in the ceiling, from which prisoners were lowered. Then take the stairs down to the level of the actual prison floor. As you descend, you'll walk past a supposedly miraculous image of Peter's face, created when a guard pushed him into the wall. Downstairs, you'll see the column to which Peter was chained. It's said that a miraculous fountain sprang up in this room so Peter could baptize other prisoners. The upside-down cross commemorates Peter's upside-down crucifixion.

Imagine humans, amid fat rats and rotting corpses, awaiting slow deaths. On the walls near the entry are lists of notable prisoners (Christian and non-Christian) and the ways they were executed: *strangolati, decapitato, morto di fame* (died of hunger) . . . .

▲Trajan's Column, Forum, and Market—This is the grandest column and best example of "continuous narration" we have from antiquity (free, always open and viewable, on Piazza Venezia across street from Victor Emmanuel Monument.) For a fee, you can go inside Trajan's Market (boring) and part of Trajan's Forum (€6.20, summer Tue–Sun 09:00–18:30, winter 09:00–16:30, closed Mon, entrance is uphill from the column on Via IV Novembre, tel. 06-3600-4399). ✪ See Trajan's Column and Forum Tour on page 83.

Capitol Hill Area

There are several ways to get to the top of Capitol Hill. If you're coming from the north (Piazza Venezia), take the grand stairs located to the right of the big, white Victor Emmanuel Monument (described below). Coming from the south (the Forum), take either the steep staircase or the winding road, which converge at a great Forum overlook and a refreshing water fountain. Block the spout with your fingers; water spurts up for drinking. Romans, who call this *il nasone* (the nose), joke that a cheap Roman boy takes his date out for a drink at *il nasone*.

▲▲**Capitol Hill (Campidoglio)**—This hill was the religious and political center of ancient Rome. It's still the home of the city's government. Michelangelo's Renaissance square is bounded by two fine museums and the mayoral palace. Its centerpiece is a copy of the famous equestrian statue of Marcus Aurelius (the original is behind glass in the adjacent museum).

Michelangelo intended that people approach the square from the grand stairway off Piazza Venezia. From the top of the stairway, you see the new Renaissance face of Rome with its back to the Forum, facing the new city. Notice how Michelangelo gave the buildings the "giant order"—huge pilasters make the existing two-story buildings feel one-storied and more harmonious with the new square. Notice also how the statues atop these buildings welcome you and then draw you in. The terraces just downhill (past either side of the mayor's palace) offer fine views of the Forum.

▲▲**Capitol Hill Museum**—This museum encompasses two buildings (Palazzo dei Conservatori and Palazzo Nuovo) connected by an underground passage that leads to the vacant Tabularium and a panoramic overlook of the Forum (€8, free on last Sun of month, Sun and Tue–Fri 09:00–19:00, Sat 09:30–23:00, last entry 60 min before closing, closed Mon, tel. 06-3996-7800). ✪ See Capitol Hill Museum Tour on page 114.

From Capitol Hill to Piazza Venezia—Leaving Capitol Hill, descend the stairs leading to Piazza Venezia. At the bottom of the stairs, look left several blocks down the street to see a condominium actually built around surviving ancient pillars and arches of Teatro Marcello—perhaps the oldest inhabited building in Europe.

Still at the bottom of the stairs, look up the long stairway to your right (which pilgrims climb on their knees) for a good example of the earliest style of Christian church. While pilgrims find it worth the climb, sightseers can skip it. As you walk toward Piazza Venezia, look down into the ditch on your right and see how modern Rome is built on the forgotten frescoes and mangled mosaics of ancient Rome.

Piazza Venezia—This vast square is the focal point of modern Rome. The Via del Corso, which starts here, is the city's axis, surrounded by Rome's classiest shopping district. In the 1930s, Mussolini whipped up Italy's nationalistic fervor here from a balcony above the square (to your right with back to Victor Emmanuel Monument). Fascist masses filled the square screaming,

"Four more years!"—or something like that. Fifteen years later, they hung Mussolini from a meat hook in Milan.

Victor Emmanuel Monument—This oversized monument to an Italian king was part of Italy's rush to overcome the new country's strong regionalism and to create a national identity after unification in 1870. It's now open to the public, offering a new view of the Eternal City (free, just climb the big stairs, long hrs).

Romans think of the monument not as an altar of the fatherland, but as "the wedding cake," "the typewriter," or "the dentures." It wouldn't be so bad if it weren't sitting on a priceless acre of ancient Rome and if they had chosen better marble (this is too in-your-face white and picks up the pollution horribly), though one of this book's authors happens to like the monument. Soldiers guard Italy's *Tomb of the Unknown Soldier* as the eternal flame flickers. At this level, stand with your back to the flame and see how Via del Corso bisects Rome.

Pantheon Area

▲▲▲**Pantheon**—For the greatest look at the splendor of Rome, antiquity's best-preserved interior is a must. Built two millennia ago, this influential domed temple served as the model for Michelangelo's dome of St. Peter's and many others (free, Mon–Sat 08:30–19:30, Sun 09:00–13:00 and 14:00–18:00, tel. 06-6830-0230). ✪ See Pantheon Tour on page 87.

▲▲**Churches near the Pantheon**—✪ For more information on the following churches, see page 89. The **Church of San Luigi dei Francesi** has a magnificent chapel painted by Caravaggio (free, Fri–Wed 07:30–12:30, 15:30–19:00, Thu 07:30–12:30, sightseers should avoid Mass at 07:30 and 19:00). The only Gothic church in Rome is **Santa Maria sopra Minerva**, with a little-known Michelangelo statue, *Christ Bearing the Cross* (the church is on a little square behind the Pantheon, to the east). The **Church of St. Ignazio**, several blocks east of the Pantheon, is a riot of Baroque illusions with a false dome. (Both Sopra Minerva and St. Ignazio churches open early; take a siesta: Sopra Minerva closes at 12:00, St. Ignazio at 12:30; and reopen from around 15:30–19:00). A few blocks away, back across Corso Vittorio Emmanuele, is the rich and Baroque **Gesu Church**, headquarters of the Jesuits in Rome (daily 06:00–12:30, 16:00–19:15). Modest dress is recommended at all churches.

Walk out the Gesu Church and two blocks down Corso V. Emmanuele to the **Sacred Area** (Largo Argentina), an excavated square facing the boulevard, about four blocks south of the Pantheon. Walk around this square and look into the excavated pit at some of the oldest ruins in Rome. Julius Caesar was assassinated near here. Today it's a refuge for cats—some 250 of them are

── HEART OF ROME ──

cared for by volunteers. You'll see them (and their refuge) at the far (west) side of the square.

▲**Trevi Fountain**—This bubbly Baroque fountain of Neptune with his entourage is a minor sight to art scholars but a major nighttime gathering spot for teens on the make and tourists tossing coins. ✪ See Night Walk across Rome on page 54.

East Rome: Near the Train Station

These sights are within a 10-minute walk of the train station. By Metro, use the Termini stop for the National Museum and the Piazza Repubblica stop for the rest.

▲▲▲**National Museum of Rome in Palazzo Massimo**—This museum houses the greatest collection of ancient Roman art anywhere, including busts of emperors and a Roman copy of the *Greek Discus Thrower* (€6.20, covered by €16 combo-ticket, Tue–Sun 09:00–19:45, some summer Sat until 23:00, last entry 45 min before closing, closed Mon, audioguide-€3.60, Metro: Termini, tel. 06-481-5576). The museum is about 100 meters from the Termini train station. As you leave the station, it's the

EAST ROME

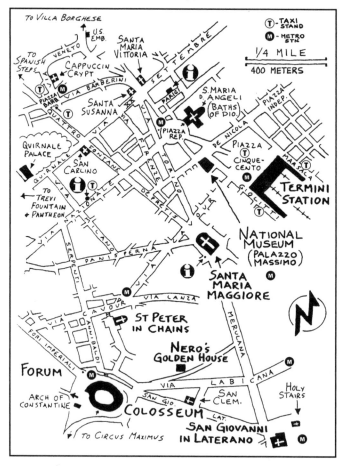

sandstone-brick building on your left. Enter at the far end, at Largo di Villa Peretti. ⚫ See National Museum of Rome Tour on page 101.

Baths of Diocletian—Around A.D. 300, Emperor Diocletian built the largest baths in Rome. This sprawling meeting place, with baths and schmoozing spaces to accommodate 3,000 bathers at a time, was a big deal in ancient times. While much of it is still closed, three sections are open: the **Church of Santa Maria degli Angeli**, once the great central hall of the baths (faces Piazza Repubblica); the **Octagonal Hall**, once a gymnasium, now a free gallery showing off fine bronze and marble statues—the kind that decorated the baths of imperial Rome (free, Tue–Sat 09:00–14:00, Sun 09:00–13:00, closed Mon, faces Piazza Repubblica); and the **Museum of the Bath**, which displays ancient Roman inscriptions on tons of tombs, steles, and tablets, but has nothing on the Baths despite its name (€4.20, covered by €16 combo-ticket, Tue–Sun 09:00–19:45, closed Mon, Viale E. De Nicola 79, entrance faces Termini station, tel. 06-488-0530). ⚫ See Baths of Diocletian Tour on page 95.

▲**Santa Maria della Vittoria**—This church houses Bernini's statue of a swooning *St. Teresa in Ecstasy* (free, daily 07:00–12:00, 16:00–19:00, on Largo Susanna, about 5 blocks northwest of train station, Metro: Repubblica). Once inside the church, you'll find St. Teresa to the left of the altar.

Teresa has just been stabbed with God's arrow of fire. Now, the angel pulls it out and watches her reaction. Teresa swoons, her eyes roll up, her hand goes limp, she parts her lips...and moans. The smiling, cherubic angel understands just how she feels. Teresa, a 16th-century Spanish nun, later talked of the "sweetness" of "this intense pain," describing her oneness with God in ecstatic, even erotic, terms.

Bernini, the master of multimedia, pulls out all the stops to make this mystical vision real. Actual sunlight pours through the alabaster windows; bronze sunbeams shine on a marble angel holding a golden arrow. Teresa leans back on a cloud and her robe ripples from within, charged with her spiritual arousal. Bernini has created a little stage-setting of heaven. And watching from the "theater boxes" on either side are members of the family that commissioned the work.

North Rome: Villa Borghese and nearby Via Veneto

▲**Villa Borghese**—Rome's scruffy "Central Park" is great for people-watching (plenty of modern-day Romeos and Juliets). Take a row on the lake or visit its fine museums.

▲▲▲**Borghese Gallery**—This private museum, filling a cardinal's mansion in the park, is newly restored and offers one of Europe's most sumptuous art experiences. Observe its slick mandatory reservation system, and you'll enjoy a collection of world-class Baroque sculpture, including Bernini's *David* and his excited statue of Apollo chasing Daphne, as well as paintings by Caravaggio, Raphael, Titian, and Rubens—with manageable crowds.

Cost, Hours, and Reservations: €7.25, Tuesday through Sunday 09:00 to 19:00, June through September may be open Saturday until 23:00, closed Monday. No photos are allowed. Reservations are mandatory and easy to get in English over the

Internet (www.ticketeria.it) or by phone: call 06-32810 (if you get an Italian recording, press 2 for English; office hours: Mon–Fri 09:00–18:00, Sat 09:00–13:00). Reserve a *minimum* of several days in advance for a weekday visit, at least a week ahead for weekends. ● For more on reservations, as well as a self-guided tour, see Borghese Gallery Tour on page 120.

Etruscan Museum (Villa Giulia Museo Nazionale Etrusco)— The Etruscan civilization thrived in this part of Italy around 600 B.C., when Rome was an Etruscan town. The Etruscan civilization is fascinating, but the Villa Giulia Museum is extremely low-tech and in a state of disarray. I don't like it, and Etruscan fans will prefer the Vatican Museum's Etruscan section. Still, the Villa Giulia does have the famous "husband and wife sarcophagus" (a dead couple seeming to enjoy an everlasting banquet from atop their tomb; 6th century B.C from Cerveteri), the *Apollo from Veio* statue (of textbook fame), and an impressive room filled with gold sheets of Etruscan printing and temple statuary from the Sanctuary of Pyrgi (€4.20, Tue–Sun 09:00–19:00, plus June–Sept Sat 21:00–23:45, closed Mon, closes earlier off-season, Piazzale di Villa Giulia 9, tel. 06-320-1951).

▲**Cappuccin Crypt**—If you want bones, this is it. The crypt is below the church of Santa Maria della Immaculata Concezione on Via Veneto, just up from Piazza Barberini. The bones of more than 4,000 monks who died between 1528 and 1870 are in the basement, all artistically arranged for the delight—or disgust— of the always-wide-eyed visitor. The soil in the crypt was brought from Jerusalem 400 years ago, and the monastic message on the wall explains that this is more than just a macabre exercise. Pick up a few of Rome's most interesting postcards (donation, Fri– Wed 09:00–12:00, 15:00–18:00, closed Thu, Metro: Barberini). A painting of St. Francis by Caravaggio is upstairs. Just up the street you'll find the American embassy, Federal Express, and fancy Via Veneto cafés filled with the poor and envious looking for the rich and famous.

Ara Pacis (Altar of Peace)—This will reopen in 2005, once restoration is complete. In 9 B.C, after victories in Gaul and Spain, Emperor Augustus celebrated the beginning of the Pax Romana by building this altar of peace. Peace is almost worshiped here. The north and south walls show a procession with realistic portraits of the imperial family in Greek Hellen- istic style. It's a fine combination of Roman grandeur and Greek elegance. Even during restoration, the altar can some- times be seen through the windows (a long block west of Via del Corso on Via di Ara Pacis, on east bank of river near Ponte Cavour, nearest Metro: Spagna).

West Rome: Vatican City Neighborhood

Vatican City, a tiny independent country, contains the Vatican Museum (with Michelangelo's Sistine Chapel) and St. Peter's Basilica (with Michelangelo's exquisite *Pietà*). A helpful tourist office is just to the left of St. Peter's Basilica (Mon–Sat 08:30–18:30, closed Sun, tel. 06-6988-1662, Vatican switchboard tel. 06-6982, www.vatican.va). The entrances to St. Peter's and to the Vatican Museum are a 15-minute walk apart (follow the outside of the Vatican wall, which links the 2 sights). The nearest Metro stops still involve a 10-minute walk to either sight: for St. Peter's, the closest stop is Ottaviano; for the Vatican Museum, it's Cipro-Musei-Vaticani. For information on Vatican tours, post offices, and the pope's schedule, see page 129.

▲▲▲**St. Peter's Basilica**—There is no doubt: This is the richest and most impressive church on earth. To call it vast is like calling God smart. The church strictly enforces its dress code. Dress modestly—a dress or long pants, shoulders covered (men and women).

Hours: May through September daily 07:00 to 19:00, October through April daily until 18:00. All are welcome to join in the hour-long Mass at the front altar (Mon–Sat at 17:00, Sun at 17:45). The view from the dome is worth the climb (€4.20 elevator plus 300-step climb, allow an hr to go up and down, May–Sept daily 08:00–18:00, Oct–April daily 08:30–17:00). ✪ See St. Peter's Basilica Tour on page 155.

▲▲▲**Vatican Museum**—The six kilometers of displays in this immense museum—from ancient statues to Christian frescoes to modern paintings—are topped by the Raphael Rooms and Michelangelo's glorious Sistine Chapel.

Cost and Hours: €9.30, March through October Monday through Friday 08:45 to 16:45, Saturday 08:45 to 13:45; November through February Monday through Saturday 08:45 to 13:45; closed Sunday except last Sunday of the month when it's free and crowded. The last entry is 75 minutes before closing time. The Sistine Chapel shuts down 30 minutes early. The museum is closed on many holidays (mainly religious ones), including—for 2002: January 1 and 6, February 11, March 19, Easter and Easter Monday, May 1, 9, and 30, June 29, August 14 and 15, November 1, and December 8, 25, and 26. Modest dress (no short shorts or bare shoulders for men or women) is appropriate and often required. ✪ See Vatican Museum Tour on page 129.

▲**Castel Sant' Angelo**—Built as a tomb for the emperor; used through the Middle Ages as a castle, prison, and place of last refuge for popes under attack; and today, a museum, this giant pile of ancient bricks is packed with history.

Ancient Rome allowed no tombs, not even the emperor's,

VATICAN CITY

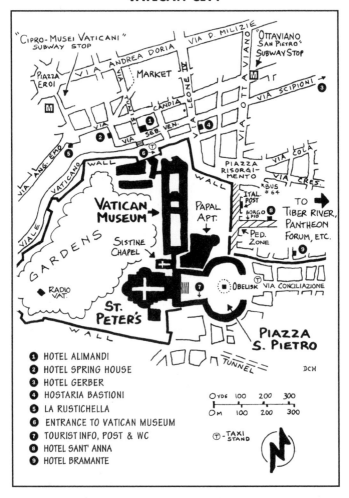

1. HOTEL ALIMANDI
2. HOTEL SPRING HOUSE
3. HOTEL GERBER
4. HOSTARIA BASTIONI
5. LA RUSTICHELLA
6. ENTRANCE TO VATICAN MUSEUM
7. TOURIST INFO, POST & WC
8. HOTEL SANT' ANNA
9. HOTEL BRAMANTE

within its walls. So Hadrian grabbed the most commanding position just outside the walls and across the river and built a towering tomb (circa A.D. 139) well within view of the city. His mausoleum was a huge cylinder (64 meters wide, 21 meters high) topped by a cypress grove and crowned by a huge statue of Hadrian himself riding a chariot. For nearly a hundred years, Roman emperors (from Hadrian to Caracalla in A.D. 217) were buried here.

In the year 590, the Archangel Michael appeared above the

mausoleum to Pope Gregory the Great. Sheathing his sword, the angel signaled the end of a plague. The fortress that was Hadrian's mausoleum eventually became a fortified palace, renamed for the "holy angel."

After Dark Age centuries as a fortress and prison, the pope built the elevated corridor connecting Castel Sant' Angelo with the Vatican (1277). Since Rome was repeatedly plundered by invaders, Castel Sant' Angelo was a handy place of last refuge for threatened popes. In anticipation of long sieges, rooms were decorated with papal splendor (you'll see paintings by Crivelli, Signorelli, and Mantegna). In the 16th century, during a sack of Rome by troops of Charles V of Spain, the pope lived inside the castle for months with his entourage of hundreds (an unimaginable ordeal, considering the food service at the top-floor bar).

After you walk around the entire base of the castle, take the small staircase down to the original Roman floor. In the atrium, study the model of the castle in Roman times and imagine the niche in the wall filled with a towering "welcome to my tomb" statue of Hadrian. From here, a ramp leads to the right, spiraling 125 meters. While some of the fine brickwork and bits of mosaic survive, the marble veneer is long gone (notice the holes in the wall which held it in place). At the end of the ramp, stairs climb to the room where the ashes of the emperors were kept. These stairs continue to the top, where you'll find the papal apartments. Don't miss the Sala del Tesoro (treasury), where the wealth of the Vatican was locked up in a huge chest. Do miss the 58 rooms of the military museum. The views from the top are great—pick out landmarks as you stroll around—and a restful coffee with a view of St. Peter's is worth the price.

Cost, Hours, Tours: €5, Tuesday through Sunday 09:00 to 19:00, plus June through September Saturday 21:00 to 23:45, closed Monday. You can take an English-language tour with an audioguide (€3.60) or live guide (€4.20, Tue–Fri at 15:00, Sat at 12:15 and 16:30, confirm times, tel. 06-3996-7600, Metro: Lepanto or bus #64, near Vatican City).

Ponte Sant' Angelo—The bridge leading to Castel Sant' Angelo was built by Hadrian for quick and regal access from downtown to his tomb. The three middle arches are actually Roman originals and a fine example of the empire's engineering expertise. The angels were designed by Bernini and finished by his students.

Southwest Rome: Trastevere

Trastevere is the colorful neighborhood across (*tras*) the Tiber (*tevere*) River. Trastevere offers the best look at medieval-village Rome. The action marches to the chime of the church bells. Go there and wander. Wonder. Be a poet. This is Rome's Left Bank.

TRASTEVERE

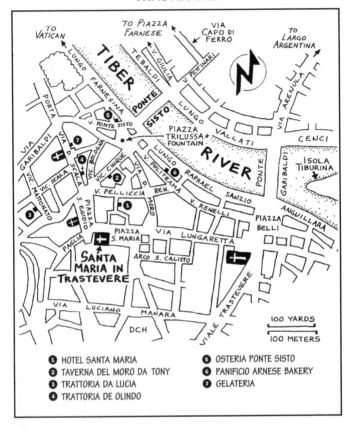

① HOTEL SANTA MARIA
② TAVERNA DEL MORO DA TONY
③ TRATTORIA DA LUCIA
④ TRATTORIA DE OLINDO
⑤ OSTERIA PONTE SISTO
⑥ PANIFICIO ARNESE BAKERY
⑦ GELATERIA

   This proud neighborhood was long a working-class area.
Now that it's becoming trendy, high rents are driving out the
source of so much color. Still, it's a great people scene, especially at
night. Wander the back streets (for restaurant recommendations,
see the Eating chapter).

   To get to Trastevere, taxi or ride the bus (from Vatican area—
#23; from Via Nazionale hotels—take #64, #70, #115, or #640 to
Largo Argentina, then transfer to #8 and get off at Piazza Mastai).
Santa Maria in Trastevere: The Church and Square—Start
your exploratory stroll at Piazza di Santa Maria in Trastevere.
While today's fountain is from the 17th century, there has been
a fountain here since Roman times.

   Santa Maria in Trastevere, one of Rome's oldest churches,

was made a basilica in the fourth century, when Christianity was legalized (free, daily 07:30–13:00, 15:00–19:00). It was the first church dedicated to the Virgin Mary. The portico (covered area just outside the door) is decorated with fascinating ancient fragments filled with early Christian symbolism. Most of what you see today dates from around the 12th century, but the granite columns come from an ancient Roman temple, and the ancient basilica floor plan (and ambience) survive. The 12th-century mosaics behind the altar are striking and notable for their portrayal of Mary—the first to show her at the throne with Jesus in Heaven. Look below the scenes from the life of Mary to see ahead-of-their-time paintings (by Cavallini, from 1300), predating the Renaissance by 100 years.

Gianicolo Hill Viewpoint—From this park atop a hill, the city views are superb, and the walk to the top holds a treat for architects. Start your walk at Trastevere's Piazza di San Cosimato, and follow Via Luciano Manara to Via Garibaldi, at the base of the hill. Via Garibaldi winds its way up the side of the hill to the church of San Pietro in Montorio. To the right of the church, in a small courtyard, is the Tempietto by Bramante. This tiny church, built to commemorate the spot where St. Peter was martyred, is considered a jewel of Italian Renaissance architecture. Continuing up the hill, Via Garibaldi connects to Passeggiata del Gianicolo. From here, you'll find a pleasant park with panoramic city views. Ponder the many Victorian-era statues, including that of baby-carrying, gun-wielding, horse-riding Anita Garibaldi. She was the Brazilian wife of the revolutionary General Giuseppe Garibaldi, who helped forge a united Italy in the late 19th century.

Linking Trastevere with "Night Walk Across Rome"—You can easily walk from Trastevere to Campo de' Fiori to link up with the beginning of the Night Walk across Rome (page 54): From Trastevere's church square (Piazza di Santa Maria), take Via del Moro to the river and cross at Ponte Sisto, a pedestrian bridge with a good view of St. Peter's dome. Continue straight ahead for one block. Take the first left, which leads down Via di Capo di Ferro through the scary and narrow darkness to Piazza Farnese, with the imposing Palazzo Farnese. Michelangelo contributed to the facade of this palace, now the French embassy. The fountains on the square feature huge, one-piece granite hot tubs from the ancient Roman Baths of Caracalla. One block from there (opposite the palace) is the atmospheric square of Campo de' Fiori.

South Rome
Baths of Caracalla (Terme di Caracalla)—Today it's just a shell—a huge shell—with all of its sculptures and most of its mosaics moved to museums. Inaugurated by Emperor Caracalla

in A.D. 216, this massive complex could accommodate 1,600 visitors at a time. Today you'll see a two-story, roofless brick building surrounded by a garden, bordered by ruined walls. The two large rooms at either end of the building were used for exercise. In between the exercise rooms was a pool flanked by two small mosaic-floored dressing rooms. Niches in the walls once held statues. In its day, this was a remarkable place to hang out. For ancient Romans, the baths were a social experience.

The Baths of Caracalla functioned until Goths severed the aqueducts in the sixth century. In modern times, operas were performed here from 1938 to 1993. For the same reason concerts no longer take place in the Forum—to keep the ruins from becoming more ruined—the performances were discontinued (€4.20, covered by €16 combo-ticket, Mon 09:00–14:00, Tue–Sun 09:00–19:15, ask if audioguides are available, fine €8 guidebook—can read in shaded garden while sitting on a chunk of column, Metro: Circus Maximus, and a 5-min walk south along Via delle Terme di Caracalla, tel. 06-5745748). Several of the Baths' statues are now in Rome's Octagonal Hall; the immense *Toro Farnese* (a marble sculpture of a bull surrounded by people) snorts in Naples' Archaeological Museum.

Testaccio—Four fascinating but lesser sights cluster at the Piramide Metro stop between the Colosseum and E.U.R., in the gritty Testaccio neighborhood. (This is a quick and easy stop as you return from E.U.R. or when changing trains en route to Ostia Antica.)

Working-class since ancient times, Testaccio has recently gone trendy-bohemian, and visitors will wander through an awkward mix of yuppie and proletarian worlds, not noticing—but perhaps feeling—the "keep Testaccio for the Testaccians" graffiti.

Pyramid of Gaius Cestius: The Marc Antony/Cleopatra scandal (around the time of Christ) brought exotic Egyptian styles into vogue. A rich Roman magistrate, Gaius Cestius, had a pyramid built as his tomb. Made of brick covered in marble, it was completed in just 330 days (as stated in its Latin inscription) and fell far short of Egyptian pyramid standards. It was later incorporated into the Aurelian Wall (located next to Piramide Metro stop).

Porta Ostiense: This formidable gate (also next to Piramide Metro stop) is from the Aurelian Wall, begun in the third century under Emperor Aurelius. The wall, which encircled the city, was 20 kilometers long and eight meters high, with 14 main gates and 380 22-meter-tall towers. Most of what you'll see today is circa A.D. 400. This gate was reconstructed by the barbarians in the sixth century. (For more on the wall, visit the Museum of the Walls at Porta San Sebastian; see "Ancient Appian Way," below.)

TESTACCIO

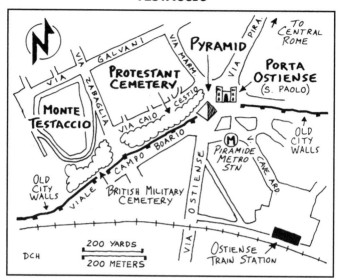

Protestant Cemetery: The *Cimitero Acattolico per gli Stranieri al Testaccio* (cemetery for the burial of non-Catholic foreigners) is a Romantic tomb-filled park, running along the wall just beyond the pyramid. From the Piramide Metro stop, walk between the pyramid and the Roman gate on Via Persichetti, then go left on Caio Cestio to the gate of the cemetery. Ring the bell (donation box, April–Sept Tue–Sun 09:00–18:00, Oct–March 09:00–17:00, closed Mon).

Originally, none of the Protestant epitaphs were allowed to make any mention of heaven. Signs direct visitors to the graves of notable non-Catholics who died in Rome since 1738. Many of the buried were diplomats. And many, such as poets Shelley and Keats, were from the Romantic Age; they came on the Grand Tour and—"captivated by the fatal charms of Rome," as Shelley wrote—never left. Head left toward the pyramid to find Keats' tomb, in the far corner. At the pyramid, look down on Matilde Talli's cat hospice (flier at the gate). Volunteers use donations to care for these "Guardians of the Departed" who "provide loyal companionship to these dead."

Monte Testaccio: Just behind the Protestant Cemetery (as you leave, turn left and continue 2 blocks down Caio Cestio) is a 35-meter-tall ancient trash mountain. It's made of broken *testae*—broken earthenware jars used to haul mostly wine 2,000 years ago, when this was a gritty port warehouse district. After 500 years of sloppy dock work, Rome's lowly eighth hill was built. Because the caves dug into the hill stay cool, trendy bars, clubs, and restaurants compete with gritty car-repair places for a spot. The neighborhood was once known for a huge slaughterhouse and a Gypsy camp that squatted inside an old military base. Now it's home to the Villagio Globale, a site for concerts and techno-raves. For a youthful and lively night scene, adventurers might consider a trip out to Monte Testaccio (Metro: Piramide).

Ancient Appian Way (Via Appia Antica)

Since the fourth century B.C., this has been Rome's gateway to the East. The first section was perfectly straight. It was the largest, widest, fastest road ever, the wonder of its day, called the "Queen of Roads." Eventually, this most important of Roman roads stretched 700 kilometers to the port of Brindisi—where boats sailed for Greece and Egypt. Twenty-nine such roads fanned out from Rome. Just as Hitler built the autobahn system in anticipation of empire maintenance, the emperors realized the military and political value of a good road system. A central strip accommodated animal-powered vehicles, and elevated sidewalks served pedestrians. As it left Rome, the road was lined with tombs and funerary monuments. Imagine a funeral procession passing under the pines and cypress and past a long line of pyramids, private mini-temples, altars, and tombs.

Hollywood created the famous image of the Appian Way lined with Spartacus and his gang of defeated and crucified slave rebels. This image is only partially accurate. Spartacus was killed in battle.

Tourist's Appian Way: The road starts about three kilometers south of the Colosseum at the massive San Sebastian Gate. The Museum of the Walls, located at the gate, offers an interesting look at Roman defense and a chance to scramble along a stretch of the ramparts (€2.60, Tue–Sun 09:00–19:00, closed Mon, tel. 06-7047-5284). A kilometer down the road are the two most historic and popular catacombs, those of San Callisto and San Sebastian (described below). Beyond that, the road becomes pristine and traffic-free, popular for biking and hiking.

To reach the Appian Way, you can hop on the new Archeobus (see "Tours of Rome," page 30) or take the Metro to the Colli Albani stop, then catch bus #660 to Via Appia Antica—its last stop and the start of an interesting stretch of the ancient road (the café next to the stop sometimes rents bikes). The segment between the third and 11th milestones is most interesting.

▲▲**Catacombs**—The catacombs are burial places for (mostly) Christians who died in ancient Roman times. By law, no one was allowed to be buried within the walls of Rome. While pagan

Romans were into cremation, Christians preferred to be buried. But land was expensive and most Christians were poor. A few wealthy, landowning Christians allowed their land to be used as burial places.

The 40 or so known catacombs circle Rome about five kilometers from its center. From the first through the fifth centuries, Christians dug an estimated 600 kilometers of tomb-lined tunnels, with networks of galleries as many as five layers deep. The tufa—soft and easy to cut, but becoming very hard when exposed to air—is perfect for the job. The Christians burrowed many layers deep for two reasons: to get more mileage out of the donated land and to be near martyrs and saints already buried there. Bodies were wrapped in linen (like Christ's). Since they figured the Second Coming was imminent, there was no interest in embalming the body.

When Emperor Constantine legalized Christianity in 313, Christians had a new, interesting problem. There would be no more persecuted martyrs to bind them and inspire them. Thus the early martyrs and popes assumed more importance, and Christians began making pilgrimages to their burial places in the catacombs.

In the 800s, when barbarian invaders started ransacking the tombs, Christians moved the relics of saints and martyrs to the safety of churches in the city center. For a thousand years, the catacombs were forgotten. Around 1850, they were excavated and became part of the romantic Grand Tour of Europe.

Finding abandoned plates and utensils from ritual meals in the candlelit galleries led 18th- and 19th-century Romantics to guess that persecuted Christians hid out and lived in these catacombs. This Romantic legend grew. But catacombs were not used for hiding out. They are simply early Christian burial grounds. With a million people in Rome, the easiest way for the 10,000 or so early Christians to hide out was not to camp in the catacombs (which everyone, including the government, knew about), but to melt into the city.

The underground tunnels, while empty of bones, are rich in early Christian symbolism, which functioned as a secret language. The dove symbolized the soul. You'll see it quenching its thirst (worshiping), with an olive branch (at rest), or happily perched (in paradise). Peacocks, known for their "incorruptible flesh," symbolized immortality. The shepherd with a lamb on his shoulders was the "good shepherd," the first portrayal of Christ as a kindly leader of his flock. The fish was used because the first letters of these words—"Jesus Christ, Son of God, Savior"—spelled "fish" in Greek. And the anchor is a cross in disguise. A second-century bishop had written on his tomb: "All who understand these things, pray for me." You'll see pictures of people praying with their hands raised up—the custom at the time.

Catacomb tours are essentially the same. Which one you take is not important. The **Catacombs of San Callisto** (a.k.a. Callixtus), the official cemetery for the Christians of Rome and burial place of third-century popes, is the most historic. Sixteen bishops (early popes) were buried here. Buy your €4.20 ticket and wait for your language to be called. They move lots of people quickly. If one group seems ridiculously large (over 50 people), wait for the next English tour (Thu–Tue 08:30–12:00, 14:30–17:30, closed Wed and Feb, closes at 17:00 in winter, Via Appia Antica 110, tel. 06-5130-1580). Dig this: The catacombs have a Web site—www.catacombe.roma.it—focusing mainly on San Callisto, featuring photos, site info, and a history.

The **Catacombs of San Sebastian** (Sebastiano) are 300 meters farther down the road (€4.20, Mon–Sat 08:30–12:00, 14:30–17:30, closed Sun and Nov, closes at 17:00 in winter, Via Appia Antica 136, tel. 06-5130-1580).

E.U.R.

In the late 1930s, Italy's dictator, Benito Mussolini, planned an international exhibition to show off the wonders of his fascist society. But these wonders brought us World War II, and Il Duce's celebration never happened. The unfinished mega-project was completed in the 1950s and now houses government offices and big, obscure museums.

If Hitler and Mussolini won the war, our world might look like E.U.R. (pronounced "ay-oor"). Hike down E.U.R.'s wide, pedestrian-mean boulevards. Patriotic murals, aren't-you-proud-to-be-an-extreme-right-winger pillars, and stern squares decorate the soulless, planned grid and stark office blocks. Boulevards named for Astronomy, Electronics, Social Security, and Beethoven are more exhausting than inspirational. Today E.U.R. is worth a trip for its Museum of Roman Civilization (described below).

The Metro skirts E.U.R. with three stops (10 min from the Colosseum). Use E.U.R. Magliana for the "Square Colosseum" and E.U.R. Fermi for the Museum of Roman Civilization (both described below). Consider walking 30 minutes from the palace to the museum through the center of E.U.R.

From the Magliana subway stop, stairs lead uphill to the **Palace of the Civilization of Labor (Palazzo del Civilta del Lavoro)**, the essence of fascist architecture. With its giant, no-questions-asked, patriotic statues and its black-and-white simplicity, this is E.U.R.'s tallest building and landmark. It's understandably nicknamed the "Square Colosseum." Around the corner, Café Palombini is still decorated in a 1930s style and is now quite

E.U.R.

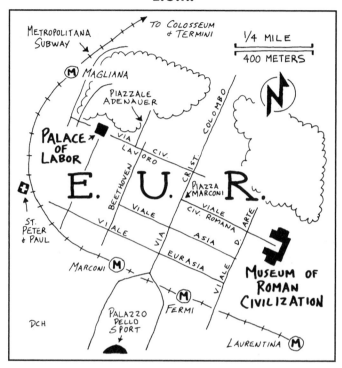

TO COLOSSEUM & TERMINI

METROPOLITANA SUBWAY

1/4 MILE

400 METERS

N

Ⓜ MAGLIANA

PIAZZALE ADENAUER

COLOMBO

PALACE OF LABOR

VIA LAVORO

CIV.

E. U. R.

BEETHOVEN

CRIST

PIAZZA MARCONI

ST. PETER & PAUL

VIALE

VIALE

VIA

VIALE CIV. ROMANA

ARTE

ASIA

D.

EURASIA

VIALE

MARCONI Ⓜ

MUSEUM OF ROMAN CIVILIZATION

DCH

PALAZZO DELLO SPORT

FERMI Ⓜ

LAURENTINA Ⓜ

trendy with young Romans (daily 07:00–24:00, good *gelato*, pastries, and snacks, Piazzale Adenauer 12, tel. 06-591-1700).

▲**Museum of Roman Civilization (Museo della Civilta Romana)**—With 59 rooms filled with plaster casts and models illustrating the greatness of classical Rome, this vast and heavy museum gives a strangely lifeless, close-up look at Rome. Each room has a theme, from military tricks to musical instruments. One long hall is filled with casts of the reliefs of Trajan's Column. The highlight is the 1:250-scale model of Constantine's Rome—circa A.D. 300 (€4.20, Tue–Sat 09:00–18:45, Sun 09:00–13:00, closed Mon, Piazza G. Agnelli, from Metro: E.U.R. Fermi, walk 10 min up Via dell Arte, you'll see its colonnade on the right, tel. 06-592-6041).

NIGHT WALK ACROSS ROME

Rome can be grueling. But a fine way to enjoy this historian's rite of passage is an evening walk lacing together Rome's floodlit night spots and fine urban spaces with real-life theater vignettes.

Sitting so close to a Bernini fountain that traffic noises evaporate; jostling with local teenagers to see all the *gelato* flavors; enjoying lovers straddling more than the bench; jaywalking past flak-proof-vested *polizia*; and marveling at the ramshackle elegance that softens this brutal city for those who were born here and can imagine living nowhere else—these are the flavors of Rome best tasted after dark.

Campo de' Fiori

Start at the Campo de' Fiori (Field of Flowers), my favorite outdoor dining room after dark (see the Eating chapter). The statue of Giordano Bruno, a heretic who was burned in 1600 for believing the world was round and not the center of the universe, marks the center of this great and colorful square. Bruno overlooks a busy produce market in the morning and strollers after sundown. This neighborhood is still known for its free spirit and occasional demonstrations. When the statue of Bruno was erected in 1889, local riots overcame Vatican protests against honoring a heretic. Bruno faces his executioner, the Vatican Chancellory (the big white building in the corner a bit to his right), while his pedestal reads: "And the flames rose up."

At the east end of the square (behind Bruno), the ramshackle apartments are built right into the old outer wall of ancient Rome's mammoth Theater of Pompey. This entertainment complex covered several city blocks, stretching from here to Largo Argentina. Julius Caesar was assassinated in the Theater of Pompey, where the Senate was renting meeting space.

NIGHT WALK ACROSS ROME

The square is lined with and surrounded by fun eateries. Bruno faces La Carbonara, the only real restaurant on the square. The Forno, next door, is a popular place for hot and tasty take-out *pizza bianco* (plain but spicy pizza bread).

•*If Bruno did a hop, step, and jump forward, then turned right on Via dei Baullari and marched 200 meters, he'd cross the busy Corso Vittorio Emanuele and find...*

Piazza Navona

Rome's most interesting night scene features street music, artists, fire-eaters, local Casanovas, ice cream, fountains by Bernini, and outdoor cafés (worthy of a splurge if you've got time to sit and enjoy the human river of Italy).

This oblong square retains the shape of the original racetrack

that was built by the emperor Domitian. (You can still see the ruins of the original entrance. Exit the square at the north end, take an immediate left, and look down to the left 7 meters below the current street level.) Since ancient times, the square has been a center of Roman life. In the 1800s, the city would flood the square to cool off the neighborhood.

The **Four Rivers fountain** in the center is the most famous fountain by the man who remade Rome in Baroque style, Gian Lorenzo Bernini. Four burly river gods (representing the four continents that existed in 1650) support an obelisk, while the water of the world gushes everywhere. The Nile has his head covered (since the headwaters were unknown then). The Ganges holds an oar. The Danube turns to admire the obelisk, which originally stood here in Domitian's stadium. And the Rio de la Plata from Uruguay tumbles backward in shock, wondering how he ever made the top four. Bernini enlivens the fountain with exotic flora and fauna from these newly discovered lands. Homesick Texans may want to find the armadillo.

The Plata river god is gazing upward at the church of Saint Agnes, worked on by Bernini's former student turned rival, Borromini. Borromini's concave facade helps reveal the dome and epitomizes the curved symmetry of Baroque. Tour guides say that Bernini designed his river god to look horrified at Borromini's work. Or he may be shielding his eyes from St. Agnes' nakedness, as she was stripped before being martyred. But the fountain was completed two years before Borromini even started work on the church.

At the **Tre Scalini** café (near the fountain), sample some *tartufo* "death-by-chocolate" ice cream, world-famous among connoisseurs of ice cream and chocolate alike (€3 to go, €6.50 at a table, closed Wed). Seriously admire a painting by a struggling artist. Request "Country Roads" from an Italian guitar player, and don't be surprised when he knows it. Listen to the white noise of gushing water and exuberant humans.

• *Leave Piazza Navona directly across from Tre Scalini café, go east past rose peddlers and palm readers, jog left around the guarded building, and follow the brown sign to the Pantheon. The Pantheon is straight down Via del Salvatore (cheap pizza place on left just before the Pantheon, WC at McDonald's).*

The Pantheon

Sit for a while under the floodlit and moonlit Pantheon's portico.

The 12-meter single-piece granite columns of the Pantheon's entrance show the scale the ancient Romans built on. The columns support a triangular, Greek-style roof with an inscription that says that "M. Agrippa" built it. In fact, it was built *("fecit")* by Emperor Hadrian (A.D. 120), who gave credit to the builder of an earlier structure. This impressive entranceway gives no clue that the greatest wonder of the building is inside—a domed room that inspired later domes, including Michelangelo's St. Peter's and Brunelleschi's Duomo (in Florence). Notice how the pavement slants down from McDonald's to the Pantheon, showing how high modern Rome has built on ancient rubble.

⭐ For more information, see Pantheon Tour on page 87.

• *With your back to the Pantheon, veer to the right down Via Olfeni.*

From the Pantheon to Piazza Colonna

After passing Bar Pantheon, you'll see **Tazza d'Oro Casa del Caffè**, one of Rome's top coffee shops, dating back to the days when this area was licensed to roast coffee beans. Look back at the fine view of the Pantheon from here. Via Olfeni leads to Piazza Capranica.

Piazza Capranica is home to the big, plain, Florentine Renaissance-style Palazzo Capranica. Big shots, like the Capranica family, built stubby towers on their palaces—not for any military use, but just to show off. Leave the piazza to the right of the palace, between the palace and the church. Via in Aquiro leads to a sixth-century B.C. **Egyptian obelisk** (taken as a trophy by Augustus after his victory in Egypt over Mark Antony and Cleopatra). Walk into the guarded square past the obelisk and face the huge parliament building.

A short detour to the left (past Albergo National) brings you to Rome's most famous gelateria. **Gelateria Caffè Pasticceria Giolitti** is cheap to go or elegant and splurge-worthy for a sit among classy locals (open daily until very late, Via Uffici del Vicario 40); get your gelato in a cone *(cono)* or cup *(bicchierini)*. You'll find better *gelato* at the nearby **Gelateria della Palma** (2 blocks in front of Pantheon, Via della Maddalena 20/23). Or head directly from the parliament into the next, even grander square.

Piazza Colonna features a huge second-century column honoring Marcus Aurelius. The big, important-looking palace is the prime minister's residence.

• *Cross Via del Corso, Rome's noisy main drag, jog right (around the Y-shaped shopping gallery from 1928), and head down Via dei Sabini to the roar of the water, light, and people of the Trevi Fountain.*

The Trevi Fountain

The Trevi Fountain shows how Rome took full advantage of the abundance of water brought into the city by its great aqueducts. This watery Baroque avalanche was built in 1762 by Nicola Salvi, hired by a pope celebrating his reopening of the ancient aqueduct that powers it. Salvi used the palace behind the fountain as a theatrical backdrop for Neptune's "entrance" into the square. Neptune surfs through his watery kingdom while Triton blows his conch shell.

The square is always lively, with lucky Romeos clutching dates while unlucky ones clutch beers. Romantics toss a coin over their shoulder, thinking it will give them a wish and assure their return to Rome. That may sound silly, but every year I go through this touristic ritual ... and it actually seems to work.

Take some time to people-watch (whisper a few breathy *bellos* or *bellas*) before leaving.

• *Face the fountain, then go past it on the right down Via delle Stamperia to Via del Triton. Cross the busy street and continue to the Spanish Steps (ask, "Dov'è Piazza di Spagna?"—Spagna rhymes with "lasagna"), a few blocks and thousands of dollars of shopping opportunities away.*

Spanish Steps (Piazza di Spagna)

The Piazza di Spagna, with the very popular Spanish Steps, got its name 300 years ago when this was the site of the Spanish Embassy. It's been the hangout of many Romantics over the years (Keats, Wagner, Openshaw, Goethe, and others). The British poet John Keats pondered his mortality, then died in the building on the right side of the steps.

The Boat Fountain at the foot of the steps, which was done by Bernini's father, Pietro Bernini, is powered by an aqueduct. All of Rome's fountains are aqueduct-powered; their spurts are determined by the water pressure provided by the various aqueducts. This one, for instance, is much weaker than Trevi's gush.

The piazza is a thriving night scene. Window-shop along Via Condotti, which stretches away from the Steps. This is where Gucci and other big names cater to the trendsetting jet set. Facing the Spanish Steps, you can walk right about a block to tour one of the world's biggest and most lavish McDonald's (clean WC). There's a taxi stand in the courtyard outside McDonald's; or, if you'd prefer, the Spagna Metro stop (usually open until 23:30) is just to the left of the Spanish Steps, ready to zip you home.

COLOSSEUM
TOUR

Rome has many layers—modern, Baroque, Renaissance, Christian. But let's face it, "Rome" is Caesars, gladiators, chariots, centurions, *"Et tu, Brute,"* trumpet fanfares, and thumbs up or thumbs down. That's the Rome we'll look at. Our "Caesar Shuffle" begins with the downtown core of ancient Rome, the Colosseum. A logical next stop is the Forum, just next door (and the next chapter), past the Arch of Constantine.

Orientation

Cost: €7 (exact change preferred), covered by €16 combo-ticket.
Hours: Daily 09:00 to 19:00.
Avoid Long Lines: Instead of waiting in line (sometimes an hour long) at the Colosseum to purchase a ticket, buy your Colosseum ticket at the Palatine Hill entrances nearby—inside the Forum entry and on

Via di San Gregorio (facing Forum entry, with Colosseum at your back, go left on street). The €16 combo-ticket—covering the Colosseum, Palatine Hill, Baths of Caracalla, National Museum of Rome, Museum of the Bath, and more—allows you to walk right into the Colosseum (if you've purchased it in advance at the Palatine Hill entrances or other participating sites).
Getting There: The Metro stop, Colosseo, lets you out just across the street from the monument. Look out for young street thieves (see page 27).
Information: Outside the entrance of the Colosseum, vendors sell handy little *Rome, Past and Present* books with plastic overlays to un-ruin the ruins (marked €10.50, offer €8). For a fee, the

ANCIENT ROME

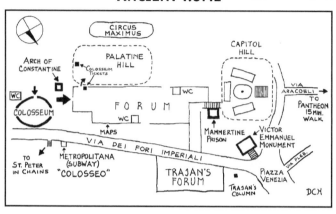

modern-day gladiators pose for photos. A WC is behind the Colosseum (facing ticket entrance, go right; WC is under stairway). Tel. 06-3974-9907.

Length of Our Tour: Allow 45 minutes.

Cuisine Art: For a quick lunch, climb the steps above the WC and cross the busy street to the cafés (with expansive views of the Colosseum). However, for a better value (but no views at all), see my listings on page 217.

Exterior of Colosseum

• *View the Colosseum from the Forum fence near the grassy patch across the street from the "Colosseo" subway station.*

Built when the Roman Empire was at its peak (A.D. 80), the Colosseum represents Rome at its grandest. The Flavian Amphitheater (its real name) was an arena for gladiator contests and public spectacles. When killing became a spectator sport, the Romans wanted to share the fun with as many people as possible. They did this by outbuilding the Greeks. The Greeks built their theaters into hillsides. The Romans, in essence, stuck two Greek theaters together to create a freestanding amphitheater. The outside (the grassy patch) was

decorated with a 33-meter-tall (100 feet) bronze statue of Nero that gleamed in the sunlight. The final structure was colossal—a "coloss-eum," the wonder of its age. It could accommodate 50,000 roaring fans (100,000 thumbs).

The Romans pioneered the use of the rounded arch and concrete, enabling them to build on this colossal scale. They made a shell of brick, then filled it in with concrete. Inside, you'll see this clearly among the ruins. Iron pegs held the larger stones together—notice the small holes that pockmark the sides. When it was done, the whole thing was faced with shining travertine marble (still visible on the top level).

The exterior says a lot about the Romans. They were great engineers, not artists. While the essential structure is Roman, the facade is Greek, decorated with the three types of Greek columns—Doric (bottom), Ionic (middle), and Corinthian (top). Originally, copies of Greek statues stood in the arches of the upper two stories. The Colosseum was designed to be functional more than beautiful. If ancient Romans visited the United States today as tourists, they'd send home postcards of our greatest works of "art"—freeways.

Only a third of the original Colosseum remains. Earthquakes destroyed some of it, but most was carted off as easy pre-cut stones for other buildings during the Middle Ages and Renaissance.

• *Enter by the south entrance—to your right, past the Arch of Constantine. Buy your ticket and go inside. Move up to a railing overlooking the arena.*

Interior of Colosseum

You're on arena level. What you see now are the underground passages beneath the playing surface. The oval-shaped arena (86 by 50 meters) was originally covered with boards, then sprinkled with sand (*arena* in Latin). Like modern stadiums, the spectators ringed
the playing area. The brick masses around you supported the first small tier of seats, and you can see two larger, slanted supports higher up. A few marble seats survive on the opposite side. Wooden beams stuck out from the top to support an enormous canvas awning that could be hoisted across by armies of sailors to provide shade for the spectators—the first domed stadium.

"Hail, Caesar! We who are about to die salute you!" The gladiators would enter the arena from the west end (to your left), parade around to the sound of trumpets, stop at the emperor's box at the "50-yard line" (where you're standing), raise their weapons, shout this salute—and the fights would begin. The fights pitted men against men, men against beasts, and beasts against beasts.

The gladiators were usually slaves, criminals, or poor people who got their chance for freedom, wealth, and fame in the ring. They learned to fight in training schools, then battled their way up the ranks. The best were rewarded like our modern sports stars with fan clubs, great wealth, and product endorsements.

The animals came from all over the world: lions, tigers, and bears (oh my!), crocodiles, elephants, and hippos (not to mention exotic human "animals" from the "barbarian" lands). They were kept in cages beneath the arena floor, then lifted up in elevators; released at floor level, the animals would pop out from behind blinds into the arena—the gladiator didn't know where, when, or by what he'd be attacked. Nets ringed the arena to protect the crowd. The stadium was inaugurated with a 100-day festival in which 2,000 men and 9,000 animals were killed. Colosseum employees squirted perfumes around the stadium to mask the stench of blood. For a lighthearted change of pace between events, the fans watched dogs bloody themselves fighting porcupines.

If a gladiator fell helpless to the ground, his opponent would approach the emperor's box and ask: Should he live or die? Sometimes the emperor left the decision to the crowd, who would judge based on how valiantly the man had fought. They would make their decision—thumbs up (Latin word: *siskel*) or thumbs down (*ebert*).

And Christians? Did they throw Christians to the lions like in the movies? Christians were definitely thrown to the lions, made to fight gladiators, crucified, and burned alive . . . but probably not here in this particular stadium. Maybe, but probably not.

Rome was a nation of warriors that built an empire by conquest. The battles fought against Germans, Egyptians, barbarians, and strange animals were played out daily here in the Colosseum for the benefit of city-slicker bureaucrats who got vicarious thrills watching brutes battle to the death. The contests were always free, sponsored by politicians to buy votes or to keep Rome's growing mass of unemployed rabble off the streets.

• *With these scenes in mind, wander around. Climb to the upper deck for a more colossal view (stairs near the exit, at north end).*

As you exit, the Roman Forum is directly in front of you, the subway stop is on your right, and the Arch of Constantine is on your left.

Arch of Constantine

If you are a Christian, were raised a Christian, or simply belong to a so-called "Christian nation," ponder this arch. It marks one of the great turning points in history—the military coup that made Christianity mainstream. In A.D. 312, Emperor Constantine defeated his rival Maxentius in one crucial battle. The night before, he had seen a vision of a cross in the sky. Constantine became

sole emperor and promptly
legalized Christianity.
With this one battle, a once-
obscure Jewish sect with a
handful of followers was now
the state religion of the entire
Western world. In A.D. 300,
you could be killed for being
a Christian; later, you could

be killed for not being one. Church enrollment boomed.

By the way, don't look too closely at the reliefs decorating
this arch. By the fourth century, Rome was on its way down.
Rather than struggle with original carvings, the makers of this
arch plugged in bits and pieces scavenged from existing monuments. The arch is newly restored and looking great. But any
meaning read into the stone will be very jumbled.

• *The Roman Forum* (Foro Romano) *is to the right of the Arch,
100 meters west. If you're ready for a visit, see the next chapter.*

rome

ROMAN FORUM TOUR

Heart of the Empire

The Forum was the political, religious, and commercial center of the city. Rome's most important temples and halls of justice were here. This was the place for religious processions, elections, important speeches, and parades by conquering generals. As Rome's empire expanded, these few acres of land became the center of the civilized world.

Orientation

Cost: Free. (There's a €6.20 charge to visit the Palatine Hill above the Forum; see next chapter.)

Hours: Daily 09:00 to 09:15 or an hour before dark.

Getting There: The closest Metro stop is Colosseo. The Forum's main entrance—where this tour begins—is near the Arch of Constantine and the Colosseum.

Information: Street vendors between the Colosseum and Forum sell small *Rome, Past and Present* books with plastic overlays that restore the ruins (marked €10.50, offer €8). Tel. 06-3974-9907.

Length of Our Tour: Allow one hour.

Overview

• *Walk through the entrance nearest the Colosseum. Hike up the ramp marked "Via Sacra." Stand next to the triumphal Arch of Titus and look out over the rubble-littered valley called the Forum.*

The hill in the distance with the bell tower is Capitol Hill. Immediately to your left, with all the trees, is Palatine Hill. The valley in-between is rectangular, running roughly east (the Colosseum end) to west (Capitol Hill). The rocky path at your feet is the Via Sacra, which runs through the trees, past the large brick Senate building, under the Arch of Septimius Severus—#13 on map on page 65—and (originally) up Capitol Hill.

THE FORUM

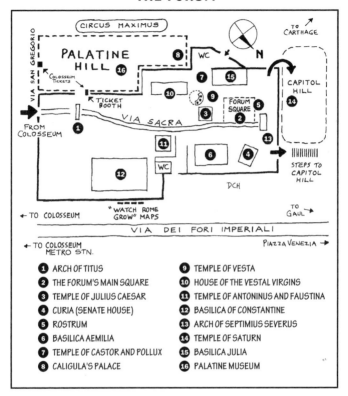

1 ARCH OF TITUS
2 THE FORUM'S MAIN SQUARE
3 TEMPLE OF JULIUS CAESAR
4 CURIA (SENATE HOUSE)
5 ROSTRUM
6 BASILICA AEMILIA
7 TEMPLE OF CASTOR AND POLLUX
8 CALIGULA'S PALACE
9 TEMPLE OF VESTA
10 HOUSE OF THE VESTAL VIRGINS
11 TEMPLE OF ANTONINUS AND FAUSTINA
12 BASILICA OF CONSTANTINE
13 ARCH OF SEPTIMIUS SEVERUS
14 TEMPLE OF SATURN
15 BASILICA JULIA
16 PALATINE MUSEUM

Picture being here when a conquering general returned to Rome with crates of booty. The valley was full of gleaming white buildings topped with bronze roofs. The Via Sacra—Main Street of the Forum—would be lined with citizens waving branches and carrying torches. The trumpets would sound as the parade began. First came porters, carrying chests full of gold and jewels. Then came a parade of exotic animals from the conquered lands—elephants, giraffes, hippopot-amuses—for the crowd to "ooh" and "ahh" at. Next were the prisoners in chains, with the captive king on a wheeled platform so the people could jeer and spit at him. Finally, the conquering hero himself

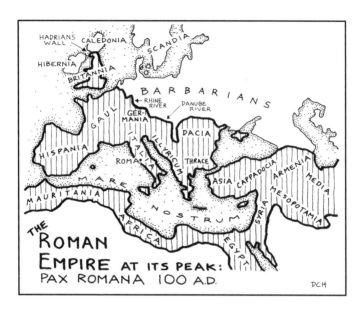

THE
**ROMAN
EMPIRE** AT ITS PEAK:
PAX ROMANA 100 A.D.

would drive down in his four-horse chariot, with rose petals strewn in his path. The whole procession would go the length of the Forum and up the face of Capitol Hill to the Temple of Saturn (the 8 big columns midway up the hill—#14 on map on page 65), where they'd place the booty in Rome's coffers. They'd continue up to the summit to the Temple of Jupiter (not visible today) to dedicate the victory to the King of the Gods.

1. Arch of Titus (Arco di Tito)

The Arch of Titus commemorated the Roman victory over the province of Judea (Israel) in A.D. 70. The Romans had a reputation as benevolent conquerors who tolerated the local customs and

rulers. All they required was allegiance to the Empire, which could be shown by worshiping the current emperor as a god. No problem for most con-quered people, who already had half a dozen gods on their prayer lists. But the Israelites' god was jealous and refused to let his people worship the emperor. Israel revolted. After a short but bitter war, the Romans defeated the rebels, took Jerusalem, and sacked their temple.

Rome—Republic and Empire (500 B.C.–A.D. 500)

Ancient Rome spanned about a thousand years, from 500 B.C. to A.D. 500. During that time, Rome expanded from a small tribe of barbarians to a vast empire, then dwindled slowly to city size again. For the first 500 years, when Rome's armies made her ruler of the Italian peninsula and beyond, Rome was a republic governed by elected senators. Over the next 500 years, a time of world conquest and eventual decline, Rome was an empire ruled by a military-backed dictator.

Julius Caesar bridged the gap between republic and empire. This ambitious general and politician, popular with the people because of his military victories and charisma, suspended the Roman constitution and assumed dictatorial powers around 50 B.C., until he was assassinated by a conspiracy of senators. His adopted son, Augustus, succeeded him, and soon "Caesar" was not just a name but a title.

Emperor Augustus ushered in the Pax Romana, or Roman peace (from A.D. 1–200), a time when Rome reached her peak and controlled an empire that stretched even beyond Eurail—from Scotland to Egypt, from Turkey to Morocco.

The propaganda value of Roman art is demonstrated on the inside of this arch, where a relief shows the emperor Titus in a chariot being crowned by the Goddess Victory. (Thanks to the tolls of modern pollution, they both look like they've been through the wars.) The other side shows the sacking of the temple—soldiers carrying a Jewish candelabrum and other plunder. The two (unfinished) plaques on poles were to have listed the conquered cities.

The brutal crushing of this rebellion (and another one 60 years later) devastated the nation of Israel. With no temple as a center for their faith, the Jews scattered throughout the world (the Diaspora). There would be no Jewish political entity again for two thousand years, until modern Israel was created after World War II.

• *Stroll into the Forum, down the Via Sacra. Pass through the trees and between ruined buildings until it opens up to a flat, grassy area.*

2. The Forum's Main Square

The original Forum, or main square, was this flat patch about the size of a football field, stretching to the foot of Capitol Hill. Surrounding it were temples, law courts, government buildings, and triumphal arches.

Rome was born right here. According to legend, twin brothers Romulus (Rome) and Remus were orphaned in infancy and raised by a she-wolf on top of the Palatine. Growing up, they found it hard to get dates. So they and their cohorts attacked the nearby Sabine tribe, fought them here in this valley, and kidnapped their women. After they made peace, the marshy valley became the meeting place and then the trading center for the scattered tribes on the surrounding hillsides.

The square was the busiest and most crowded—and often the seediest—section of town. Besides the senators, politicians, and currency exchangers, there were even sleazier types—souvenir hawkers, fortune-tellers, gamblers, slave marketers, drunks, hookers, lawyers, and tour guides.

The Forum is now rubble, no denying it, but imagine it in its prime: blinding white marble buildings with 13-meter-high columns and shining bronze roofs; rows of statues painted in realistic colors; chariots rattling down the Via Sacra. Mentally replace tourists in T-shirts with tribunes in togas. Imagine the buildings towering and the people buzzing around you while an orator gives a rabble-rousing speech from the Rostrum. If things still look like just a pile of rocks, at least tell yourself, "But Julius Caesar once leaned against these rocks."

• *At the east end of the main square sit the foundations of a temple now capped with a peaked wood-and-metal roof...*

3. The Temple of Julius Caesar (Templo del Divo Giulio, or "Ara di Cesare")

Julius Caesar's body was burned on this spot—right under the metal roof—after his assassination.

Caesar (100–44 B.C.) changed Rome—and the Forum—dramatically. He cleared out many of the wooden market stalls and began to ring the square with even grander buildings. (Caesar's house was located behind the temple, near that clump of trees.)

However, not every-
one liked his urban design
or his politics. When he
assumed dictatorial powers,
he was ambushed and
stabbed to death by a conspiracy of senators, including his adopted son, Brutus
(*Et tu, Brute?*).

The funeral was held
here, facing the main square. The citizens gathered and speeches
were made. Mark Antony stood up to say (in Shakespeare's words),
"Friends, Romans, countrymen, lend me your ears. I come to bury
Caesar, not to praise him." When Caesar's body was burned, the
citizens who still loved him threw anything at hand on the fire,
requiring the fire department to come put it out. Later, Emperor
Augustus dedicated this temple in his name, making Caesar the
first Roman to be a god.

• *Head down the Via Sacra toward the arch of Septimius Severus.*
Stop at the big, well-preserved brick building with the triangular roof.
If the door's open, look in.

4. The Curia

The Senate House (Curia) was the most important political building in the Forum. Three hundred senators, elected by the citizens
of Rome, met here to debate and create the laws of the land.
Their wooden seats once circled the building in three tiers; the
Senate president's podium sat at the far end. The marble floor is
from ancient times. Listen to the echoes in this vast room—the
acoustics are great.

Rome prided itself on being a republic. Early in the city's history,
its people threw out the king and established rule by elected
representatives. Each Roman citizen was free to speak his mind
and have a say in public policy. Even when emperors became the
supreme authority, the Senate was a power to be reckoned with.

(Note: Although Julius
Caesar was assassinated
in "the Senate," it wasn't
here—the Senate was
temporarily meeting
across town.)

A statue and two
reliefs inside the Curia
help build our mental
image of the Forum.

The statue, made of porphyry marble in about A.D. 100, with its plugged-in head, arms, and feet missing, was a tribute to an emperor, probably Hadrian or Trajan. The two relief panels may have decorated the Rostrum. One shows a government amnesty on debt, with people burning their debt records, while the other shows intact architecture and the latest fashion in togas.

• *Go back down the Senate steps to the metal guardrail and look right to a three-meter-high wall marked . . .*

5. Rostrum (Rostri)

Nowhere was Roman freedom more apparent than at this "Speaker's Corner." The Rostrum was a raised platform, three meters high and 25 meters long, decorated with statues, columns, and the prows of ships (*rostra*). Rome's orators, great and small, came here trying to draw a crowd and sway public opinion. Mark Antony rose to offer Caesar the laurel-leaf crown of kingship, which Caesar publicly (and hypocritically) refused while privately becoming a dictator. Men such as Cicero railed against the corruption and decadence that came with the city's newfound wealth. In later years, daring citizens even spoke out against the emperors, reminding them that Rome was once free.

Picture the backdrop these speakers would have had—a mountain of marble buildings piling up on Capitol Hill. The impressive Temple of Saturn (eight remaining columns) stood to the left. And, in imperial times, these voices of democracy would have been dwarfed by images of empire such as the huge Arch of Septimius Severus (A.D. 203). The tall Column of Phocas nearby, one of the last great monuments erected in the Forum, was originally topped by a bronze statue.

In front of the Rostrum are trees bearing fruits that were sacred to the ancient Romans: olives (provided food, light, and preservatives), figs (tasty), and wine grapes (made a popular export product).

• *Return to the Temple of Julius Caesar and turn left up the exit ramp. From here, you can look down at the remains of . . .*

6. Basilica Aemilia

A basilica was a Roman hall of justice. In a society that was as legal-minded as America is today, you needed a lot of lawyers and a big place to put them. Citizens came here to work out matters such as inheritances and building permits, or to sue somebody.

Notice the layout. It was a long, rectangular building. The stubby columns all in a row form one long, central hall flanked by two side aisles. Medieval Christian churches adopted this basilica floor plan.

• *Return again to the Temple of Julius Caesar. Notice the ruts in the stone street in front of the temple—carved by chariot wheels. To the right of the temple are the three tall Corinthian columns of the Temple of Castor and Pollux—#7 on map on page 65. Beyond that is Palatine Hill.*

8. Caligula's Palace

Emperor Caligula (ruled A.D. 37–41) had a huge palace on Palatine Hill overlooking the Forum. It actually sprawled down the hill into the Forum (some supporting arches remain in the hillside), with an entrance by the Temple of Castor and Pollux.

Caligula was not a nice person. He tortured enemies, stole senators' wives, and parked his chariot in handicap spaces. But Rome's luxury-loving emperors only added to the glory of the Forum, with each one trying to make his mark on history.

• *To the left of the Temple of Castor and Pollux, find the remains of a small white circular temple . . .*

9. The Temple of Vesta

This was Rome's most sacred spot. Rome considered itself one big family, and this temple represented a circular hut, like the kind Rome's first families lived in. Inside, a fire burned, just as in a Roman home. And back in the days before lighters and matches, you never wanted your fire to go out. As long as the sacred flame burned, Rome would stand. The flame was tended by priestesses known as Vestal Virgins.

• *Around the back of the Temple of Vesta you'll find two rectangular brick pools. These stood in the courtyard of . . .*

10. The House of the Vestal Virgins

The Vestal Virgins lived in a two-story building surrounding a central courtyard with these two pools at one end. Rows of statues to the left and right marked the long sides of the building. This place was the model—both architecturally and sexually— for medieval convents and monasteries.

The six Vestal Virgins, chosen from noble families before they reached the age of 10, served a 30-year term. Honored and revered by the Romans, the Vestals even had their own box opposite the emperor in the Colosseum.

As the name implies, a Vestal took a vow of chastity. If she served her term faithfully—abstaining for 30 years—she was given a huge dowry, honored with a statue (like the ones at left), and allowed to marry (life begins at 40?). But if they found any Virgin who wasn't, she was strapped to a funeral car, paraded through the streets of the Forum, taken to a crypt, given a loaf of bread and a lamp... and buried alive. Many women suffered the latter fate.

• *Return to the Via Sacra. Pause at the well-preserved Temple of Antoninus and Faustina.*

11. Temple of Antoninus and Faustina

These 17-meter-tall Corinthian (leafy) columns must have been awe-inspiring to out-of-towners who grew up in thatched huts. Although the temple has been reconstructed as a church, you can still see the basic layout—a staircase led to a shaded porch (the columns), which admitted you to the main building (now a church) where the statue of the god sat. Originally, these columns supported a triangular pediment decorated with sculptures.

• *Now head uphill, back up the Via Sacra, in the direction of the Colosseum. Many of the large basalt stones under your feet were walked on by Caesar Augustus 2,000 years ago. Veer left on the path leading to the three enormous arches.*

12. Basilica of Constantine

Yes, these are big arches. But they represent only one third of the original Basilica of Constantine, a mammoth hall of justice. The arches were matched by a similar set along the Via Sacra side (only a few squat brick piers remain). Between them ran the central hall,

which was spanned by a roof 40 meters high—about 17 meters higher than the side arches you see. (The stub of brick you see sticking up once spanned the central hall.) The hall itself was as long as a football field, lavishly furnished with colorful inlaid marble, fountains, and statues, and filled with strolling Romans. At the far (west) end was an enormous marble statue of Emperor Constantine on a throne (pieces of this statue are on display in Rome's Capitol Hill Museum).

This building was larger than Basilica Aemilia but had the same general shape—rectangular, with a long central hall flanked by two side halls.

Rome Falls

This peak of Roman grandeur is a good place to talk about the Fall of Rome. Again, Rome lasted 1,000 years—500 years of growth, 200 years of peak power, and 300 years of gradual decay. The Fall had many causes, among them the barbarians that pecked away at Rome's borders. Christians blame the Fall on moral decay. Pagans blamed it on Christians. Marxists blame it on a shallow economy based on spoils of war. (Pat Buchanan blamed it on Marxists.) Whatever the reasons, the far-flung Empire could no longer keep its grip on conquered lands, and it pulled back. Barbarian tribes from Germany and Asia attacked the Italian peninsula and even looted Rome itself in A.D. 410, leveling many of the buildings in the Forum. In 476, when the last emperor checked out and switched off the lights, Europe plunged into centuries of ignorance, poverty, and weak government—the Dark Ages.

But Rome lived on in the Catholic Church. Catholicism was the state religion of Rome's last generations. Emperors became popes (both called themselves Pontifex Maximus), senators became bishops, orators became priests, and basilicas became churches. Christian worship services required a larger meeting hall than

Roman temples provided, so they used the spacious Roman basilica (hall of justice) as the model for their churches. Cathedrals from France to Spain to England, from Romanesque to Gothic to Renaissance, all have the same basic floor plan as a Roman basilica. And remember that the goal for the greatest church building project ever—that of St. Peter's—was to "put the dome of the Pantheon atop the Basilica of Constantine." The glory of Rome never quite died.

PALATINE
HILL
TOUR

If you found the Forum absolutely enthralling, you'll be mildly entertained by Palatine Hill. It's certainly jam-packed with history— "the huts of Romulus and Remus," the huge Imperial Palace, a view of the Circus Maximus—but there's only the barest skeleton of rubble left to support all that history. Palatine Hill is highly recommended for serious sightseers with low expectations.

Orientation

Cost: €6.20, covered by €16 combo-ticket.
Hours: Daily 09:00 to 19:15 or an hour before dark.
Getting There: Enter the Palatine Hill from within the Forum (the entrance closest to the Colosseum; Metro: Colosseo). Buy your ticket at the booth about 30 meters uphill from the Arch of Titus.
Length of Our Tour: Allow 90 minutes.
• *After you buy your ticket, follow the path the ancients walked, straight up the hill. At the top of the hill, keep heading to the gray, modern building housing the museum ("Antaquario Palatino"). Orient with your back to the museum, so you're facing the Forum (roughly north).*

THE IMPERIAL PALACE

You're standing at the center of a huge palace, the residence of emperors for three centuries. Orgies, royal weddings, assassinations, concerts, intrigues, births, funerals, banquets, and the occasional Tupperware party took place within these walls.

What walls? The row of umbrella pines to the east (to your right as you face the Forum) now marks one edge of the palace. The reconstructed brick tower (at about 11 o'clock, as you face the Forum) was the northwest corner. The palace also stretched behind you (the area behind the museum) and beneath you, since some of the palace had a lower floor. The area to your left was

PALATINE HILL

- **1** MAIN COURTYARD
- **2** THRONE ROOM
- **3** BANQUET HALL
- **4** STADIUM
- **5** PRIVATE WING OF PALACE
- **6** "LOGGIA STATI MATTEI" MUSEUM
- **7** LOWER COURTYARD
- **8** CIRCUS MAXIMUS
- **9** MUSEUM (ANTAQUARIO PALATINO)
- **10** HOUSE OF LIVIA AND AUGUSTUS
- **11** PALACE OF TIBERIUS AND CALIGULA (AND CRYPTOPORTICUS TUNNEL)
- **12** IRON AGE HUTS
- **13** TEMPLE OF CYBELE

the official wing of the palace; to your right were the private quarters. All in all, it made a cozy little 150,000-square-foot pad.

The palace was built by Emperor Domitian around A.D. 81. His family was trying to rid Rome of the bitter taste of Nero, and this palace was a way of one-upping Nero and his Golden House.

• *To your left (as you face the Forum) is a big rectangular field with an octagonal brick design in the center. Let's start with the Official Wing (Domus Flavia) of the palace: its main courtyard, throne room, and banquet hall.*

1. Main Courtyard (Peristilio)

The brick octagon was a sunken fountain in the middle of an open-air courtyard. Like even the humblest Roman homes, this palace was built around an oasis of peace where you could enjoy the sun, catch the precious rain, and listen to the babble of moving water. The courtyard was lined with columns (notice the fragments) supporting an arcade for shade. Originally, the floor and walls of the courtyard were faced with shiny white marble.

• *Step between the big, brick wall-stumps at the north (Forum) end of the courtyard and enter the...*

2. Throne Room

The Throne Room was the official center of power, the nerve center of an empire that controlled some 50 million people from Scotland to Africa. The curved apse of the largest brick stump (there's now a plaque on it) marks the spot where the emperor sat on his throne for official business.

Imagine being a Roman citizen summoned by the emperor. You'd enter the palace through the main doorway (now a gap) at the far (Forum) end of the room, having climbed up three flights of a monumental staircase. The floor and walls dazzled with green, purple, red, white, and yellow marble. Along the walls were 12 colossal statues of Roman gods. The ceiling towered seven stories overhead. On either side were doorways leading to a basilica and the emperor's private temple. Ahead of you, in the apse, sat the emperor on a raised throne, dressed in royal purple, with a crown of laurel leaves on his head and a sceptre cradled in his arm. Big braziers burned on either side, throwing off a flickering light. As you approached, you'd raise your arm to greet him, saying, "*Ave, Cesare!*" The words would echo through the great hall.

• *From the Throne Room, return to the courtyard and walk to the far (south) end, to the square area with a sunken floor now covered with gravel.*

3. Banquet Hall (Triclinium)

The floor level of the banquet hall was a foot higher than the sunken level we see. It was raised on brick pillars (some of the raised floor still remains) and heated by air from underground stoves. At the far end of the room, the platform and curved apse mark the spot where the emperor ate while looking down on his subjects. On either side of the room are windows that the guests could look through to see oval-shaped fountains (these still remain) bubbling in an artificial cavern.

Here, the wealthiest Romans enjoyed the spoils that poured

into Rome from their vast empire. Reclining on a couch, waited on by slaves, you'd order bowls of larks' tongues or a roast pig stuffed with live birds, then wash it down with wine. When you were stuffed, but the waiters brought yet another delicacy, you could call for a feather, vomit, and start all over. Dancing, dark-skinned slave girls from Egypt or flute players from Greece entertained. If you fancied one, he or she was yours—the bedrooms were just down the hall.

Or so went the stories. In fact, many emperors were just and simple men, continuing the old Roman traditions of hard work and moderate tastes. But just as many were power-mad scoundrels who used their power to indulge their every urge.

• *The palace's stadium is 100 meters to the east. Belly up to the railing and look down on the elliptical track.*

4. Stadium (Hippodromo)

One-hundred-fifty meters long, this cigar-shaped, sunken stadium was the palace's rec room. It looks like a race track and may have

been used for foot and horse races, but it also held gardens with strolling paths. The oval running track at the south end was added later. The emperor had a raised box on the 50-yard line, in the curved apse across from you. At the north end were changing rooms, and the marble fragments that litter the ground once held up an arcade.

5. Private Wing (Domus Augustana) of the Palace

The area between the stadium and official wing held the private rooms of the emperor and his extended family. Today, a lone umbrella pine on a mound marks the courtyard of this wing. Wander through the maze of rooms (many of them reconstructed), noticing:

• The typical Roman building method: Build a brick shell, fill it with concrete, then finish it with either plaster (you'll see an occasional faded fresco) or slabs of marble. The small, round pockmarks on many walls show where the marble was fastened.

• Some brick walls have brick arches incorporated within

them. These "blind arches" were structural elements that allowed the walls to be built higher. The iron bar clamps are recent additions and hold the crumbling walls together.

• Niches and apses once held statues. Every family had their own household gods and displayed small images of these guardian spirits, as well as busts of honored ancestors.

• The fragments of columns, reliefs, and sculpture scattered about suggest the wealth of this great palace.

• Finally, notice the floor plan—a complex, fantasyland maze of small, private, sometimes even curved rooms.

6. "Loggia Stati Mattei" Museum

This museum is located in one of the rooms of the Domus Augustana. From the balcony of this reconstructed room, look down on the original frescoes dug out from the ancient Temple of Isis (located near where the Throne Room was later built).

• *In the south part of the Domus Augustana, you can look down on the ruins of the lower story.*

7. Lower Courtyard (Peristilio)

This open-air courtyard has the concave-convex remains of a large fountain that must have been a marvel. Try to mentally reconstruct the palace that surrounded this fountain. The emperors could look down on it from the upper story (where you're standing) or view it from the rooms around it on the lower story, where the emperor and his family ate their meals in private.

The lower story was built into the slope of the hill. The southern part of the palace was an extension of the hillside, supported beneath your feet by big arches.

• *Head to the southern edge of the hill, overlooking the Circus Maximus. Lean over the railing and you can see the concave shape of the palace's southern facade.*

8. Circus Maximus

If the gladiator show at the Colosseum was sold out, you could always get a seat at the Circus Max. In an early version of today's demolition derby, Ben Hur and his fellow charioteers once raced recklessly around this oblong course.

The chariots circled around the cigar-shaped mound in the center (notice the lone cypress tree that now marks one

end of the mound). Bleachers (now grassy banks) originally
surrounded the track (see artist's reconstruction on this page).

The track was 400 meters long, while the whole stadium measured 650 by 220 meters and seated—get this—250,000 people.
The wooden bleachers once collapsed during a race, killing 13,000.

The horses started
from a starting gate at the
west end (to your right),
while the public entered at
the other end. Races consisted of seven laps (about
1.5 km total). In such a
small space, collisions and
overturned chariots were common. The charioteers were usually
poor low-borns who used this dangerous sport to get rich and
famous. Many succeeded.

The public was crazy about the races. There were 12 per day,
240 days a year. Four teams dominated the competition—Reds,
Whites, Blues, and Greens—and every citizen was fanatically
devoted to one of them. Obviously, the emperors had the best
seats in the house; built into the palace's curved facade was a box
overlooking the track. For their pleasure, emperors occasionally
had the circus floor carpeted with designs in colored powders.

Picture the scene: intact palace; emperor watching; a quarter
of a million Romans cheering, jeering, and furiously betting.

Horses raced here for over a thousand years. The track was
originally built by Rome's Etruscan kings (c. 600 B.C.), and the
spectacles continued into the Christian era, until 549, despite
church disapproval.

From this viewpoint, looking to the left, you can see the ruins
of the Baths of Caracalla rising above the trees a kilometer away.
About 1.5 kilometers beyond that, the Appian Way led from a
grand gate in the ancient wall, past the catacombs, to Brindisi.

9. Museum (Antaquario Palatino)

The museum contains statues and frescoes that help you imagine
the luxury of the Imperial Palatine. Upstairs, pause at the statue
of "Magna Mater" on her throne. This Great Mother brought
life and fertility to the Roman people, who worshiped her at the
Temple of Cybele (which we'll see later). Her arms and foot
were destroyed by time, but there was always a cavity where her
head should be—this was a standard Roman device in which
interchangeable heads could be inserted. In this case, the Magna
Mater's "head" was actually a sacred, black, cone-shaped meteorite
that caused astonishment when it fell from the sky.

Downstairs, there's a helpful model of the Iron Age huts of Romulus (and a WC).

• *From the museum, head west, crossing the octagonal brick courtyard and continuing through ruins. As you exit the ruins of the Imperial Palace, you'll run into a railing overlooking the sunken remains (with modern corrugated roof) of . . .*

10. House of Livia and Augustus (Casa di Livia)

Augustus, the first emperor, lived in this house (and the neighboring house to the left) with his wife, Livia. Peer down the hallways at the small rooms with honeycomb brick walls that surrounded a small courtyard. This relatively humble dwelling is a far cry from the later Imperial Palace. There are some fine frescoes inside (usually closed for restoration), but Casa di Livia had little of the lavish marble found in most homes of the wealthy.

Augustus was a modest man who believed in traditional Roman values. His wife and daughter wove the clothes he wore. He slept in the same small bedroom for 40 years. He burned the midnight oil in his study, reading and writing his memoirs. Augustus set a standard for emperors' conduct that would last . . . until his death.

• *To the right of Casa di Livia are the Farnese Gardens. These grow over the remains of what was the . . .*

11. Palace of Tiberius and Caligula (and the Cryptoporticus Tunnel)

Augustus' successors started the trend of fancy imperial homes with a palace that sprawled all the way from here to the Forum. Virtually nothing is visible today. One feature that remains is the underground passageway (Cripto Portico) that runs from near Casa di Livia toward the Forum—140 meters long. Look down and see some of the mosaic floor of this once marbled and stuccoed passageway, which is lit by windows along the side. Emperors used it as a private, convenient way to get around the hill. Caligula may have been murdered in it.

• *Circle clockwise around Casa di Livia to an area with several archaeological sites. Head for the far, southwest corner. Under a corrugated roof are the scant outlines of . . .*

12. Iron Age Huts—"The Huts of Romulus and Remus"

Looking down into the pit from the railing (stand at the far right), you can make out some elliptical and rectangular shapes carved into the stony ground—the partial outlines of huts from around 850 B.C. Some have holes that once held the wooden posts of round, thatched huts.

Romulus and Remus were babies orphaned when their mother, a disgraced Vestal Virgin, was executed. (She claimed she was raped by Mars, the War God.) Set adrift on the flooding Tiber, the babes washed ashore at the foot of Palatine Hill. A shepherd discovered them in a cave just downhill from here, being suckled by a mother wolf. He took them home—maybe right here—and raised them as his own. When Romulus grew up, he killed his brother and built a square wall (Roma Quadrata) around the tiny hill town, founding the city of Rome. (The dusty-orange blocks of volcanic tufa stone may be part of that wall.)

For centuries, the Romans believed this legend. They honored the wolf's cave (called the "Lupercal," where every February 15th men dressed up in animal skins and whipped women), as well as the spot where Romulus lived. Lo and behold, in the 1940s, these huts were unearthed, and the legend became history.

• *Over your right shoulder are the rectangular walls of the...*

13. Temple of Cybele (Templo di Cibele), or Temple of the Magna Mater

The statue of the Mother of the Gods, built to thank her for saving Rome from Hannibal and his elephants (c. 200 B.C.), once sat at the far end of this temple. (It's now in the museum.)

March 22 was a festive day at the temple, as new priests joined the Magna Mater's cult by castrating themselves and draping their testicles over the altar, helping the goddess fertilize the world.

Here at Rome's birthplace, reflect on the rise of this great culture—from thatched hut to the modest house of Augustus to the massive Imperial Palace of Domitian, with its stadium and view over the Circus Maximus. It's no wonder that the hill's name gave us our English word "palace."

• *A good way to complete your Palatine visit is to stroll through the Farnese Gardens (Horti Farnesini), admiring its exotic plants, fountains, underground grotto, and pavilions. When you see the view of the Forum from here, you'll know why the Palatine was Rome's best address.*

TRAJAN'S COLUMN, FORUM & MARKET

Rome's expansion peaked under Emperor Trajan (ruled A.D. 98–117)— the empire stretched from Scotland to the Sahara, from Spain to Asia. A triumphant Trajan returned to Rome with his booty and shook it all over the city. He extended the Forum by building his own commercial, political, and religious center nearby, complete with temples, law courts, squares lined with shops, and a monumental column.

Orientation

Cost and Hours: Trajan's Column and Forum are free and always viewable; Trajan's Market, including access to part of the Forum, costs €6.20 (summer Tue–Sun 09:00–18:30, winter 09:00–16:30, closed Mon, tel. 06-3600-4399).

Getting There: Trajan's Column is just a few steps off Piazza Venezia, on Via dei Fori Imperiali, across the street from the Victor Emmanuel Monument. Trajan's Forum stretches southeast of the Column toward the Colosseum. The entrance to Trajan's (dull) Market is uphill from the Column on Via IV Novembre.

Length of Our Tour: Thirty minutes, or an hour if you also enter Trajan's Market.

Trajan's Column

Rising 42 meters and decorated with a spiral relief of 2,500 figures trumpeting Trajan's exploits, this is the world's grandest column from antiquity. The ashes of Trajan and his wife were once held in the base, and the sun once glinted off a polished bronze statue of Trajan at the top. (Today, St. Peter is on top.) Built as a stack of 17 marble doughnuts, the column is hollow (note the small window slots) with a spiral staircase inside, leading up to the balcony.

The relief unfolds like a scroll, telling the story of Trajan's

conquest of Dacia (modern-day Romania). It starts at the bottom
with a trickle of water that becomes a river and soon picks up boats
full of supplies. Then come the soldiers themselves, who spill out
from the gates of the city. A river god (bottom band, south side)

surfaces to bless the journey. Along
the way (second band), they build
roads and forts to sustain the vast
enterprise, including (third band,
south side) Trajan's kilometer-long
bridge over the Danube, the longest
for a thousand years. (Find the 3
tiny, crisscross rectangles representing the wooden span.) Trajan himself (fourth band, in military skirt
with toga over his arm) mounts a
podium to fire up the troops. They hop into a Roman galley ship
(fifth band) and head off to fight the valiant Dacians in the middle
of a forest (eighth band). Finally, at the very top, the Romans
hold a sacrifice to give thanks for the victory, while the captured
armor is displayed on the pedestal. Originally, the entire story was
painted in bright colors. If you unwound the scroll, it would stretch
over two football fields—it's far longer than the frieze around the
Greek Parthenon. (An unscrolled copy is in E.U.R.'s Museum of
Roman Civilization.)

Trajan's Forum
The best place to view the ruins of the Forum is on the
pedestrian-only Via Alessandrina, which cuts right through
the heart of the Forum.

Trajan's Forum starts at Trajan's Column and runs about
100 meters southeast toward the Colosseum. It's mostly rubble
today. The highlight of the Forum, then and now, is Trajan's
Market—the big, crescent-shaped brick structure that rises up
the flank of Quirinal Hill.

Trajan's Forum was a crucial expansion of the old Roman
Forum, which was too small and ceremonial to fill the commercial
needs of a booming city of over a million people. Built with the
staggering haul of gold plundered from Dacia (Romania), this
was the largest Forum ever—its opulence astounded even the
jaded Romans. You entered at the Colosseum end through a
triumphal arch and were greeted in the main square by a large
statue of the soldier-king on a horse. Continuing on, you'd
enter the Basilica Ulpia (the gray granite columns near Trajan's
Column), the largest law court of its day. Finally, at the far end
was Trajan's Column, flanked by two libraries that contained the

— TRAJAN'S FORUM —

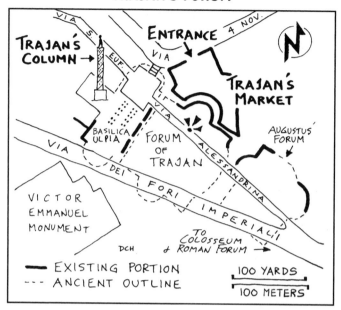

EXISTING PORTION
ANCIENT OUTLINE

100 YARDS
100 METERS

world's knowledge in Greek and Latin. Balconies on the libraries gave close-up looks at the upper reliefs of the Column, in case anyone doubted the outcome of Trajan's war.

To build his Forum, Trajan literally moved mountains. He cut away a ridge that once connected the Quirinal and Capitol Hills, creating this artificial valley. Trajan's Column marks the hill's original height—42 meters (125 feet).

Trajan's Market

Nestled into the cut-away curve of the hill is the semicircular brick complex of Trajan's Market. Part shopping mall, part warehouse, part administration office, it was a place Romans gravitated to and a popular spot to bring out-of-town guests.

At ground level, the 11 tall arches housed (shallow) shops selling fresh fruit, vegetables, and flowers to shoppers who passed by on the street. The 26 windows (above) lighted a covered walkway lined with shops that sold wine and olive oil. On the roof runs a street that held still more shops, making about 150 in all. Shoppers could browse through goods from every corner of Rome's vast empire—exotic fruits from Africa, spices from Asia, fish and chips from Britain.

Above the semicircle, the upper floors of the complex housed bureaucrats in charge of a crucial element of city life—doling out free grain to unemployed citizens, who lived off the wealth plundered from distant lands. Better to pacify them than risk a riot. Above the offices, at the very top, rises a tower added in the Middle Ages.

Going inside the Market (which costs €6.20) is worth it only for those with a good imagination and stamina for stairs. As you walk by the shops in the welcome shade of the arcade, you'll get a better sense of how inviting the Market must have been in its heyday. Today, only one shop is "furnished"—crammed with the clay jugs used to store olive oil (upstairs from ticket booth). Throughout the Market, you'll get expansive views of the ancient Forum and modern Victor Emmanuel Monument.

The Market was beautiful and functional, filling the space of the curved hill perfectly and echoing the curved side of the Forum's main courtyard. (The wall of rough tufa stones in the left foreground once extended into a semicircle.) Unlike most Roman buildings, the brick facade was never covered with plaster or marble. The architect liked the simple contrast between warm brick and the white stone lining the arches and windows.

Trajan's conquest of the Dacians was Rome's last and greatest foreign conquest. It produced this Forum, which stood for centuries as a symbol of a truly cosmopolitan civilization.

PANTHEON
TOUR

The Pantheon was a Roman temple dedicated to all *(pan)* the gods *(theos)*. First built in 27 B.C. (under "M. Agrippa"—as you'll see on the facade), it was completely rebuilt around A.D. 120 by the emperor Hadrian.

Several interesting churches are clustered near the Pantheon. These are described below, after the Pantheon Tour.

Orientation

Cost: Free.

Hours: Monday through Saturday 08:30 to 19:30, Sunday and holidays 09:00 to 13:00 and 14:00 to 18:00.

Getting There: Walk (it's a 10- to 15-min walk from the Forum), take a taxi, or catch a bus. Bus #64 runs daily and frequently between the train station and Vatican City, stopping at Largo Argentina, a few blocks south of the Pantheon. The *electrico* mini-bus #116 runs between Campo de' Fiori and Piazza Barberini via the Pantheon (daily except Sun).

Information: Tel. 06-6830-0230. Small gift shop inside entrance. Nearest WCs at bars and McDonald's on the square.

Length of Our Tour: Allow 45 minutes.

Cuisine Art: You'll find Rome's best *gelato* at Gelateria della Palma, two blocks in front of the Pantheon (Via della Maddalena 20); for lunch or dinner ideas, see page 216.

Exterior

The Pantheon doesn't look like much from the outside, but this is perhaps the most influential building in art history. Its dome was the model for the Florence cathedral dome, which

launched the Renaissance, and for Michelangelo's dome of
St. Peter's, which capped it all off. Even Washington, D.C.'s
Capitol Building was inspired by this dome.

• *Pass between the enormous, one-piece granite columns (most are original) and through the enormous, original bronze door. Stand awestruck
for a moment, then take a seat on the bench to your right.*

Interior

The dome, which was the largest
made until the Renaissance, is
set on a circular base. The mathematical perfection of this dome-
on-a-base design is a testament to
Roman engineering. The dome is
as high as it is wide—44 meters
(142 feet). To picture it, imagine
a basketball set inside a waste-
basket so that it just touches bottom.

The dome is made from concrete that gets lighter and thinner
as it reaches the top. The walls at the base are seven meters thick
and made from heavy travertine concrete, while near the top they're
less than two meters thick and made of a light volcanic rock. Both
Brunelleschi and Michelangelo studied this dome before building
their own (in Florence and in the Vatican). Remember, St. Peter's
Cathedral is really only "the dome of the Pantheon atop the Basilica
of Constantine."

The oculus, or eye-in-the-sky,
at the top, the building's only light
source, is almost 10 meters across.
The 1,800-year-old floor has holes
in it and slants toward the edges to
let the rainwater drain. The marble
floor is largely restored, though the
designs are close to the originals.

In ancient times, this was a
one-stop-shopping temple where you could worship any of the
gods whose statues decorated the niches. Early in the Middle Ages
the Pantheon became a Christian church (from "all the gods" to
"all the martyrs"), which saved it from architectural cannibalism
and ensured its upkeep through the Dark Ages. The only major
destruction came in the 17th century, when the pope took the
bronze plating and melted it down to build the huge bronze
canopy over the altar at St. Peter's. About the only new things in the
interior are the decorative statues and the tombs of famous
people, such as the artist Raphael (to the left of the main altar,

in the glass case) and modern Italy's first two kings, Victor Emmanuel II and Umberto I (to the right).

The Pantheon is the only continuously used ancient building in Rome. When you leave, you'll notice how the rest of the city has risen on 20 centuries of rubble.

The Pantheon also contains the world's greatest Roman column. There it is, spanning the entire 44 meters from heaven to earth—the pillar of light from the oculus.

CHURCHES NEAR THE PANTHEON
Francesi, Gesu, Sopra Minerva, and St. Ignazio
Church of San Luigi dei Francesi

The one truly *magnifique* sight in the French national church is the chapel in the far left corner, which was decorated by Caravaggio (free, but bring coins to buy light, Fri–Wed 07:30–12:30, 15:30–19:00, Thu 07:30–12:30, sightseers should avoid Mass at 07:30 and 19:00, modest dress recommended).

The Calling of St. Matthew (left wall)

Matthew and his well-dressed, tax-collecting cronies sit in a dingy bar and count the money they've extorted. Suddenly, two men in robes and bare feet enter from the right—Jesus and Peter. Jesus' "Creation-of-Adam" hand emerges from the darkness to point at Matthew. A shaft of light extends the gesture, lighting up the face of bearded Matthew, who points to himself Last Supper–style to ask, "You talking to me?" Jesus came to convince Matthew to leave his sleazy job and preach Love. Matthew did.

In this, his first large-scale work, 29-year-old Caravaggio (1571–1610) shocked critics and clerics by showing a holy scene in a down-to-earth location. Lower-class people in everyday clothes were his models; his setting was a dive bar (which he knew well). Christ's teeny gold halo is the only hint of the supernatural, as Caravaggio makes a bold proclamation—that miracles are natural events experienced in a profound way.

St. Matthew and the Angel (center wall)

Matthew followed Christ's call, traveled with Him, and (supposedly) wrote His life's story (the Gospel of Matthew). Here, Matthew is hard at work when he's interrupted by an angel with a few suggestions. Matthew's bald head, wrinkled face, and grizzled beard make him an all-too-human saint. Even the teen angel lacks a holy glow—he just hangs there. Caravaggio paints a dark background, then shines a dramatic spotlight on the few things that tell the story.

The Martyrdom of St. Matthew (right wall)

Matthew lies prone, while a truly scary man straddles him and brandishes a sword. The bystanders shrink away from this angry executioner. Caravaggio shines his harsh third-degree spotlight on Matthew and the killer, who are the focus of the painting. The other figures swirl around them in a circle (with the executioner's arm as the radius). Matthew, who thought he had given up everything to follow Christ, now gives up his life as well.

When the chapel was unveiled in 1600, Caravaggio's ultra-realism shocked Rome. (Find his bearded self-portrait in the background.) Although he died only 10 years later, his uncompromising details, emotional subjects, odd compositions, and dramatic lighting set the tone for later Baroque painters.

Il Gesu Church

The center of the Jesuit order and the best symbol of the Catholic Counter-Reformation, the Gesu Church is packed with overblown art and underappreciated history (free, daily 06:00–12:30, 16:00–19:15, modest dress recommended).

Exterior

The facade looks ho-hum, like a thousand no-name Catholic churches scattered from Europe to Southern California ... until you realize that this was the first, the model for the others. Its scroll-like shoulders  were revolutionary, breaking up the rigid rectangles of Renaissance architecture and signaling the coming of Baroque.

The building to the right of the church is where Ignatius of Loyola, the founder of the Jesuits, lived, worked, and died.

• *Step inside the church and look up at the huge painting on the ceiling.*

1. Ceiling Fresco and Stucco—The Triumph of the Name of Jesus (by Il Baciccia)

A twisted tangle of bodies—the Damned—spills over the edge of the ceiling, plunging downward on the way to Hell. The painted bodies become 3-D stucco bodies in a classic example of Baroque multimedia.

During the Counter-Reformation, when Catholics fought Protestants for the hearts and minds of the world's Christians, art became propaganda. The moral here is clear—this is the fate of Protestant heretics who dared pervert the true teachings of Jesus.

2. The Nave

When the church was originally built (1568), the walls were white and the decor was simple. It was designed for what the Jesuits did best—teaching. The Jesuits wanted to educate Catholics to prepare them for the onslaught of probing Protestant questions. The church's nave is like one big lecture hall, with no traditional side aisles.

In the 1500s, the best way to keep Protestants from stealing your church members was to reason with them. By the 1600s, it was easier to kill them, and the Thirty Years' War raged across Europe. The church became crusted over with the colorful, bombastic, jingoistic Baroque you see today.

3. Tomb and Altarpiece of St. Ignatius of Loyola
(left transept)

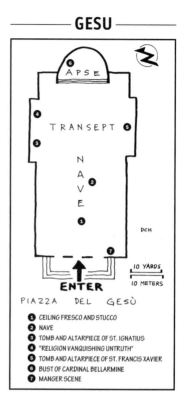

GESU

- **1** CEILING FRESCO AND STUCCO
- **2** NAVE
- **3** TOMB AND ALTARPIECE OF ST. IGNATIUS
- **4** "RELIGION VANQUISHING UNTRUTH"
- **5** TOMB AND ALTARPIECE OF ST. FRANCIS XAVIER
- **6** BUST OF CARDINAL BELLARMINE
- **7** MANGER SCENE

The gleaming statue of Ignatius spreads his arms wide and gazes up, receiving a vision from on high. Ignatius (1491–1556) was a Spanish soldier during the era of conquistadores. Then, at age 30, he was struck down by a cannonball. While convalescing, he was seized by the burning desire to change his life. He wandered Europe and traveled to Jerusalem. He meditated with monks. He lived in a cave. At 33, he enrolled in a school for boys to pick up the knowledge he'd missed. He studied in Paris and in Rome. Finally, after almost two decades of learning and seeking, he found a way to combine his military training with his spiritual aspirations.

In 1540, the pope gave approval to Ignatius and his small band of followers—the Society of Jesus (Jesuits). These monks, organized like a military company, vowed complete obedience to their "General," and placed themselves at the service of the pope. Their mission? To be the intellectual warriors doing battle with heretics. They were in the right place at the right time—Ignatius and Luther were almost exact contemporaries.

Ignatius' body lies in the small coffin beneath the statue (near ground level). This simple, intense man might have been embarrassed by the lavish memorial to him, with its silver, gold, green marble, and lapis lazuli columns. Above Ignatius, a statue of God stands near a lapis lazuli globe (the biggest in the world) and gestures as though to say, "Go and spread the Word to every land"... which the Jesuits tried to do.

4. "Religion Vanquishing Untruth"
(marble statue group to the right of Ignatius)
This statue (and a similar one to the left of Ignatius) shows the Church as a woman hauling back and punching out a bunch of miserable Protestants. Not too subtle.

Yes, the Jesuits got a reputation for unfeeling dedication to truth above all else, but their weapons were words, ideas, and critical reasoning. They taught and defended the recently revamped doctrines of the Council of Trent (1545–1563).

5. Tomb and Altarpiece of St. Francis Xavier
(right transept)
This was also the Age of Discovery, when Spain and Portugal were colonizing and Christianizing the world, using force if necessary. Francis Xavier joined a Portuguese expedition and headed out to convert the heathen. He touched down in Africa, India, Indonesia, China, and Japan. Along the way, he learned new languages and customs as he tried to communicate a strange, monotheistic religion to puzzled polytheists.

He had been on the road more than a decade (1552) when he died on an island off China (see the painting over the altar). Thanks largely to zealous Jesuits such as Francis, Catholicism became a truly worldwide religion.

6. Bust of Cardinal Roberto Bellarmine—
by Gian Lorenzo Bernini
The great sculptor Bernini attended this church and honored Bellarmine with a bust. The Jesuits produced some great, open-minded thinkers, from the poet Gerard Manley Hopkins to modern mystic Teilhard de Chardin. But they also caught flak for being closed-minded to new ideas. In the 1700s, several countries expelled them, and finally

(1773), the pope even banned the Society. Chastened, they were brought back (1814) and today fill the staff of many a Catholic college.

7. Manger Scene
Don't leave before pressing the button to see water run, comets shoot, and angels fly. It's cheesy, but it carries on the Baroque tradition of using whiz-bang effects to make the supernatural seem tangible to the masses.

Church of Santa Maria sopra Minerva

This is the only Gothic church you'll see in Rome (free, daily 07:00–12:00, 15:30–19:00, modest dress recommended). On a little square behind the Pantheon to the east, past the Bernini statue of an elephant carrying an Egyptian obelisk, this Dominican church was built *sopra* (over) a pre-Christian temple of Minerva. Before stepping in, notice the high-water marks on the wall (right of the door). Inside, you'll see that the lower parts of the frescoes were lost to floods. (After the last great flood, in 1870, Rome built the present embankments, finally breaking the spirit of the Tiber River.)

When this Gothic-style church was built, Rome was almost a ghost town. Little was built during this time. Much of what was built during this period was redone in the Baroque style. This church is a refreshing exception.

St. Catherine's body lies under the altar (her head is in Siena). In the 1300s, she convinced the pope to return from France to Rome, thus saving Italy from untold chaos.

Left of the altar stands a little-known Michelangelo statue, *Christ Bearing the Cross*. Michelangelo gave Jesus an athlete's body (a striking contrast to the docile Christ of medieval art), but he left the face to one of his pupils. Fra Angelico's simple tomb is farther to the left, near the back door. Head over to the right (south transept), pop in a coin for light, and enjoy a Filippo Lippi fresco showing scenes of St. Thomas Aquinas (big man in black and white).

Exit the church via its rear door (behind the Michelangelo statue), walk down Fra Angelico lane (spy any artisans at work), turn left, and walk to the next square. On your right, you'll find the...

Church of St. Ignazio

This church is a riot of Baroque illusions (free, daily 07:00–12:30, 15:30–19:00, modest dress recommended). Study the fresco over the door and the ceiling in the nave. Then stand on the yellow disk on the floor, between the two stars. Look at the (black) dome. Watching the dome, walk under and past it. Building project runs out of money? Hire a painter to paint a fake, flat dome.

Back outside, the church faces the yellow headquarters of the Carabinieri police force, forming a square that has been compared to a stage set, with several converging streets. Sit on the church steps, admire the theatrical yellow backdrop, and watch the "actors" enter one way and exit another, in the human opera that is modern Rome.

BATHS OF DIOCLETIAN TOUR

rome

Of all the marvelous structures built by the Romans, their public baths were the grandest, and the Baths of Diocletian were the granddaddy of them all. These baths sprawled over 10 acres—roughly twice the area of the entire Forum—and could cleanse 3,000 Romans at once. Today, there are several sections you can visit:

The **Church of Santa Maria degli Angeli**, housed in the former main hall of the baths, is the single most impressive place. The entrance is on Piazza Repubblica (free).

The **Octagonal Hall**, also facing Piazza Repubblica, is a well-preserved rotunda that now displays sculpture from the baths. As you face the church entrance, the Octagonal Hall is 100 meters to your left (free, Tue–Sat 09:00–14:00, Sun 09:00–13:00, closed Mon, borrow the English-description booklet, handy WC hidden in the back corner through an unmarked door).

The **Museum of the Bath** (Museo Nazionale Romano Terme di Diocleziano) contains tons of Roman tombstones and inscriptions. The entrance faces the Termini train station (€4.20, covered by €16 combo-ticket, Tue–Sun 09:00–19:45, closed Mon, Viale E. De Nicola 79, tel. 06-488-0530).

Energetic architecture wonks can even walk the perimeter of the baths: from Via Torino to Piazza dei Cinquecento to Via Volturno to Via XX Settembre.

SANTA MARIA DEGLI ANGELI

From Piazza Repubblica, step through the curved brick wall of the ancient baths and into a church.

The Church's Entry Hall—The Baths' Tepidarium

This round-domed room with an oculus (open skylight) was once the cooling-off room of the baths where medium, "tepid"

— BATHS OF DIOCLETIAN —

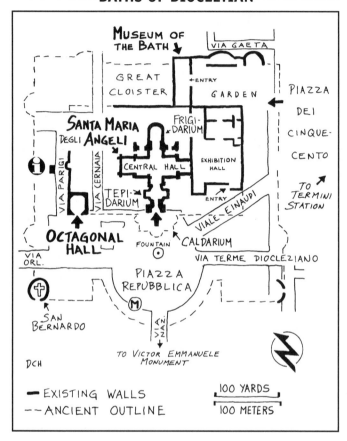

MUSEUM OF THE BATH

VIA GAETA

GREAT CLOISTER

←ENTRY

GARDEN

PIAZZA DEI CINQUE- CENTO

SANTA MARIA DEGLI ANGELI

FRIGI- DARIUM

VIA PARIGI

VIA CERNAIA

CENTRAL HALL

EXHIBITION HALL

TO TERMINI STATION

TEPI- DARIUM

ENTRY

VIALE EINAUDI

OCTAGONAL HALL

FOUNTAIN

CALDARIUM

VIA ORL.

VIA TERME DIOCLEZIANO

PIAZZA REPUBBLICA

M

SAN BERNARDO

N
W E
S

TO VICTOR EMMANUELE MONUMENT

DCH

— EXISTING WALLS
-- ANCIENT OUTLINE

100 YARDS
100 METERS

temperatures were maintained. Romans loved to sweat out last night's indulgences at the baths. After stripping in the locker rooms, they'd enter the steam baths of the *caldarium*, located where Piazza Repubblica is today. The *caldarium* had wood furnaces, stoked by slaves, under the raised floors to heat the floors and hot tubs. The ceiling was low to keep the room steamy.

Next, you'd pass into this *tepidarium*, where masseuses would rub you down and scrape you off with a stick (Romans didn't use soap). Finally, you'd continue on to the central area of the baths...

The Church's Large Transept— The Baths' Central Hall

This hall retains the grandeur of the ancient baths. It's the size of a football field and seven stories high—originally higher, since the old floor was five meters below its present level. The ceiling's crisscross arches were an architectural feat unmatched for a thousand years. The eight red granite columns are original—stand next to one and feel its 1.5-meter girth. (Only the 8 in the transept proper are original. The others are made of plastered-over brick.) The original hall was covered with mosaics, marble, and gold, and lined with statues.

From here, Romans could continue (through what is now the apse, near altar) into a large, open-air courtyard to take a dip in the huge swimming pool (in the *frigidarium*) that paralleled this huge hall. Many other rooms, gardens, and courtyards extended beyond what we see here. The baths were built in only 10 years (around A.D. 300)—amazing when you think of the centuries it took builders of puny medieval cathedrals, such as Paris' Notre-Dame.

Mentally undress your fellow tourists and churchgoers, and imagine hundreds of naked or togaed Romans wrestling, doing jumping jacks, singing in the baths, networking, or just milling about.

The baths were more than washrooms. They were health clubs with exercising areas, equipment, and swimming pools. They had gardens for socializing. Libraries, shops, bars, fast-food vendors, pedicurists, depilators, and brothels catered to every Roman need. Most important, perhaps, the baths offered a spacious, cool-in-summer/warm-in-winter place for Romans to get out of their stuffy apartments, schmooze, or simply hang out.

Admission was virtually free, requiring only the smallest coin. Baths were open to men and women—and during Nero's reign, coed bathing was popular—but generally there were either separate rooms or separate entry times. Most Romans went daily.

The church we see today was designed by Michelangelo (1561), who placed the entry at the right end of the transept and used the long hall as the nave. Later, when Piazza Repubblica became an important Roman intersection, another architect reoriented it, turning Michelangelo's nave into a long transept, so people could enter from the piazza.

Step into the sacristy (free, left of main altar) for an

explanation of the church's architectural history and copies of Michelangelo's drawings.

Notice the immensity and power of the Roman brickwork in this room (and just outside in the courtyard). Large building projects like this were political security: They provided employment and fed the masses.

Diocletian (ruled A.D. 285–305) struggled with a system to rule his unwieldy empire. He broke it into zones ruled by four "tetrarchs." Later, Constantine divided the empire into east and west halves. During Diocletian's "tetrarchs" period, architecture and art were grandiose, but almost a caricature of greatness—meant to proclaim to Romans that their city was still the power it no longer was.

The baths were one of the last great structures built before Rome's 200-year fall. They functioned until A.D. 537, when barbarians cut the city's aqueducts, plunging Rome into a thousand years of B.O.

OCTAGONAL HALL (AULA OTTAGONA)

This octagonal building, capped by a dome with a hole in the top, may have served as a cool room (*frigidarium*), with small pools of cold water for plunging into. Or, because of its many doors, it may simply have been a large intersection, connecting other parts of the baths. Either way, it's one of the best-preserved rooms. Originally, the floor was seven meters lower—as you can see through the glass-covered hole in the floor. The graceful iron grid supported the canopy of a 1928 planetarium. Today, the hall's a free gallery showing off fine bronze and marble statues, some of which once decorated the Baths of Caracalla. Of the statues (mostly Roman copies of Greek originals—athletes, gods, Herculeses, satyrs, and portraits), two merit a close look:

The Boxer at Rest—Pugilatore, First Century B.C.

An exhausted boxer sits between rounds and gasps for air. See the brass-knuckle-type Roman boxing gloves. Textbook Hellenistic, this bronze statue is realistic and full of emotion. His face is scarred, his back muscles are knotted, and he's got cauliflower ears. He's losing.

Slumped over, he turns with a questioning look ("Why am I losing again?"), and eyes that once held glass now make him look empty indeed. I coulda been a contender.

Roman Aristocrat
The aristocrat's face is older than his body. This bronze-casted statue is typical of the day: Take a body of Alexander the Great and pop on a portrait bust.

MUSEUM OF THE BATH

The museum is separated into three parts: Epigraphy (most interesting), History of the Proto-Latin People (dull pre-Roman vases, etc.), and the Michelangelesque cloister (yawn).

Epigraphy

Epigraphy means the study of inscribed objects, and ancient Rome was big on writing, from tombs to laws to graffiti to propaganda. This museum is difficult to appreciate quickly, and most travelers will find more history presented on a grander scale at the nearby National Museum of Rome. Here, you'll see many fragments, and it takes time and patience to read the English descriptions.

The building, with its white walls and suspended walkways, has a light, airy feeling, but the only reminder of the Baths is in the museum's name.

The first room contains pottery, bronze vases, and votive offerings found in tombs and at altars. Notice the display case containing the artifacts from a warrior's grave: swords, a helmet, and a remarkably well-preserved anatomical breastplate (475 B.C.).

In the side hall (loaded with tombstones), look for the two pottery cups in a small glass case titled "Catiline and Cato Seeking Votes" (63 B.C.). In hopes of getting elected, candidates would write their names on cups, fill the cups with food or drink, then pass them out to people on the street. Politicians—and voters—haven't changed much.

On the second floor (which holds more tombstones), follow the walkways—lined with even more tombstones—to a room holding several statues and the sarcophagus of a man who supervised gladiators (A.D. 270). On his tomb, the peaceful country scene of sheep and shepherds is disturbed by huge, hungry lions gobbling sheep (at the sides of the tomb), while gladiators race along the top.

On the third-floor walkway, you'll find some early Christian inscriptions (3rd century), one showing the sign of the fish (symbolizing Jesus) and an anchor (representing the cross). Also on the third floor, near the back of the hall (and the WCs), are tombs showing Romans in action: cobbling shoes, spinning yarn, dancing, working with marble, and fighting gladiators.

In the uppermost room, a painted marble bas-relief shows the god Mithras stabbing a bull. The cult of Mithras believed this act brought life to the universe (though it didn't do much for the bull). It's thought that much marble sculpture was once painted.

History of the Proto-Latin People

The two wings of this section, which overlook the cloister, would be more interesting if air-conditioned. One wing tells the history of the pre-Roman people and the other displays articles found in tombs (from the 11th to 6th century B.C.). Although ancient Rome was impressive, this part of the museum reminds us that the Roman civilization built upon a solid foundation.

Michelangelesque Cloister

So named because it was based on a drawing by the great Renaissance artist, this large, elegant cloister was built in 1565. As you enter the courtyard, look left to see the lifelike monk. There's no need to walk around the cloisters, unless you like mediocre statuary.

PIAZZA REPUBBLICA

The piazza, shaped like an exedra (a semicircular recess in a wall or building), echoes a wall of the original baths. It was called Piazza Exedra until Italian unification. The thundering Via Nazionale starts at what was an ancient door. Look down it (past the almost erotic nymphs of the Naiad fountain) to the Victor Emmanuel Monument. The Art Nouveau fountain of the four water nymphs created quite a stir when unveiled in 1911. The nymphs were modeled after a set of twins, who kept coming to visit as late as the 1960s for a reminder of their nubile youth.

NATIONAL MUSEUM OF ROME
TOUR

Museo Nazionale Romano
Palazzo Massimo alla Terme

rome

Rome lasted a thousand years, and so do most Roman history courses. But if you want a breezy overview of this fascinating society, there's no better place than the Palazzo Massimo.

Rome took Greek culture and wrote it in capital letters. Thanks to this lack of originality, ancient Greek statues were preserved for our enjoyment today. But the Romans also pioneered an unheard-of path in art—sculpting painfully realistic portraits of emperors and important citizens.

Think of this museum as a walk back in time. As you gaze at the same statues the Romans swooned over, Rome comes alive—from Romulus sucking a wolf's teat to Julius Caesar's murder to Caligula's incest to the coming of Christianity.

Orientation

Cost: €6.20, covered by €16 combo-ticket.

Hours: Tuesday through Sunday 09:00 to 19:45, closed Monday, open some summer Saturdays until 23:00.

Getting There: The museum is about 100 meters from the Termini train station (Metro: Termini). As you leave the station, it's the sandstone-brick building on your left. Enter at the far end, at Largo di Villa Peretti.

Information: Tel. 06-481-5576.

Tours: An audioguide costs €3.60 (buy ticket first, then get audioguide at bookshop). To see the fresco collection on the second floor, you must reserve an entry time for a free, 45-minute tour led by an Italian-speaking guide. If interested, book the next available tour when you buy your ticket.

Length of Our Tour: Allow two hours.

Starring: The Discus Thrower, Roman emperor busts, original Greek statues, and fine Roman copies.

THE MUSEUM

The Palazzo Massimo is now the permanent home of the major Greek and Roman statues that were formerly scattered in other museums. However, some famous statues once in the collection (*The Boxer at Rest*, *Gaul Killing His Wife*, and *Ludovisi Throne*) are still located elsewhere. With its long name, Palazzo Massimo seems to be searching for a convenient nickname to distinguish it from other "Museo Nazionales" around town.

The museum is rectangular, with rooms and hallways built around a central courtyard. The ground-floor displays follow Rome's history as it changes from democratic republic to dictatorial empire. The first-floor exhibits take Rome from its peak to its slow fall. The second floor houses rare frescoes and fine mosaics (reservation for a free tour required), and the basement displays coins and everyday objects. As you tour this museum, note that "room" is *sala* in Italian and "hall" is *galleria*.

GROUND FLOOR—FROM SENATORS TO CAESARS

• *Buy your ticket and pass through the turnstile, where you'll find . . .*

Minerva

It's big, it's gaudy, it's a weird goddess from a pagan cult. Welcome to the Roman world. The statue is also a good reminder that all the statues in this museum—now missing limbs, scarred by erosion, or weathered down to the bare stone—were once whole and painted to look as lifelike as possible.

• *Continuing to the right, you'll stand at the head of . . .*

Gallery I—Portrait Heads from the Republic, 500–1 B.C.

Stare into the eyes of these stern, hardy, no-nonsense, farmer-stock people who founded Rome. The wrinkles and crags of these original "ugly Republicans" tell the story of Rome's roots as a small agricultural tribe that fought neighboring tribes for survival.

These faces are brutally realistic, unlike more idealized Greek statues. Romans honored their ancestors and worthy citizens in the "family" (*gens*) of Rome. They wanted lifelike statues to remember them by, and to instruct the young with their air of moral rectitude.

In its first 500 years, Rome was a republic ruled by a Senate of wealthy landowners. But as Rome expanded throughout Italy and the economy shifted from farming to booty, changes were needed.

• *Enter room I (Sala I) and find the bust of . . .*

——— NATIONAL MUSEUM—GROUND FLOOR ———

- **1** MINERVA
- **2** PORTRAIT HEADS
- **3** JULIUS CAESAR
- **4** OCTAVIAN
- **5** LIVIA
- **6** TIBERIUS
- **7** CALIGULA
- **8** AUGUSTUS
- **9** FOUR FRESCOES
- **10** ALEXANDER THE GREAT
- **11** SOCRATES
- **12** NIOBID
- **13** GREEK-MANIA

Julius Caesar (Rilievo con Ritratto c.d. Cesare), c. 100–44 B.C.

The prominent brow, the strong nose, the male-pattern baldness with the forward comb-over—these features identify the man who changed Rome forever. (Or some think it may be a lookalike.)

When this charismatic general swept onto the scene, Rome was in chaos. Rich landowners were fighting middle-class plebs, who wanted their slice of the plunder. Slaves such as Spartacus were picking up hoes and hacking up masters. And renegade generals—the new providers of wealth and security in a booty economy—were becoming dictators. (Notice the life-size statue of an unknown but obviously once-renowned general.)

Caesar was a people's favorite. He conquered Gaul (France), then sacked Egypt, then impregnated Cleopatra. He defeated rivals and made them his allies. He gave great speeches. Chicks dug him.

With the army at his back and the people in awe, he took the reins of government, instituted sweeping changes, made himself the center of power... and antagonized lovers of freedom everywhere.

A band of Republican assassins surrounded him in a Senate meeting. He called out for help as one by one they stepped up to take turns stabbing him. The senators sat and watched in silence. One of the killers was his adopted son, Brutus, and Caesar died saying, "*Et tu, Brute?*"

• *At the end of the hall, enter into...*

Room IV—The Julio-Claudian Family: Rome's First Emperors, c. 50 B.C.–A.D. 68

Julius Caesar died, but his family name, his politics, and his flamboyance lived on, turning Rome into a dictatorship ruled by an emperor.

• *In this room, look at the busts along the wall (to the right as you enter), and find the "scalped" bust of...*

Octavian, later called Augustus (Ritratto di Ottaviano), ruled 27 B.C.–A.D. 14

Julius Caesar adopted his grandnephew, Octavian. After the assassination, 18-year-old Octavian got revenge against Brutus and the others, then eliminated his own rivals, Mark Antony and wife Cleopatra. For the first time in almost a century of fighting, one general reigned supreme. Octavian took the title "Augustus" ("He who just keeps getting bigger"), becoming the first of the emperors who would rule Rome for the next 500 years. (More on Augustus later.)

Livia (Ritratto di Livia)

Augustus/Octavian's wife, Livia, was a major power behind the throne. Her stern, thin-lipped gaze withered rivals at court. Her hairstyle—bunched up in a peak, braided down the center, and tied in back—became the rage of Europe, as her face appeared everywhere in statues and on coins. Notice that by the next generation (Antonia Minore, Livia's daughter-in-law), a simpler bun was chic. And by the following generation, it was tight curls. Empresses dictated fashion like emperors dictated policy.

Livia bore Augustus no sons. She lobbied hard for Tiberius, her own son by a first marriage, to succeed as emperor. Augustus didn't like him, but Livia was persuasive. He relented, ate some bad figs, and died—the gossip was that Livia poisoned him to seal the bargain. The pattern of succession was established—adopt a son from within the extended family—and Tiberius was proclaimed emperor.

Tiberius (Ritratto de Tiberio), ruled A.D. 14–37

Acne may have soured Tiberius to the world. Shy and sullen but diligent, he worked hard to be the easygoing leader of men Augustus had been. Early on, he was wise and patient, but he suffered personal setbacks. Politics forced him to divorce his only beloved and marry a slut. His favorite brother died, then his son. Embittered, he let subordinates run things and retired to Capri, where he built a villa with underground dungeons. There he hosted orgies of sex, drugs, torture, really loud music, and execution. At his side was his young grandnephew, whom he adopted as next emperor.

Caligula (Caligola; in the glass case), ruled A.D. 37–41

This emperor had sex with his sisters, tortured his enemies, stole friends' wives during dinner, then returned to rate their performance in bed, crucified Christians, tore up parking tickets, and had men kneel before him as a god. Caligula has become the archetype of a man with enough power to act out his basest fantasies.

Politically, he squandered Rome's money, then taxed and extorted from the citizens. Perhaps he was made mad by illness, perhaps he was the victim of vindictive historians, but still, no one mourned when assassins ambushed him and ran a sword through his privates. Rome was tiring of this family dynasty's dysfunction. Augustus must have been rolling in his grave... and they hadn't even seen Nero yet.

Before leaving the room, look around and see if you can spot a family resemblance. Livia's thin lips and Augustus' strong nose? Maybe.

Room V—Augustus and Rome's Legendary Birth

Statue of Augustus as Pontifex Maximus
(Ritratto di Augusto in Vesta di Offerente)

Here, 50-year-old Emperor Augustus takes off his armor and laurel-leaf crown and dons the simple hooded robes of a priest. In fact, Augustus was a down-to-earth man who lived simply, worked hard, read books, listened to underlings, and tried to restore traditional Roman values after the turbulence of Julius Caesar's time. He outwardly praised and defended the Senate and the Republic while actually becoming its emperor. Despite the excesses of his descendants, Augustus' reign marked the start of 200 years of peace and prosperity, the "Pax Romana."

See if the statue matches a

description of Augustus by a contemporary—the historian Seutonius: "He was unusually handsome. His expression was calm and mild. He had clear, bright eyes, in which was a kind of divine power. His eyebrows met. His hair was slightly curly and somewhat golden." Any variations were made by sculptors who idealized features to make him almost godlike.

Augustus proclaimed himself a god—not arrogantly or blasphemously, as Caligula later did, but as the honored "father" of the "family" of Rome. As the empire expanded, the vanquished had to worship the emperor's statue as a show of loyalty. Augustus even claimed he was descended from Romulus and Remus. Such propaganda solidified the emperor's hold over Rome as both political and spiritual head.

Four Frescoes of Rome's Mythical Origins (Fregio Pittorico, etc.)

These cartoon-strip frescoes (read right to left) tell the story of Augustus' legendary forebears.

1. Upper right fresco: Aeneas (red skin) arrives in Italy from Troy and fights the locals for a place to live.

2. Upper left: His wife (far left, seated, in purple) and son build a city wall around Rome. The womenfolk are safe and the city prospers.

3. Lower right: Several generations later, the God of War (in center, with red skin) lies in wait to rape and impregnate a Vestal Virgin.

4. Lower left: Her disgraced babies, Romulus and Remus, are placed in a basket (center) and set adrift on the Tiber River. They wash ashore, are suckled by a wolf, and finally (far left) taken in by a shepherd. These legendary babies, of course, grow up to found the city which makes real history.

• *Exit the room and go round the corner to busts of . . .*

Gallery III—Rome's Greek Mentors

Alexander the Great (Alessandro Magno)

Alexander the Great (356–323 B.C.) single-handedly created an empire by conquering, in just a few short years, lands from Greece to Egypt to Persia, spreading Greek culture and language along the way. Later, when the Romans conquered Greece (c. 200 B.C.), they inherited this preexisting collection of cultured, Greek-speaking cities ringing the Mediterranean.

Alexander's handsome statues set the standard for those of later Roman emperors. His features were chiseled and youthful, and he was adorned with pompous decorations, like a golden sunburst aura (which was fitted into holes). The greatest man of his day, he ruled the known world by the age of 30.

Alexander, a Macedonian, had learned Greek culture from his teacher, none other than the philosopher Aristotle. Aristotle's teacher was Plato, whose mentor was...

Socrates (Socrate)

This nonconformist critic of complacent thinking is the father of philosophy. The Greeks were an intellectual, introspective, sensitive, and artistic people. The Romans were practical, no-nonsense soldiers, salesmen, and bureaucrats. Many a Greek slave—warning a Roman Senator not to wear a plaid toga with a polka-dot robe—was more cultured than his master.

Room VII—Pure Greek Beauty in Greek Originals

Niobid (Niobide Ferita), 440 B.C.

The Romans were astonished by the beauty of Greek statues. This woman's smooth skin contrasts with the rough folds of her clothing. Her pose is angular but still balanced—notice how she twists naturally around an axis running straight up and down. She looks like a classical goddess awakening from a beautiful dream. But...

Circle around back. The hole bored in her back, right in that itchy place you can't quite reach, once held a golden arrow. The woman has been shot by Artemis, goddess of hunting, because her mother dared to boast to the gods about her kids. The Niobid reaches back in vain, trying to remove the arrow before it drains her of life.

Romans ate this stuff up: the sensual beauty, the underplayed pathos, the very Greekness of it. They crated up centuries-old statues like this and brought them home to their gardens and palaces. Appreciate the beauty in this room, since these are some of the world's rare, surviving Greek originals.

Room VIII—Greek Mania

By Julius Caesar's time, Rome was in the grip of a "Neo-Attic" craze, and there weren't enough old statues to meet the demand. Crafty Greeks began cranking out knock-offs of Greek originals for mass consumption. The works in this room were of extremely high quality, while others were more like cheesy fake *Davids* in a garden store.

To the Romans, this "art" was just furniture for their homes. An altar from a Greek temple became a place to set your wine, a sacred basin was a rain catcher, a statue of Athena took your olive pits. Different styles from different historical periods were mixed and matched to suit Roman tastes. The rich Roman who bought *Afrodite Pudica*, signed along the base by "Menophantos," would not have known or cared that the artist was copying a one-of-a-kind original done by the great Praxiteles 400 years before, back when Greece was Golden.

Rome conquered Greece, but the Greeks conquered the Romans.

• *Take a break, then head upstairs to the first floor.*

FIRST FLOOR

As we saw, Augustus' family did not always rule wisely. Under Nero (ruled A.D. 54–68), the debauchery, violence, and paranoia typical of the Julio-Claudians festered to a head. When the city burned in the great fire of 64, the Romans suspected Nero of torching it himself to clear land for his enormous luxury palace.

Enough. Facing a death sentence, Nero committed suicide with the help of a servant. An outsider was brought in to rule.

Room I—The Flavian Family

Vespasian (Vespasianus), ruled A.D. 69–79

Balding and wrinkled, with a big head, a double chin, and a shy smile, Vespasian was a common man. The son of a tax collector, he rose through the military ranks with a reputation as a competent drudge. As emperor, he restored integrity, raised taxes, started the Colosseum, and suppressed the Jewish rebellion in Palestine.

Domitian (Domitianus)

Vespasian's son, Domitian (emperor A.D. 81–96), used his father's tax revenues to construct the massive Imperial Palace on Palatine Hill, home to emperors for the next three centuries. Shown with his lips curled in a sneering smile, he was a moralistic prude who executed several Vestal ex-Virgins, while in private he took one mistress after another. Until...

Domitia

...until his stern wife found out and hired a servant to stab him in the groin. Domitia's hairstyle is a far cry from the "Livia" cut, with a high crown of tight curls.

NATIONAL MUSEUM—FIRST FLOOR

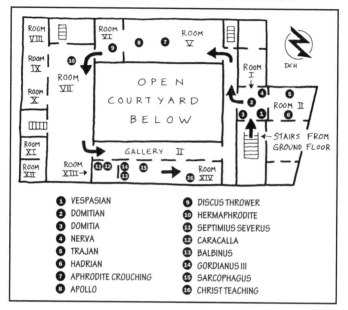

- **1** VESPASIAN
- **2** DOMITIAN
- **3** DOMITIA
- **4** NERVA
- **5** TRAJAN
- **6** HADRIAN
- **7** APHRODITE CROUCHING
- **8** APOLLO
- **9** DISCUS THROWER
- **10** HERMAPHRODITE
- **11** SEPTIMIUS SEVERUS
- **12** CARACALLA
- **13** BALBINUS
- **14** GORDIANUS III
- **15** SARCOPHAGUS
- **16** CHRIST TEACHING

Nerva

The Flavian dynasty was no better than its predecessors. Nerva, old and childless, made a bold, far-sighted move—he adopted a son from outside of Rome's corrupting influence.

Room II—A Cosmopolitan Culture

Trajan (Traianus-Hercules), ruled A.D. 98–117

Born in Spain, this conquering hero pushed Rome's borders to their greatest extent, creating a truly worldwide empire. The spoils of three continents funneled into a city of a million-plus people. Trajan could present himself as a "new Hercules," and no one found it funny. Romans felt a spirit of Manifest Destiny: "The gods desire that the City of Rome shall be the capital of all the countries of the world." (Livy)

Hadrian (Hadrianus), ruled A.D. 117–138

Hadrian was a fully cosmopolitan man. His beard—the first we've seen—shows his taste for foreign things; he poses like the Greek philosopher he imagined himself to be.

Hadrian was a voracious tourist, personally visiting almost

every corner of the vast empire, from Britain (where he built
Hadrian's Wall) to Egypt (where he sailed the Nile), from
Jerusalem (where he suppressed another Jewish revolt) to Athens
(where he soaked up classical culture). An omnivorous learner,
he scaled Mount Etna just to see what made a volcano tick. Back
home, he beautified Rome with the Pantheon and his Villa at
Tivoli, a microcosm of places he'd visited.

Hadrian is flanked here by the two loves of his life. His wife,
Sabina, with modest hairstyle and scarf, kept the home fires burning for her traveling husband. Hadrian was 50 years old when he
became captivated by the teenage boy, Antinous, with his curly
hair and full, sensual lips. Together they traveled the Nile, where
Antinous drowned. Hadrian wept. This public display of emotion,
somewhat embarrassing to the stoic Romans, became a legend
among Greeks, who erected Antinous statues everywhere.

Hadrian spent his last years at his lavish villa outside Rome,
surrounded by buildings and souvenirs that reminded him of his
traveling days.

Rooms V and VI—Rome's Grandeur

Pause at Rome's peak to admire the things the Romans found
beautiful. Imagine these statues in their original locations, in the
pleasure gardens of the Roman rich—surrounded by greenery,
with the splashing sound of fountains, the statues all painted in
bright, lifelike colors. Though executed by Romans, the themes
are mostly Greek, with godlike humans and human-looking gods.

Aphrodite Crouching (Afrodite Accovacciata)

Hadrian had good taste—he ordered a copy of this Greek classic for
his bathroom. The goddess of beauty crouches while bathing, then
turns to admire herself. This sets her whole body in motion—one
thigh goes down, one up; her head turns clockwise while her body
goes reverse—yet she's perfectly still. The crouch creates a series of
symmetrical love handles, molded by the sculp-
tor into the marble like wax.

Apollo

The god of light appears as a slender youth,
not some burly, powerful, autocratic god. He
stands *contrapposto*—originally he was leaning
against the tree—in a relaxed and very human
way. His curled hair is tied with a headband,
with strands that tumble down his neck.
His muscles and skin are smooth. (The rusty
stains come from the centuries Apollo spent

submerged in the Tiber.) Apollo is in a reflective mood, and the serenity and intelligence in his face show off classical Greece as a nation of thinkers.

The Discus Thrower (Discobolo)

An athlete winds up, about to unleash his pent-up energy and hurl the discus. The sculptor has frozen the moment for us, so we can examine the inner workings of the wonder called man. The perfect pecs and washboard abs make this human godlike. Geometrically, you could draw a perfect circle around him, with his hipbone at the center. He's natural yet ideal, twisting yet balanced, moving while at rest. For the Greeks, the universe was a rational place, and the human body was the perfect em-bodi-ment of the order found in nature.

This statue is the best-preserved Roman copy (not 1 member is missing—I checked) of the original Greek work by Myron (450 B.C.). Statues of athletes like this commonly stood in the baths, where Romans cultivated healthy bodies, minds, and social skills, hoping to live well-rounded lives. *The Discus Thrower*, with his geometrical perfection and godlike air, sums up all that is best in the classical world.

Room VII

Hermaphrodite Sleeping (Ermafrodito Dormiente)

After leaving the baths, a well-rounded Roman may head post-haste to an orgy, where he might see a reclining nude like this, be titillated, circle around for a closer look, and say, "Hey! (Insert your reaction here)!"

Room XIII—Beginning of the End

Septimius Severus, ruled A.D. 193–211

Rome's sprawling empire was starting to unravel, and it took a disciplined, emperor-general like this African to keep it together. Severus' victories on the frontier earned him a grand triumphal arch in the Forum, but here he seems to be rolling his eyes at the chaos growing around him.

Caracalla, ruled A.D. 211–217

The stubbly beard, cruel frown, and glaring eyes tell us that Severus' son was bad news. He murdered his little brother, Geta, to seize power, then proceeded to massacre thousands of loyal citizens on a whim. The army came to distrust rulers whose personal agenda got in their way, and Caracalla was stabbed in the back by a man whose brother had just been executed.

Room XIV—The Fall

There are a lot of scared faces in this room. People who grew up in the lap of luxury and security were witnessing the unthinkable— the disintegration of a thousand years of tradition. Rome never recovered from the chaos of the third century. Disease, corruption, revolts from within, and "barbarians" pecking away at the borders were body blows that sapped Rome's strength.

Balbinus, ruled A.D. 238

This old man was appointed emperor by the Senate, but he was no soldier, and the army didn't like him. He was one of some 20 emperors in the space of 40 years who were saluted, then mur- dered, at the whim of soldiers of fortune. At one point, the office of emperor was literally auctioned to the highest bidder. Balbinus, with his stubbly beard and forlorn look, knows he's lost the army's confidence, and he waits for the ax to fall. Next.

Gordianus III, ruled A.D. 238–244

The 13-year-old Gordianus, with barely a wisp of facial hair, was naive and pliable, the perfect choice—until he got old enough to question the generals. His assassins had no problem sneaking up on him because, as you can see, he had no ears.

Sarcophagus of a Procession (Sarcofago con Corteo, etc.), A.D. 270

This coffin shows a parade of digni- taries accompanying a new Roman leader. As they march up Capitol Hill, they huddle together, their backs to the wall, looking around suspiciously for assassins. Their faces reflect the fear of the age. Rome would stagger on for another 200 years, but the glory of old Rome was gone. The city was becoming a den of thugs, thieves, prostitutes, barbarians... and Christians.

Small Statuette of Christ Teaching (Cristo Docente), A.D. 350

Christ sits like a Roman senator—in a toga, holding a scroll, dispensing wisdom like the law of the land. The statue comes from those delirious days when formerly persecuted Christians could now "come out" and worship in public. Emperor Constantine (ruled 306–337) legalized Christianity, and within two generations it was Rome's official religion.

Whether Christianity invigorated or ruined Rome is debated, but the Fall was inevitable. Rome's once-great legions backpedaled, until even the city itself was raped and plundered by foreigners (410). In 476, the last emperor sold his title for a comfy pension plan, and "Rome" was just another dirty city with a big history. The barely flickering torch of ancient Rome was passed on to medieval Christians: Senators became bishops, basilicas became churches, and the Pontifex Maximus (Emperor) became the Pontifex Maximus (Pope).

THE REST OF THE MUSEUM

The second floor contains frescoes and mosaics that once deco-rated the walls and floors of Roman villas. The frescoes (in black, red, yellow, and blue) show a few scenes of people and animals but are mostly archi-tectural designs, with fake columns and "windows" that "look out" on landscape scenes. Granted, the collection is impressive, but the tour is in Italian (the guides *might* speak a little English), and it's a 45-minute commitment.

More interesting stuff is in the basement, housing coins and everyday objects from ancient Rome. In A.D. 300, one *denar* bought one egg. Evaluate Roman life by studying Diocletian's wage and price controls. Find your favorite emperor or empress on the coins using remote-controlled magnifying glasses.

CAPITOL HILL MUSEUM TOUR

Recently reopened, this museum is a joy. Perched on the top of Capitol Hill Square, its two buildings (Palazzo dei Conservatori and Palazzo Nuovo) are now connected by an underground passage—which leads to the Tabularium and panoramic views of the Roman Forum.

Orientation

Cost: €8, free on the last Sunday of the month.

Hours: Tuesday through Friday and Sunday 09:00 to 19:00, Saturday 09:30 to 23:00, closed Monday, January 1, May 1, and December 25.

Getting There: From Piazza Venezia or the Forum, walk uphill to the top of Capitol Hill (Campidoglio in Italian; pron. cahm-pee-dohl-yoh).

Information: You'll find some English descriptions within the museum. Free baggage check. Tel. 06-3996-7800.

Tour: The €3.60 audioguide, available only at the Palazzo dei Conservatori entrance, is good.

Length of Our Tour: Allow one hour.

Cuisine Art: Great view café—called Café Capitolino—upstairs in Palazzo dei Conservatori (also has an exterior entrance for public).

Starring: Ancient Greek and Roman statuary, plus 14th- to 17th-century paintings and Forum views.

MUSEUM OVERVIEW

To identify the museum's two buildings, face the equestrian statue on Capitol Hill Square (with your back to the grand stairway leading up to the square). The Palazzo Nuovo is on your left, the Palazzo dei Conservatori is on your right (closer to the river). Ahead is the Palazzo Senatorio (mayoral palace, not open to public); below it—and out of sight—are the Tabularium and underground passage connecting the two museum buildings.

The Palazzo dei Conservatori, built in the 16th century, originally housed city offices, as well as ancient statuary (such as the *She-Wolf* and *Boy Extracting a Thorn*) given by popes through-out the years to the city of Rome.

The Palazzo Nuovo, built across the square in the 17th century, was filled with the art that was, by then, overcrowding Palazzo dei Conservatori. The Palazzo Nuovo opened as a museum in 1737. When the painting gallery was added in the 18th century to the Palazzo dei Conservatori, art filled both buildings.

You can buy a ticket at either building (but if you want to rent an audioguide, go to Palazzo dei Conservatori). And, with your ticket, you can enter either museum (or connect the buildings underground). The ticket, valid for three hours, "starts" when it's scanned by the ticket taker.

Note that this museum is also referred to as the Capitoline Museums or Musei Capitolini. Same place.

•*Start at the...*

PALAZZO NUOVO

•*After your ticket is scanned, walk down the hall to the small courtyard on your left. Behind the glass is...*

Marcus Aurelius

This is the greatest surviving equestrian statue of antiquity. Marcus Aurelius was a Roman philosopher-emperor (ruled A.D. 161–180), known more for his *Meditations* than his prowess on the battlefield. Notice that he doesn't use stirrups. An Asian invention, those newfangled devices wouldn't arrive in Europe for another 500 years.

Dark-Age Christians thought the statue's hand was raised in blessing, which probably led to their misidentifying him as Constantine, the first Christian emperor. While most pagan statues were destroyed by Christians, "Constantine" was spared.

In 1538, Michelangelo placed this gilded bronze statue in the center of the square he designed, Capitol Hill Square, directly out-side this museum. During the last few years, the statue was moved inside and restored, while a copy was placed on the square.

• *Go up the stairs. The first room at the top contains one of the most famous pieces in the museum.*

Dying Gaul

A first-century-B.C. copy of a Greek original, this was sculpted to celebrate the
Greeks' victory over the Galatians. It's
thought this statue may have been part of a
larger sculpture group (long since lost).

Wounded in battle, the dying Gaul
holds himself upright, but barely. Minutes
earlier, before he was stabbed in the chest,
he'd been in his prime. Now he can only
watch helplessly as his life ebbs away. His
sword is useless against this last battle. With his messy hair, down-
cast eyes, and crumpled position, he poignantly reminds us that
every victory means a defeat.

• *In the next few rooms, take a quick look at...*

Ancient Roman Statues and Busts

A reddish faun glories in grapes and life, oblivious to the loss of his
penis (at least he still has his tail). The statue, found in a couple
dozen pieces in Hadrian's Villa, was skillfully restored. Check out
the ceilings in this room and elsewhere; this building is truly a
palazzo (palace).

More sculpture from Hadrian's
Villa (and elsewhere) fills the next
room, the large hall. Notice the
Wounded Amazon (near the window)
plucking her delicate dress away from
her breast. This is a Roman copy
of a fifth-century Greek original
by Polycletus.

Roll through the Room of
Philosophers (Socrates, Homer,
Euripdedes, Cicero, and many more) and the Room of Emperors
(Constantine's mom Helena rests center stage)—both rooms are
lined with rows of busts. In this 3-D yearbook of ancient history,
there are few labels. If you knock into anything, heads will roll,
but you won't know whose.

• *Enter the hallway and start down the hall. The small octagonal room—
off to your left—contains one of the museum's treasures.*

Capitoline Venus

This is a Roman copy of a Greek fourth-century original
by the master Praxiteles. Venus leaves the bath, modestly
covering herself (nearly). Unaware of being observed, with a
reason for being unclothed, she's nude instead of naked. Her

blank eyes hold no personality or emotion. Her fancy hairstyle is the only complicated thing about her. She is simply beautiful—generically erotic.

• *Farther down the hallway, enter the small room to your left.*

Mosaic of Doves

Four doves perch on the rim of a bronze bowl as one drinks water from the bowl. Minute bits make up this small, exquisite work. Found in the center of a floor in one of the rooms in Hadrian's Villa, this second-century A.D. mosaic was based on an earlier work done, of course, by the Greeks.

• *Head down the stairs to reach the underground passage (and WC). Follow signs to the . . .*

TABULARIUM

Built in the first century A.D., these sturdy, vacant rooms once held the archives of ancient Rome. The word Tabularium comes from "tablet," on which laws were written. Inside the Tabularium, you can look to your right to see the remains of an earlier temple, look up to see two huge white hunks of a temple overhang, and look down to see an underground passage, but the irresistible urge is to look out—at the Forum. This head-on view does justice to the Forum, giving you a more complete picture of the sprawl of ancient Rome.

The arcade of the Tabularium used to have more overlooks, but some of the arches were bricked up during the Middle Ages.

• *Leave the Tabularium, taking the underground passage and stairs up to Palazzo Conservatori.*

PALAZZO DEI CONSERVATORI

In the courtyard, enjoy the massive chunks of Constantine: his head, hand, and foot. When intact, this giant held the place of honor in the Basilica of Constantine in the Forum.

• *Go up to the room at the top of the stairs.*

Huge Statues, Huge Art—Roman Style

Here are more hunks of another statue of Constantine: head, finger, and a globe he held in his hand. The large wall paintings in this room commemorate the founding of Rome, from its wolfish origins (the twins Romulus and Remus nursed by a she-wolf) to the bloody battles fought with nearby tribes for supremacy. Everything about this room—the gargantuan Constantine, the gilded Hercules, and even the larger-than-life pope—is about power wielded by men.

• *For a contrast, power yourself straight ahead into the corner room to see one of the museum's highlights.*

Boy Extracting a Thorn (Spinario)

He's just a boy, intent only on picking a thorn out of his foot. As he bends over to reach his foot, his body sticks out at all angles, like a bony chicken wing. He's even scuffed up, the way small boys get. At this moment, nothing matters to him but that splinter. Our lives are filled with these mundane moments (when we'd give anything for a tweezers) rarely captured in art.
• *In the next room . . .*

Capitoline *She-Wolf*

The original bronze She-Wolf suckles the twins Romulus and Remus. The wolf is Etruscan from the fifth century B.C., the boys an invention of the Renaissance, the result—the symbol of Rome. Look into the eyes of the wolf. An animal looks back, with ragged ears, sharp teeth, and staring eyes. This wild animal, teamed with the wildest creatures of all—hungry babies—makes a powerful symbol for the tenacious city/empire of Rome.

• *In the next room . . .*

From Michelangelo to Medusa

Along with a kindly bust of Michelangelo, this room contains Bernini's scary bust of Medusa—even she looks distressed by the writhing snakes on her head. This goes way beyond a bad hair day.
• *Walk between Michelangelo and Medusa to the next room to discover the remarkable bust of . . .*

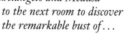

Commodus as Hercules

This dull-eyed emperor brat used to run around the palace in animal skins. Here he wears a lion's head over his own, and drapes the lion's paws over his chest. This lion king made a bad emperor.
• *Go upstairs to the . . .*

Painting Gallery

Wander among works by van Dyck, Velázquez (self-portrait near entry), Titian, Tintoretto, and Bellini. The highlights are two Caravaggios: *St. John the Baptist* and an earlier work, *The Fortune Teller* (both in the Santa Petronilla room).

• *Head upstairs to the café.*

VIEW CAFÉ

You've earned the café. Its huge outdoor view patio overlooks the domes of Rome. From the Tabularium, you saw the Forum, the heart of ancient Rome. From here, you see the churches, representing the religion that remained after Rome fell. Be here at sunset—it's divine.

r o m e

BORGHESE GALLERY TOUR

Galleria Borghese

More than just a great museum, Galleria Borghese is a beautiful villa set in the greenery of surrounding gardens. You get to see art commissioned by the luxury-loving Borghese family displayed in the very rooms they were created for. Frescoes, marble, stucco, and interior design enhance the masterpieces. This is a place where—regardless of whether you learn a darn thing—you can sit back and enjoy the sheer beauty of the palace and its art.

Orientation

Cost: €7.25.

Hours: Tuesday through Sunday 09:00 to 19:00, sometimes until 23:00 on Saturdays June through September, closed Monday.

Reservations: Reservations are mandatory and easy to get in English over the Internet (www.ticketeria.it) or by phone: Call 06-32810 (if you get an Italian recording, press 2 for English; office hours: Mon–Fri 09:00–19:00, Sat 09:00–13:00, office closed Sat in Aug). Every two hours, 360 people are allowed to enter the museum. Entry times are 09:00, 11:00, 13:00, 15:00, and 17:00 (plus 19:00 and 21:00 if open late on Sat June–Sept). Reserve a *minimum* of several days in advance for a weekday visit, at least a week ahead for weekends. When you reserve, request a day and time (which you'll be given if available), and you'll get a claim number. While you'll be advised to come 30 minutes before your appointed time, you can arrive a few minutes beforehand. But don't be late, as no-show tickets are sold to stand-bys.

Visits are strictly limited to two hours. Concentrate on the first floor, but leave yourself 30 minutes for the paintings of the Pinacoteca upstairs; highlights are marked by the audioguide icons. The fine bookshop and cafeteria are best visited outside your two-hour entry window.

— BORGHESE GALLERY—GROUND FLOOR —

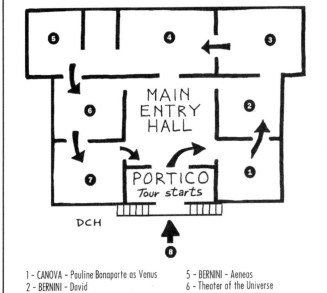

MAIN
ENTRY
HALL

PORTICO
Tour starts

DCH

1 - CANOVA - Pauline Bonaparte as Venus
2 - BERNINI - David
3 - BERNINI - Apollo Chasing Daphne
4 - BERNINI - Rape of Proserpine,
        Diana the Hunter,
        & other marbles

5 - BERNINI - Aeneas
6 - Theater of the Universe
7 - CARAVAGGIO paintings
8 - Enter Basement below for tickets,
        info, shop, WC, and stairs up to
        Pinacoteca (Painting Gallery)

If you don't have a reservation, just show up (or call first and ask if there are openings; a late afternoon on a weekday is usually your best bet). Reservations are tightest at 11:00 and on weekends. No-shows are released a few minutes after the top of the hour.

Generally, out of 360 reservations, a few will fail to show (but more than a few may be waiting to grab them).

Guided English **tours** are offered at 09:10 and 11:10 for €4.20; reserve with entry reservation (or consider the excellent audioguide tour for €4.20).

Length of Our Tour: Two hours maximum.

Getting There: The museum is in the Villa Borghese park. A taxi (tell the cabbie your destination: gah-leh-REE-ah bor-GAY-zay)

can get you within 100 meters of the museum. Otherwise, Metro to Spagna and take a 15-minute walk through the park.
Photography: No photos are allowed.
Checkroom: Baggage check is free and mandatory.
Cuisine Art: A café is on-site.
Starring: Sculptures by Bernini and paintings by Caravaggio, Raphael, and Titian.

Portico

Ancient Roman reliefs (at either end), topped by Michelangelo-designed panels, capture the essence of the collection—a gathering of beautiful objects from every age and culture inside a lavish 17th-century villa. Cardinal Borghese built the villa, collected ancient works, and hired the best artists of his day. In pursuing the optimistic spirit of the Renaissance, they invented Baroque.

Main Entry Hall   ˙

Five Roman mosaics decorate the floor with colorful, festive scenes of slaughter. Gladiators fight animals and each other with swords, whips, and tridents. The Greek letter θ (theta) marks the dead. Notice some of the gladiators' pro-wrestler nicknames: "Cupid," "Serpent," "Licentious."

On the wall is a thrilling first-century Greek sculpture of a horse falling. The Renaissance-era rider was added by Pietro Bernini, father of the famous Bernini.

Room I

Statue of *Pauline Bonaparte as Venus* (*Paolina Borghese Bonaparte*)—Antonio Canova (1808)

Napoleon's sister went the full monty for the sculptor Canova, scandalizing Europe. ("How could you have done such a thing?!" she was asked. She replied, "The room wasn't cold.") With the

famous nose of her conqueror brother, she strikes the pose of Venus as conqueror of men's hearts. Her relaxed afterglow and slight smirk say she's already had her man. The light dent she puts in the mattress makes this goddess human.

Notice the contrasting textures that Canova gets out of the pure-white marble: the rumpled sheet versus her smooth skin. The satiny-smooth pillows and mattress versus the creases in them. Her porcelain skin versus the hint of a love handle. Canova polished and waxed the marble until it looked as soft and pliable as cloth.

The mythological pose, the Roman couch, the ancient hairdo, and the calm harmony make Pauline the epitome of the neoclassical style.

Room II

David—**Gian Lorenzo Bernini (1624)**

Duck! David twists around to put a big rock in his sling. He purses his lips, knits his brow, and winds his body like a spring as his eyes lock onto the target—Goliath, who's somewhere behind us, putting us right in the line of fire.

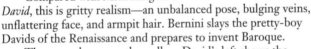

In this self-portrait, 25-year-old Bernini is ready to take on the world. He's charged with the same fighting energy that fueled the missionaries and conquistadores of the Counter-Reformation.

Compared with Michelangelo's *David*, this is gritty realism—an unbalanced pose, bulging veins, unflattering face, and armpit hair. Bernini slays the pretty-boy Davids of the Renaissance and prepares to invent Baroque.

The sarcophagus on the wall on David's left shows the Hellenistic inspiration for Baroque. Look at the *Labors of Hercules* (A.D 160, at chest level).

Room III

Apollo and Daphne (*Apollo e Dafne*)—**Bernini (1625)**

Apollo—made stupid by Cupid's arrow of love—chases after Daphne, who has been turned off by the "arrow of disgust." Just as he's about to catch her, she calls to her father to save her. Magically, her fingers begin to sprout leaves, her toes become roots, her skin turns to bark, and she transforms into a tree. Frustrated Apollo ends up with a handful of leaves.

Stand behind the statue to experience it as Bernini originally intended. It's only when you circle around to the front that he reveals the story's surprise ending.

Walk slowly around. It's as much air as stone. The back leg defies gravity. It was two years in restoration (described to me as being something like dental work). The marble leaves at the top ring like crystal when struck. Notice the same scene, colorized, painted on the ceiling above.

Bernini carves out some of the chief features of Baroque art: He makes a supernatural event seem realistic. He freezes it at the most dramatic, emotional moment. The figures move and twist in unusual poses. He turns the wind machine on, sending Apollo's cape billowing behind him. It's a sculpture group of two, forming a scene, rather than a stand-alone portrait. And the subject is classical. Even in strict Counter-Reformation times, there was always a place for groping, if the subject matter had a moral—this one taught you not to pursue fleeting earthly pleasures. And, besides, Bernini tends to show a lot of skin, but no genitals.

Room IV

The Rape of Proserpine (Il Ratto di Proserpina)—Bernini (1622)

Pluto strides into the Underworld and shows off his catch—the beautiful daughter of the earth goddess. His three-headed guard dog, Cerberus, barks triumphantly. Pluto is squat, thick, and uncouth, with knotted muscles and untrimmed beard. He's trying not to hurt her, but she pushes her divine molester away and twists to call out for help. Tears roll down her cheeks. She wishes she could turn into a tree.

Bernini was the master of marble. Look how Pluto's fingers dig into her thigh like it was real flesh. Bernini picked out this Carrara marble knowing that its relative suppleness and ivory hue would lend itself to a fleshy statue.

Diana the Hunter (Artemis)—Artist Unknown

The statues in the niches are classical originals. *Diana the Hunter* is a rare Greek original from the second century B.C. The traditional *contrapposto* pose (weight on one leg) and idealized grace were an inspiration for artists, such as Canova, who grew tired of Bernini's Baroque bombast.

The Marbles in Room IV

Appreciate the beauty of the different types of marble in the room: Bernini's ivory Carrara, Diana's translucent white, purple porphyry emperors, granite-like columns that support them, wood-grained pilasters on the walls, and the different colors on the floor—green, red, gray, lavender, and yellow, some grainy, some "marbled" like a steak. Some of the world's most beautiful and durable things have been made from the shells of sea creatures layered in sediment, fossilized into limestone, then heated and crystallized by the pressure of the earth: marble.

Room VI

Aeneas (Enea, etc.)—Bernini (1620)

Aeneas' home in Troy is in flames, and he escapes with the three most important things: his family (decrepit father on his shoulder, baby boy), his household gods (the statues in dad's hands), and the Eternal Flame (carried by son). They're all in shock, lost in thought, facing an uncertain future. Aeneas isn't even looking where he's going; he just puts one foot in front of the other. Little do they know that eventually they'll wind up in Italy, where—according to legend—Aeneas will found the city of Rome and house the flame in the Temple of Vesta.

Bernini was still a teenager when he started this, his first life-size work. He was probably helped by his dad, who nurtured the child prodigy much like Leopold mentored Mozart, but without the rivalry. Bernini's portrayal of human flesh—from baby fat to middle-age muscle to sagging decrepitude—is astonishing. Still, the composition is static—not nearly as interesting as the reliefs up at the ceiling, with their dancing, light-footed soldiers with do-si-do shields.

Room VII

The "Theater of the Universe"

The room's decor sums up the eclectic nature of the villa. There are Greek statues and Roman mosaics. There are fake "Egyptian" hieroglyphs (perfectly symmetrical in good neoclassical style). Look out the window past the sculpted gardens, at the mesh domes of the aviary once filled with exotic birds. Cardinal Borghese's vision was to make a place where art, history, music, nature, and science would come together... "a theater of the universe."

Room VIII

Caravaggio

The paintings in this room change often, but you'll likely find one or two by the Baroque innovator Caravaggio (1571–1610). Caravaggio brought Christian saints and Greek gods down to earth with gritty realism. His saints are balding and wrinkled.

His Bacchus (a self-portrait) is pale and
puffy faced. David sticks Goliath's severed head (a self-portrait) right in your
face. The Madonnas scarcely glow. Baby
Jesus is buck naked. Ordinary people
were his models. Caravaggio's straight-
forwardness can be a refreshing change
in a museum full of (sometimes overly)
refined beauty.

Pinacoteca—Painting Gallery

To reach the Pinacoteca, go outside and return to the basement
where you got your ticket, follow signs to the Pinacoteca, show your
ticket to the guard, and climb the long spiral stairway. Remember,
you're limited to only 30 minutes in the Pinacoteca, and you must
visit it within the two-hour window of time printed on your ticket.
Most visitors wait until the last half hour to see the Pinacoteca, so
that's when it's most crowded (and the ground floor is less crowded).
If you see the paintings first, remember that given a two-hour visit,
the ground floor with the sculpture is worth most of that time.

Room XIV

Bust of Cardinal Borghese (Ritr. del Card. Scipione Borghese)—Bernini (1632)

Say *grazie* to the man who built this villa, assembled the collection,
and hired Bernini to sculpt masterpieces. The cardinal is caught
turning as though to greet someone at a party. There's a twinkle in
his eye, and he opens his mouth to make a witty comment. This
man of the cloth was, in fact, a sophisticated hedonist.
• *On the table nearby, find the smaller . . .*

Bust of Pope Paul V

The cardinal's uncle was a more sober man, but also a patron of
the arts who hired Bernini's father. When Pope Paul saw sketches
made by little Lorenzo, he announced: "This boy will be the
Michelangelo of his age."
• *On the wall above the table, find these paintings . . .*

Two Bernini Self-Portraits (*Autoritratto Giovanile*, 1623; and *Autoritratto in Eta Matura*, 1630/35)

Bernini was a master of many media, including painting. The
younger Bernini looks out a bit hesitantly, as if he's still finding his
way in high-class society. But in his next self-portrait, with a few
masterpieces under his belt, Bernini showed himself with more

confidence and facial hair—the dashing and passionate man who would rebuild Rome in Baroque style, from St. Peter's Square to the fountains that dot the piazzas.

Room IX

Deposition (Deposizione di Cristo)— Raphael (Raffaelo Sanzio)

Jesus is being taken from the cross. The men support him while the women support Mary, who has fainted. The woman who commis-

sioned the painting had recently lost her son. She wanted to show the death of a son and the grief of a mother.

In true Renaissance style, Raphael orders the scene with geometrical perfection. The curve of Jesus' body is echoed by the swirl of Mary Magdalene's hair, and then by the curve of Calvary Hill, where he met his fate.

Room X

Danae—Correggio

Cupid strips Danae as she spreads her legs, most unladylike, to receive a trickle of gold from the smudgy cloud overhead—this was Zeus' idea of intercourse with a human. The sheets are rumpled, and Danae looks right where the action is with a smile on her face. It's hard to believe that a suppos-edly religious family would dis-play such an erotic work. But the

Borgheses felt that the Church was truly "catholic" (universal), and that all forms of human expression—including physical passion—glorified God.

Room XX

Sacred and Profane Love (Amor Sacrae, Amor Profane)—Titian (Tiziano Vecello)

The clothed woman at left was recently married, and she cradles a vase filled with jewels representing the riches of earthly love.

Her naked twin on the right holds the burning flame of eternal, heavenly love. Baby Cupid, between them, playfully stirs the waters.

This exquisite painting expresses the spirit of the Renaissance—that earth and heaven are two sides of the same coin. And here in the Borghese Gallery, that love of earthly beauty can be spiritually uplifting—as long as you feel it within two hours.

VATICAN MUSEUM TOUR

rome

The glories of the ancient world displayed in a lavish papal palace, decorated by the likes of Michelangelo and Raphael...the Musei Vaticani. Unfortunately, many tourists see the Vatican Museum only as an obstacle between them and its grand finale, the Sistine Chapel. True, this huge, confusing, and crowded mega-museum can be a jungle—but with this book as your vine, you should swing through with ease, enjoying the highlights and getting to the Sistine just before you collapse. On the way, you'll enjoy some of the less appreciated but equally important sections of this warehouse of Western civilization.

Orientation
Cost: €9.30, free on last Sunday of each month.
Dress Code: Modest dress (no short shorts or bare shoulders) is appropriate and often required.
Hours: March through October Monday through Friday 08:45 to 16:45, Saturday 08:45 to 13:45; November through February Monday through Saturday 08:45 to 13:45, closed Sunday except last Sunday of the month (when it's free, crowded, and open 08:45–13:45). The last entry is 75 minutes before closing time. The museum is closed on many holidays (mainly religious ones) including—in 2002: January 1 and 6, February 11, March 19, Easter and Easter Monday, May 1, 9, and 30, June 29, August 14 and 15, November 1, and December 8, 25, and 26.

The Sistine Chapel closes 30 minutes before the museum does. Some individual rooms close at odd hours, especially after 13:00. TV screens inside the entrance lists closures. The rooms described here are usually open. The museum is generally hot and crowded. Saturday, the last Sunday of the month, and Monday are the worst; afternoons are best.

───── VATICAN MUSEUM OVERVIEW ─────

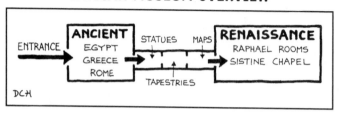

Getting There: From the nearest Metro stop, Cipro-Musei Vaticani, it's a 10-minute walk. From St. Peter's Square, it's about a 15-minute walk (follow the Vatican Wall). Taxis are reasonable (hop in and say "moo-ZAY-ee vah-tee-KAHN-ee").

Information: In the entry, look for the *i* (it's probably in the bank of windows to your left, under "Special Permits"; some English spoken). You'll find a book kiosk in the lobby, another up the stairs, and others scattered throughout the museum. Some exhibits have English explanations. The museum has signs to four color-coded self-guided visits (A—the Sistine blitz, B—highlights, C—a good tour, D—everything). Tel. 06-6988-4947 or 06-6988-3333.

Exchange windows with sinful rates are in the entry and exit. The post office is upstairs.

Tour: You can rent a €5.20 audioguide (but if you do, you lose the option of taking the shortcut from the Sistine Chapel to St. Peter's, because the audioguide must be returned at the entrance).

Length of Our Tour: Until you expire, or 2.5 hours, whichever comes first.

Photography: No photos are allowed in the Sistine Chapel. Elsewhere in the museum, photos without a flash are permitted.

Cuisine Art: A cafeteria is upstairs. Cheaper choices: The great Via Andrea Doria produce market is three blocks north of the entrance (head across the street, down the stairs, and continue straight) and inexpensive Pizza Rustica shops line Viale Giulio Cesare. Good restaurants are nearby (see page 219).

Starring: World history, Michelangelo, Raphael, *Laocoön*, the Greek masters, and their Roman copyists.

The Pope's Collection

With the fall of Rome, the Catholic (or "universal") Church became the great preserver of civilization, collecting artifacts from cultures dead and dying. Renaissance popes (15th and 16th centuries) collected most of what we'll see. Those lusty priests-as-Roman-emperors loved the ancient world. They built these palaces and decorated them with classical statues and Renaissance paintings. They combined the classical and Christian worlds, finding the divine in the creations of man.

We'll concentrate on classical sculpture and Renaissance painting. But along the way (and there's a lot of along-the-way here), we'll stop to leaf through a few yellowed pages from this 5,000-year-old scrapbook of humankind.

This heavyweight museum is shaped like a barbell—two buildings connected by a long hall. The entrance building covers the ancient world (Egypt, Greece, Rome). The one at the far end covers its "rebirth" in the Renaissance (including the Sistine Chapel). The halls there and back are a mix of old and new. Move quickly—don't burn out before the Sistine Chapel at the end—and see how each civilization borrows from and builds on the previous one.

• *Leave Italy by entering the doors. Go upstairs (or take the elevator) to buy your ticket, punch it in the turnstiles, go through a security check (just like at the airport), and then take the long escalator or spiral stairs up, up, up.*

At the top: To your right is the café and the Pinacoteca painting gallery (consider touring the Pinacoteca now if you want the option of taking the shortcut from the Sistine Chapel directly to St. Peter's; for information on the Pinacoteca, see the end of this chapter). To your left, the beginning of our tour. Go left, then take another left up a flight of stairs to reach the first-floor Egyptian Rooms (Museo Egizio). Don't stop until you find your mummy.

EGYPT (3000–1000 B.C.)

Egyptian art was for religion, not decoration. A statue or painting preserved the likeness of someone, giving him a form of eternal life. Most of the art was for tombs, where they put the mummies. Notice that the art is only realistic enough to get the job done. You can recognize that it's a man, a bird, or whatever, but these are stiff, two-dimensional, schematic figures—functional rather than beautiful.

Mummies

This woman died three millennia ago. Her corpse was disemboweled, and her organs were placed in a jar like those you see nearby. Then the body was refilled with pitch, dried with natron (a natural sodium carbonate), wrapped in linen, and placed

in a wood coffin, which went inside a stone coffin, which was placed

THE ANCIENT WORLD

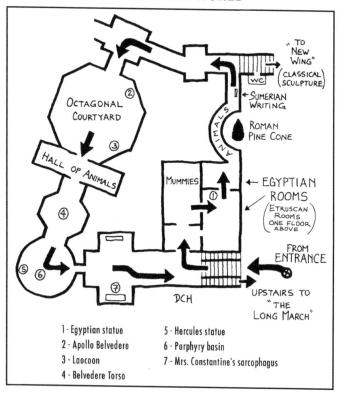

"TO NEW WING"
(CLASSICAL SCULPTURE)

WC

← SUMERIAN WRITING

ROMAN PINE CONE

OCTAGONAL COURTYARD ②

③

HALL OF ANIMALS

ANIMALS

MUMMIES ①

④

← EGYPTIAN ROOMS
(ETRUSCAN ROOMS ONE FLOOR ABOVE)

FROM ENTRANCE

⑤ ⑥

⑦

DCH

UPSTAIRS TO "THE LONG MARCH"

1 - Egyptian statue
2 - Apollo Belvedere
3 - Laocoon
4 - Belvedere Torso
5 - Hercules statue
6 - Porphyry basin
7 - Mrs. Constantine's sarcophagus

in a tomb. (Remember that the pyramids were just big tombs.) In the next life, the spirit was homeless without its body, and you wanted to look your best—notice the henna job on her hair.

Notice, painted inside the coffins, what the deceased "packed" for the journey to eternity. The coffins were decorated with magical spells to protect the body from evil and to act as crib notes for the confused soul in the netherworld.

Egyptian Statues

Even in the Romanized versions, it's clear that Egyptian statues are stiff and unnatural. They step out awkwardly, with arms straight down at their sides. Each was made according to an established set of proportions. Little changed over the centuries. These had a function and they worked. In Egyptian belief, a statue like this could be a place of refuge for the wandering soul of a dead man.

Various Egyptian Gods as Animals

Before technology made humans top dogs on earth, it was easier to appreciate our fellow creatures. The Egyptians saw the superiority of animals and worshiped them as incarnations of the gods. Wander through a pet store of Egyptian animal gods. The lioness portrays the fierce goddess Sekhmet; the clever baboon is the god of wisdom, Thot, and Horus has a falcon's head.

• *Continue through a curved corridor of animal gods, then through three more rooms, pausing at the glass case in the third room, which contains brown clay tablets.*

Sumerian Writing

Even before Egypt, civilizations flourished in the Middle East. The Sumerian culture in Mesopotamia (modern Iraq) invented writing around 3000 B.C. You can see the clay tablets with this cuneiform (wedge-shaped) script. Also notice the ingenious cylindrical seals, with which they made impressions in soft clay to seal documents and mark property.

• *Go with the flow past a view of Rome out the window, then turn left into the octagonal courtyard of the "Pio-Clementino" section.*

SCULPTURE—GREECE AND ROME (500 B.C.–A.D. 500)

This palace wouldn't be here, this sculpture wouldn't be here, and you'd be spending your vacation in South Dakota at Reptile Gardens if it weren't for a few thousand Greeks in a small city about 450 years before Christ. Athens set the tone for the rest of the West. Democracy, theater, economics, literature, and art all got their start in Athens during a 50-year "Golden Age." Greek culture was then appropriated by Rome and revived again 1,500 years later, during the Renaissance. The Renaissance popes built and decorated these palaces, re-creating the glory of the classical world.

Apollo Belvedere

Apollo, the god of the sun and of music, is hunting. He has spotted his prey and is about to go after it with his (missing) bow and arrows. The optimistic Greeks conceived of their gods in human form . . . and buck naked.

The Greek sculptor Leochares, following the style of the greater Greek sculptor Praxiteles, has fully captured the beauty

of the human form. The anatomy is perfect, his pose is natural. Instead of standing at attention, face forward with his arms at his sides (Egyptian style), Apollo is on the move, stepping forward slightly with his weight on one leg.

The Greeks loved balance. A well-rounded man was both a thinker and an athlete, a poet and a warrior. In art, the *Apollo Belvedere* balances several opposites. Apollo eyes his target, but hasn't attacked yet. He's moving, but not out of control. He's also a balance between a real person and an ideal god. And the smoothness of his muscles is balanced by the rough folds of his cloak. The only sour note: his recently added left hand. Could we try a size smaller?

During the Renaissance, when this Roman copy of the original Greek work was discovered, it was considered the most perfect work of art in the world. The handsome face, eternal youth, and the body that seems to float just above the pedestal made *Apollo Belvedere* an object of wonder and almost worship. Apollo's grace was something superhuman, divine, and godlike, even for devout Christians.

• *In the neighboring niche to the right, a bearded old Roman river god lounges in the shade. This pose inspired Michelangelo's Adam, in the Sistine Chapel (coming soon). While there are a few fancy bathtubs in this courtyard, most of the carved boxes you see are sarcophagi— Roman coffins and relic holders, carved with the deceased's epitaph in picture form.*

Laocoön

Laocoön (lay-AWK-oh-wahn) was a pagan high priest of Troy, the ancient city attacked by the Greeks. When the Greeks brought the Trojan Horse to the gates as a ploy to get inside the city walls, Laocoön tried to warn his people not to bring it inside. But the gods wanted the Greeks to win, so they sent huge snakes to crush him and his two sons to death. We see them at the height of their terror, when they realize that, no matter how hard they struggle, they—and their entire race—are doomed.

The *Laocoön* is Hellenistic, done four centuries after the Golden Age, after the scales of "balance" had been tipped. Where *Apollo* is a balance between stillness and motion, this is unbridled motion. Where *Apollo* is serene, this is emotional. Where *Apollo* is idealized grace, this is powerful and gritty realism. The figures (carved from 4 blocks of marble pieced together seamlessly) are

powerful, not light and graceful. The poses are as twisted as possible, accentuating every rippling muscle and bulging vein. Follow the line of motion from *Laocoön*'s left foot, up his leg, through his body, and out his right arm (which some historians used to think extended straight out—until the elbow was dug up early in the 1900s). Goethe used to stand here and blink his eyes rapidly, watching the statue flicker to life.

Laocoön was the most famous Greek statue in ancient Rome and considered "superior to all other sculpture or painting." It was famous in the Renaissance, too—though no one had seen it, only read about it in ancient accounts. Then, in 1506, it was unexpectedly unearthed in the ruins of Nero's Golden House near the Colosseum. The discovery caused a sensation. They cleaned it off and paraded it through the streets before an awestruck populace. No one had ever seen anything like its motion and emotion, having been raised on a white-bread diet of pretty, serene, and balanced *Apollo*s. One of those who saw it was the young Michelangelo, and it was a revelation to him. Two years later, he started work on the Sistine Chapel, and the Renaissance was about to take another turn.

• *Leave the courtyard. Swing around the Hall of Animals, a jungle of beasts real and not so real, to the limbless* Torso *in the middle of the next large hall.*

Belvedere Torso

My entire experience with statues consists of making snowmen. But standing face to face with this hunk of shaped rock makes you appreciate the sheer physical labor involved in chipping a figure out of solid rock. It takes great strength, but at the same time, great delicacy.

This is all that remains of an ancient statue of Hercules seated on a lion skin. Michelangelo loved this old rock. He knew he was the best sculptor of his day. The ancients were his only peers—and his rivals. He'd caress this statue lovingly and tell people, "I am the pupil of the *Torso*." To him, it contained all the beauty of classical sculpture. But it's not beautiful. It's ugly. Compared with the pure grace of the *Apollo*, it's downright hideous.

But Michelangelo, an ugly man himself, was looking for a new kind of beauty—not the beauty of idealized gods, but the innate beauty of every person, even so-called ugly ones. With its knotty lumps of muscle, the *Torso* has a brute power and a distinct personality despite—or because of—its rough edges. Remember this *Torso*, because we'll see it again later on.

• *Enter the next, domed room.*

Round Room

This room, modeled on the Pantheon interior, gives some idea of Roman grandeur. Romans often took Greek ideas and made them bigger, like the big bronze statue of Hercules with his club, found near Pompey's Theatre (by modern-day Campo de' Fiori). The mosaic floor recreates an ancient Roman villa, and the enormous Roman hot tub/birdbath/vase, made of purple porphyry marble, is also likely from a villa. Purple was a rare, royal, expensive, and prestigious color in pre-Crayola days.

• *Enter the next room.*

Sarcophagi

These two large porphyry marble coffins were made for the Roman Emperor Constantine's mother and daughter. They were

Christians and, therefore, outside the law until Constantine made Christianity legal (A.D. 312).

• *See how we've come full circle in this building—the Egyptian Rooms are ahead on your left. Go upstairs and prepare for the Long March down the hall lined with statues,*

toward the Sistine Chapel and Raphael Rooms.

    Overachievers may first choose to pop into the Etruscan wing—"Museo Etrusco"—located a few steps up from the "Long March" level. (Others have permission to save their aesthetic energy for the Sistine.)

THE ETRUSCANS (800–300 B.C.)

Room I

The chariot is from 550 B.C., when crude Romans were ruled by their more civilized neighbors to the north—the Etruscans. Imagine the chariot racing around the dirt track of the Circus Maximus, through the marshy valley of the newly drained Forum, or up Capitol Hill to the Temple of Jupiter—all originally built by Rome's Etruscan kings.

Room II

The golden breastplate (*Pectoral*, 650 B.C., immediately to the right), decorated with tiny winged angels and animals, shows off the sophistication of the Etruscans. Though unwarlike and politically decentralized, these people were able to "conquer" all of central Italy around 650 B.C. through trade, offering tempting metalwork goods like this.

The Etruscan vases done in the Greek style remind us of the other great pre-Roman power—the Greek colonists who settled in southern Italy (Magna Graecia). The Etruscans traded with the Greeks, adopting their fashions. Rome, cradled between the two, grew up learning from both cultures.

A Greek-style bowl (far corner of the room) depicting a man and woman in bed together would have scandalized early Roman farmers. He's peeing in a chamberpot, she's blowing a flute. Etruscan art often showed husbands and wives at ease together, giving them a reputation among the Romans as immoral, flute-playing degenerates.

Room III

This bronze warrior, whose head was sawed off by lightning, has a rare inscription that's readable (on armor below the navel). It probably refers to the statue's former owner: "Aha! Trutitis gave [this] as [a] gift." Archaeologists understand the Etruscans' Greek-style alphabet and some individual words, but they've yet to fully crack the code. As you look around at beautiful bronze pitchers, candlesticks, shields, and urns, ponder yet another of Etruria's unsolved mysteries—no one is sure where these sophisticated people came from.

Room IV

Most of our knowledge of the Etruscans is from sarcophagi and art in Etruscan tombs. Their funeral art is solemn, but hardly morbid—check out the sarcopha-guy with the bulging belly, enjoying a banquet for all eternity.

The Etruscans' origins are obscure, but their legacy is clear. In 509 B.C., the Etruscan king's son raped a Roman. The king was thrown out, the Republic was declared, Etruscan cities were conquered by Rome's legions, and their culture was swallowed

up in Roman expansion. By Julius
Caesar's time, the few remaining
ethnic Etruscans were reduced
to serving their masters as flute
players, goldsmiths, surgeons, and
street-corner soothsayers, like the
one that Caesar brushed aside
when he called out, "Beware the
ides of March..."

• *Backtrack, returning to the long hall leading to the Sistine Chapel
and Raphael Rooms.*

THE LONG MARCH—SCULPTURE, TAPESTRIES, MAPS, AND VIEWS

Remember, this building was originally a series of papal palaces.
The popes loved beautiful things, and, as heirs of Imperial Rome,
they felt they deserved such luxury. This half-kilometer walk
gives you a sense of the scale that Renaissance popes built on.
The palaces and art represent both the peak and the decline of
the Catholic Church in Europe. It was extravagant spending
like this that inspired Martin Luther to rebel, starting the
Protestant Reformation.

Gallery of the Candelabra— Classical Sculpture

In the second "room" of the long hall, stop at
the statue *Diana the Huntress* on the left. Here,
the virgin goddess goes hunting. Roman
hunters would pray and give offerings to
statues like this to get divine help in their
search for food.

Farmers might pray
to another version of the
same goddess, *Artemis*,
on the opposite wall. This billion-breasted
beauty stood for fertility. "Boobs or bulls'
balls?" Some historians say that bulls were
sacrificed and castrated, with the testicles
draped over the statues as symbols of fertility.

• *Shuffle along to the next "room" on the left and
the* Bacchus *with a baby on his shoulders.*

Fig Leaves

Why do the statues have fig leaves? Like *Bacchus*, many of these
statues originally looked much different than they do now. First off,

THE LONG MARCH

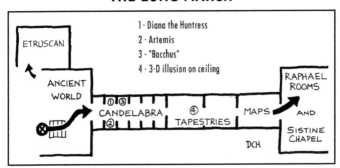

1 - Diana the Huntress
2 - Artemis
3 - "Bacchus"
4 - 3-D illusion on ceiling

ETRUSCAN

ANCIENT WORLD

CANDELABRA

TAPESTRIES

MAPS

RAPHAEL ROOMS

AND

SISTINE CHAPEL

DCH

they were painted, usually in gaudy colors. *Bacchus* may have had brown hair, rosy cheeks, purple grapes, and a leopard-skin sidekick at his feet. Even the *Apollo Belvedere*, whose cool gray tones we now admire as "classic Greek austerity," may have had a paisley pink cloak for all we know. Also, many statues had glass eyes like *Bacchus*.

And the fig leaves? Those came from the years 1550 to 1800, when the church decided that certain parts of the human anatomy were obscene. (Why they didn't pick the feet, which are universally ugly, I'll never know.) Perhaps church leaders associated these full-frontal statues with the outbreak of Renaissance humanism that reduced their power in Europe. Whatever; they reacted by covering classical crotches with plaster fig leaves, the same leaves Adam and Eve had used when the concept of "privates" was invented.

Note: The leaves could be removed at any time if the museum officials were so motivated. There are suggestion boxes around the museum. Whenever I see a fig leaf, I get the urge to pick-it. We could start an organ-ized campaign....

• *Cover your eyes in case they forgot a fig leaf or two and continue to the tapestries.*

Tapestries

Along the left wall are tapestries designed by Raphael's workshop and made in Brussels. They show scenes from the life of Christ, starting with the baby Jesus in the manger.

Check out the beautiful sculpted reliefs on the ceiling, especially the lavender panel near the end of the first tapestry room showing a centurion ordering Eskimo pies from a vendor. Admire the workmanship of this relief, then realize that it's not a relief at all—it's painted on a flat surface! Illusions like this were proof that painters had mastered the 3-D realism of ancient statues.

Map Gallery and View of Vatican City

This gallery still feels like a pope's palace. The crusted ceiling is pure papal splendor. The maps on the walls are decorations from the 16th century. You can plan the next leg of your trip with the two maps of Italy at the far end of the hall—"New Italy" and "Old Italy"—both with a smoking Mount Vesuvius next to Napoli/Neapolis/Naples. There's an interesting old map of Venice on the right as you exit.

The windows give you your best look at the tiny country of Vatican City, formed in 1929. It has its own radio station, as you see from the tower on the hill. What you see here is pretty much all there is—these gardens, the palaces you're in, and St. Peter's.

If you lean out and look left you'll see the dome of St. Peter's the way Michelangelo would have liked you to see it—without the bulky Baroque facade.

• *Exit the map room and take a breather in the next small tapestry hall before turning left into the crowded Raphael Rooms.*

RENAISSANCE ART

Raphael Rooms—Papal Wallpaper

We've seen art from the ancient world; now we'll see its rebirth in the Renaissance. We're entering the living quarters of the great Renaissance popes—where they slept, worked, and worshiped. The rooms reflect the grandeur of their position. They hired the best artists—mostly from Florence—to paint the walls and ceilings, combining classical and Christian motifs.

• *Entering, you'll immediately see . . .*

The huge non-Raphael painting shows Sobieski liberating Vienna from the Muslim Turks in 1683, finally tipping the tide in favor of a Christian Europe. See the Muslim tents on the left and the spires of Christian Vienna on the right.

The second room's paintings celebrate the doctrine of the Immaculate Conception, establishing that Mary herself was conceived free from original sin. This medieval idea wasn't actually made dogma until a century ago. The largest fresco shows how

——RAPHAEL ROOMS——

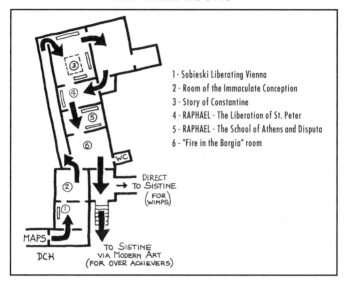

1 - Sobieski Liberating Vienna
2 - Room of the Immaculate Conception
3 - Story of Constantine
4 - RAPHAEL - The Liberation of St. Peter
5 - RAPHAEL - The School of Athens and Disputa
6 - "Fire in the Borgia" room

WC

DIRECT → TO SISTINE (FOR WIMPS)

MAPS

DCH

TO SISTINE VIA MODERN ART (FOR OVER ACHIEVERS)

the inspiration came straight from heaven (upper left) in a ray of light directly to the pope.

• *Next, you'll pass along an outside ramp overlooking a courtyard (is that the pope's Fiat?), finally ending up in the first of the Raphael Rooms—the Constantine Room.*

Constantine Room

The frescoes (by Raphael and assis-tants) celebrate the passing of the baton from one culture to the next. Remember, Rome was a pagan empire persecuting a new cult from the East—Christianity.

Then, on the night of October 27, A.D. 312 (left wall), as Constan-tine (in gold, with crown) was preparing his troops for a coup d'état, he looked up and saw something strange. A cross appeared in the sky with the words, "You will conquer in this sign."

The next day (long wall), his troops raged victoriously into battle with the Christian cross atop their Roman eagle banners. There's Constantine in the center, slashing through the enemy, with God's warrior angels riding shotgun overhead.

Constantine was supposedly baptized a Christian (right wall), even stripping and kneeling before the pope. As emperor, he legalized Christianity and worked hand in hand with the pope (window wall). When Rome fell, its glory lived on through the Dark Ages in the pomp, pageantry, and learning of the Catholic Church.

Look at the ceiling painting. A classical statue falls and crumbles before the overpowering force of the cross. Whoa! Christianity triumphs over pagan Rome. (This was painted, I believe, by Raphael's surrealist colleague, Salvadorus Dalio.)

RAPHAEL

Raphael was only 25 when Pope Julius II invited him to paint the walls of his private apartments. Julius was so impressed by Raphael's talent that he had the work of earlier masters scraped off and gave Raphael free rein to paint what he wanted.

Raphael lived a charmed life. He painted masterpieces effortlessly. He was handsome and sophisticated, and soon became Julius' favorite. In a different decade, he might have been thrown out of the Church as a great sinner, but his love affairs and devil-may-care personality seemed to epitomize the optimistic pagan spirit of the Renaissance. His works are graceful but never lightweight or frilly—they're strong, balanced, and harmonious in the best Renaissance tradition. When he died young in 1520, the High Renaissance died with him.

• *Continue through the next room and bookshop. In the following room, block the sunlight with your hand to see . . .*

The Liberation of St. Peter

Peter, Jesus' right-hand man, was thrown into prison in Jerusalem for his beliefs. In the middle of the night, an angel appeared and rescued him from the sleeping guards (Acts 12). The chains miraculously fell away (and were later brought to the St. Peter-in-Chains Church in Rome) and the angel led him to safety (right)

while the guards took hell from their captain (left). This little "play" is neatly divided into three separate acts that make a balanced composition.

Raphael makes the miraculous event even more dramatic with the use of three kinds of light illuminating the dark cell—half-moonlight, the captain's torch, and the radiant angel. Raphael's mastery of realism, rich colors, and sense of drama made him understandably famous.

• *Enter the next room . . .*

The School of Athens

In both style and subject matter, this fresco sums up the spirit of the Renaissance, which was not only the rebirth of classical art, but a rebirth of learning, discovery, and the optimistic spirit that man is a rational creature. Raphael pays respect to the great thinkers and scientists of ancient Greece, gathering them together at one time in a mythical school setting.

In the center are Plato and Aristotle, the two greatest. Plato points up, indicating his philosophy that mathematics and pure ideas are the source of truth, while Aristotle points down, showing his preference for hands-on study of the material world. There's their master, Socrates (midway to the left, in green), ticking off arguments on his fingers. And in the foreground at right, Euclid bends over a slate to demonstrate a geometrical formula.

Raphael shows that Renaissance thinkers were as good as the ancients. There's Leonardo da Vinci, whom Raphael worshiped, in the role of Plato. Raphael himself (next to last on the far right, with the black beret) looks out at us. And the "school" building is actually an early version of St. Peter's Basilica (under construction at the time).

Raphael balances everything symmetrically—thinkers to the left, scientists to the right, with Plato and Aristotle dead center—showing the geometrical order found in the world. Look at the square floor tiles in the foreground. If you laid a ruler over them and extended the line upward, it would run right to the center of the picture. Similarly, the tops of the columns all point down to the middle. All the lines of sight draw our attention to Plato and Aristotle, and to the small arch over their heads—a halo over these two secular saints in the divine pursuit of knowledge. While Raphael was painting this room, Michelangelo was at work down the hall in the Sistine Chapel. Raphael popped in on the sly to see the master at work. He was astonished. When he saw Michelangelo's powerful figures and dramatic scenes, he began to beef up his delicate, graceful style to a more heroic level. In *The School of Athens*, perhaps Raphael's greatest work, he tipped his brush to the master by adding Michelangelo to the scene—the brooding, melancholy figure in front, leaning on a block of marble.

The Disputa

As if to underline the new attitude that pre-Christian philosophy and church thinking could coexist, Raphael painted *The Disputa* facing *The School of Athens*. Christ and the saints in heaven are overseeing a discussion of the Eucharist (the communion wafer)

by mortals below. The classical-looking character in blue looks out as if to say, "There's *The School of Athens*," while pointing toward the center of *The Disputa*, as if to say, "But here's the School of Heaven." Balance and symmetry reign, from the angel trios in the upper corners to the books littering the floor.

In Catholic terms, the communion wafer miraculously becomes the body of Christ when it's consecrated by a priest, bringing a little bit of heaven into the material world. Raphael's painting also connects heaven and earth, with descending circles: Jesus in a halo, down to the dove of the Holy Spirit in a circle, which enters the communion wafer in its holder. The composition drives the point home. By the way, these rooms were the papal library, so themes featuring learning, knowledge, and debate were appropriate.

Moving along, the last Raphael Room (called the "Fire in the Borgia" Room) shows work done mostly by Raphael's students, who were influenced by the muscularity and dramatic, sculptural poses of Michelangelo.

• *Get ready. It's decision time. From here, there are two ways to get to the Sistine Chapel. Leave the final Raphael Room and you'll soon see two arrows—one pointing left to the Sistine (Cappella Sistina) and one pointing right to the Sistine. Left goes directly to the Sistine. But going right (5 min and a few staircases longer) leads to a quiet room at the foot of the stairs with a bench where you can sit in peace and read ahead before entering the hectic Sistine Chapel. Also, you get to stroll through the impressive Modern Religious Art collection on the way (signs will direct you to the Sistine). Your call.*

THE SISTINE CHAPEL

The Sistine Chapel contains Michelangelo's ceiling and his huge *Last Judgment*. The Sistine is the personal chapel of the pope and the place where new popes are elected. When Pope Julius II asked Michelangelo to take on this important project, he said, "No, *grazie*."

Michelangelo insisted he was a sculptor, not a painter. The Sistine ceiling was a vast undertaking, and he didn't want to do a half-vast job. But the pope pleaded, bribed, and threatened until Michelangelo finally consented, on the condition he be able to do it all his own way.

Julius had asked for only 12 apostles along the sides of the ceiling, but Michelangelo had a grander vision—the entire history of the world until Jesus. He spent the next four years (1508–1512) bent over on his back on scaffolding six stories up, covering the ceiling with frescoes of Bible scenes. In sheer physical terms, it's an astonishing achievement: 600 square meters (nearly 2,000 square feet), and every human figure done by his own hand. (Raphael only designed most of his rooms, letting assistants do the grunt work.)

First, he had to design and erect the scaffolding. Any materials had to be hauled up on pulleys. Then, a section of ceiling would be plastered. With fresco—painting on wet plaster—if you don't get it right the first time, you have to scrape the whole thing off and start over. And if you've ever struggled with a ceiling light fixture or worked underneath a car for even five minutes, you know how heavy your arms get. The physical effort, the paint dripping in his eyes, the creative drain, and the mental stress from a pushy pope combined to almost kill Michelangelo.

But when it was finished and revealed to the public, it simply blew 'em away. Like the *Laocoön* statue discovered six years earlier, it was unlike anything seen before. It both caps the Renaissance and turns it in a new direction. In perfect Renaissance spirit, it mixes Old Testament prophets with classical figures. But the style is more dramatic, shocking, and emotional than the balanced Renaissance works before it. This is a very personal work—the Gospel according to Michelangelo—but its themes and subject matter are universal. Almost without exception, art critics concede that the Sistine ceiling is the single greatest work of art by any one human being.

The Sistine Ceiling—Understanding What You're Standing Under

The ceiling shows the history of the world before the birth of Jesus. We see God creating the world, creating man and woman, destroying the earth by flood, and so on. Along the sides (where the ceiling starts to curve) we see the Old Testament prophets

THE SISTINE SCHEMATIC

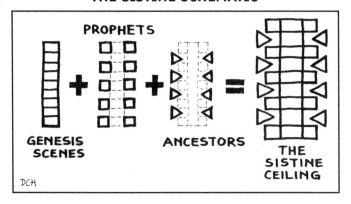

and pagan Greek prophetesses that foretold the coming of Christ. Dividing these scenes and figures is a painted architectural framework (a 3-D illusion) decorated with nude, statuelike figures with symbolic meaning.

The key is to see three simple divisions in the tangle of bodies:
(1) The central spine of nine rectangular Bible scenes
(2) The line of prophets on either side
(3) The triangles between the prophets showing the ancestors of Christ

• *Ready? Within the chapel, grab a seat along the side (if possible). Face the altar with the big* Last Judgment *on the wall (more on that later). Now look up to the ceiling and find the central panel of...*

The Creation of Adam

God and Man take centerstage in this Renaissance version of creation. Adam, newly formed in the image of God, lounges dreamily in perfect naked innocence. God, with his entourage, swoops in in a swirl of activity (which—with a little imagination—looks like a cross-section of a human brain... quite a strong humanist statement). Their reaching hands are the center of this work. Adam's is limp and passive; God's is strong and forceful, His finger twitching upward with energy. Here is the very moment of creation, as God passes the spark of life to man, the crowning work of His creation.

This is the spirit of the Renaissance. God is not a terrifying

THE SISTINE CEILING

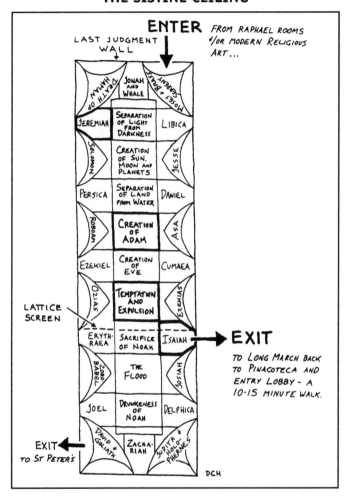

ENTER FROM RAPHAEL ROOMS ¼/OR MODERN RELIGIOUS ART...

LAST JUDGMENT WALL

MOSES + BRASS SERPENT

DEATH OF HAMAN

JONAH AND WHALE

JEREMIAH

SEPARATION OF LIGHT FROM DARKNESS

LIBICA

SOLOMON

CREATION OF SUN, MOON AND PLANETS

JESSE

PERSICA

SEPARATION OF LAND FROM WATER

DANIEL

ROBOAM

CREATION OF ADAM

ASA

EZEKIEL

CREATION OF EVE

CUMAEA

OZIAS

TEMPTATION AND EXPULSION

EZECHIAS

LATTICE SCREEN

ERYTH-RAEA

SACRIFICE OF NOAH

ISAIAH

EXIT

TO LONG MARCH BACK TO PINACOTECA AND ENTRY LOBBY - A 10-15 MINUTE WALK.

ZORO-BABEL

THE FLOOD

JOSIAH

JOEL

DRUNKENNESS OF NOAH

DELPHICA

EXIT TO ST PETER'S

DAVID & GOLIATH

ZACHA-RIAH

JUDITH & HOLOFERNES

DCH

giant reaching down to puny and helpless man from way on high. Here they are on an equal plane, divided only by the diagonal patch of sky. God's billowing robe and the patch of green upon which Adam is lying balance each other. They are like two pieces of a jigsaw puzzle, or two long-separated continents, or like the yin and yang symbols finally coming together—uniting, complementing each other, creating wholeness. God and man work together in the divine process of creation.

• *This celebration of man permeates the ceiling. Notice the Adonises-come-to-life on the pedestals that divide the central panels. And then came woman.*

The Garden of Eden: Temptation and Expulsion

In one panel, we see two scenes from the Garden of Eden. On the left is the leafy garden of paradise where Adam and Eve lie around blissfully. But the devil comes along— a serpent with a woman's torso—and winds around the forbidden Tree of Knowledge. The temptation to gain new knowledge is too great for these Renaissance people. They eat the forbidden fruit.

At right, the sword-wielding angel drives them from Paradise into the barren plains. They're grieving, but they're far from helpless. Adam's body is thick and sturdy, and we know they'll survive in the cruel world. Adam firmly gestures to the angel, like he's saying, "All right, already! We're going!"

The Nine Scenes from Genesis

Take some time with these central scenes to understand the story the ceiling tells. They run in sequence, starting at the front:

(1) God, in purple, divides the light from darkness.
(2) God creates the sun (burning orange) and the moon (pale white, to the right). Oops, I guess there's another moon.
(3) God bursts toward us to separate the land and water.
(4) *The Creation of Adam*
(5) God creates Eve, who springs out of Adam's side.
(6) *The Garden of Eden: Temptation and Expulsion*
(7) Noah kills a ram and stokes the altar fires to make a sacrifice to God.
(8) The great Flood, sent by God, destroys the wicked, who desperately head for higher ground. In the distance, the Ark carries Noah's family to safety.
(9) Noah's sons see their drunk father. (Perhaps Michelangelo chose to end it with this scene as a reminder that even the best of men are fallible.)

Prophets

By 1510, Michelangelo had finished the first half of the ceiling, the end farthest from the *Last Judgment* wall. When they took the scaffolding down and could finally see what he'd been working on for two years, everyone was awestruck—except Michelangelo. As powerful as his figures are, from the floor they didn't look dramatic enough for Michelangelo. For the other half, he pulled out all the stops.

Compare the many small figures in the Noah scenes with, say, Adam and God at the other end. Or compare an early prophet with a later one. Isaiah ("Esaias," in purple) is shown in a pose like a Roman senator. He is a stately, sturdy, balanced, composed Renaissance Man. Now look at Jeremiah ("Hieremias") in the corner by the *Last Judgment*. This prophet, who witnessed the destruction of Israel, is a dark, brooding figure. He slumps his chin in his hand and ponders the fate of his people. The difference between the small, dignified Isaiah and the large, dramatic Jeremiah is like the difference between *Apollo Belvedere* and the *Laocoön*. This sort of emotional power was a new element in Renaissance painting.

The Cleaning Project

The ceiling and the *Last Judgment* have been cleaned, removing centuries of preservatives, dirt, and soot from candles, oil lamps, and the annual Papal Barbecue (just kidding). The bright, bright colors that emerged are a bit shocking, forcing many art experts to reevaluate Michelangelo's style. Notice the very dark patches left in the corner above the Last Judgment and imagine how dreary and dark it must have been before the cleaning.

The Last Judgment

When Michelangelo was asked to paint the altar wall 23 years later (1535), the mood of Europe—and of Michelangelo—was completely different. The Protestant Reformation had forced the Catholic Church to clamp down on free thought, and religious wars raged. Rome had recently been pillaged by roving bands of mercenaries. The Renaissance spirit of optimism was fading. Michelangelo himself had begun to question the innate goodness of mankind.

It's Judgment Day, and Christ—the powerful figure in the center, raising his arm to strike down the wicked—has come to find out who's naughty and who's nice. Beneath him, a band of angels blows its trumpets Dizzy Gillespie–style to  wake the dead. The dead at lower left leave their graves and prepare to be judged. The righteous, on Christ's right hand (the left

THE LAST JUDGMENT

1 - Christ with Mary at his side
2 - Trumpeting Angels
3 - The dead come out of their graves, the righteous ascend
4 - One of the damned
5 - Charon in his boat
6 - The demon/critic of nudity
7 - St. Bartholomew with flayed skin containing Michelangelo's self-portrait

side of the picture), ascend to the glories of Heaven. The wicked on the other side are hurled down to Hell, where demons wait to torture them. Charon, from the underworld of Greek mythology, waits below to ferry the souls of the damned to Hell.

It's a grim picture. No one, but no one, is smiling. Even many of the righteous being resurrected (lower left) are either skeletons or cadavers with ghastly skin. The angels have to play tug-of-war with subterranean monsters to drag them from their graves.

Over in Hell, the wicked are tortured by gleeful demons. One of the damned (to the right of the trumpeting angels) has an utterly lost expression, as if saying, "Why did I cheat on my wife?!" Two demons grab him around the ankles to pull him down to the bowels of Hell, condemned to an eternity of constipation.

But it's the terrifying figure of Christ who dominates this scene. As he raises his arm to smite the wicked, he sends a ripple of fear through everyone, and they recoil. Even the saints around him—even Mary beneath his arm (whose interceding days are clearly over)—shrink back in terror. His expression is completely closed, and he turns his head, refusing to even listen to the whining alibis of the damned. Look at Christ's bicep. If this muscular figure looks familiar to you, it's because you've seen it before—the *Belvedere Torso*.

When *The Last Judgment* was unveiled to the public in 1544, it caused a sensation. The pope is said to have dropped to his knees and cried, "Lord, charge me not with my sins when thou shalt come on the Day of Judgment." And it changed the course of art. The complex composition, with more than 300 figures swirling around the figure of Christ, was far beyond traditional Renaissance balance. The twisted figures shown from every imaginable angle challenged other painters to try and top this master of 3-D illusion.

And the sheer terror and drama of the scene was a striking contrast to the placid optimism of, say, Raphael's *School of Athens*. Michelangelo had Baroque-en all the rules of the Renaissance, signaling a new era of art.

With the Renaissance fading, the fleshy figures in *The Last Judgment* aroused murmurs of discontent from Church authorities. Michelangelo rebelled by painting his chief critic into the scene—in Hell. He's the demon in the bottom right corner wrapped in a serpent. Look how Michelangelo covered his privates. Sweet revenge.

(After Michelangelo's death, there was no defense, and prudish church authorities painted the wisps of clothing we see today.)

Now move up close. Study the details of the lower part of the painting from right to left. Charon, with Dr. Spock ears and a Dalí moustache, paddles the damned in a boat full of human turbulence. Look more closely at the J-Day band. Are they reading music, or is it the Judgment Day tally? Before the cleaning, these details were lost in murk.

The Last Judgment marks the end of Renaissance optimism epitomized in *The Creation of Adam*, with its innocence and exaltation of man. There, he was the wakening man-child of a fatherly God. Here, man cowers in fear and unworthiness before a terrifying, wrathful deity.

Michelangelo himself must have wondered how he would be judged—had he used his God-given talents wisely? Look at St. Bartholomew, the bald-bearded guy at Christ's left foot (our right). In the flayed skin he's holding is a barely recognizable face—the twisted self-portrait of a self-questioning Michelangelo.

• *If you exit the Sistine Chapel through the side door next to the screen, you'll soon find yourself facing the Long March back to the museum's entrance. You're one floor below the long corridor you walked to get here.*

Or consider the Sistine–St. Peter's shortcut: In the back corner of the Sistine Chapel, there's an exit that shortcuts directly to St. Peter's Basilica. If you're planning on going to the basilica next, you can exit here and save yourself a 30-minute walk (10–15 minutes back to Vatican Museum entry/exit, then a 15-minute walk to St. Peter's). Note that if you take this shortcut, you'll miss the Pinacoteca—unless you saw it at the beginning.

THE LONG MARCH BACK

Along this corridor, you'll see some of the wealth amassed by the popes, mostly gifts from royalty. Find your hometown on the map of the world from 1529—look in the land called "Terra Incognita." The elaborately decorated library that branches off to the right contains rare manuscripts.

• *The corridor eventually spills out back outside. Follow signs to the ...*

PINACOTECA (PAINTING GALLERY)

How would you like to be Lou Gehrig—always batting behind Babe Ruth? That's the Pinacoteca's lot in life, following Sistine & Co. But after the Vatican's artistic feast, this little collection of paintings is a delicious, 15-minute after-dinner mint.

See this gallery of paintings as you'd view a time-lapse blossoming of a flower, walking through the evolution of painting from medieval to Baroque with just four stops.

• *Enter and stroll up to Room IV.*

Melozzo Da Forli—Musician Angels

Salvaged from a condemned church, this playful series of frescoes shows the delicate grace and nobility of Italy during the time known fondly as the *quattro-centro* (1400s). Notice the detail and the classical purity given these religious figures.

───── PINACOTECA ─────

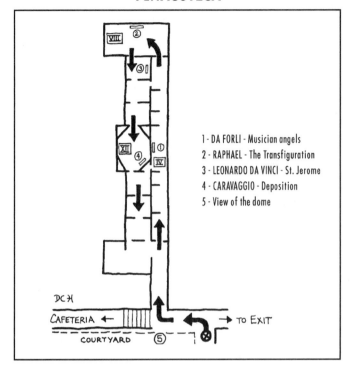

1 - DA FORLI - Musician angels
2 - RAPHAEL - The Transfiguration
3 - LEONARDO DA VINCI - St. Jerome
4 - CARAVAGGIO - Deposition
5 - View of the dome

• *Walk on to the end room (Room VIII) where they've turned on the dark to let Raphael's* Transfiguration *shine. Take a seat.*

Raphael—*The Transfiguration*

Raphael's *Transfiguration* shows Christ on a mountaintop visited in a vision by the prophets Moses and Elijah. Peter, James, and John cower in awe under Jesus, "transfigured before them, his face shining as the sun, his rainment white as light." (As
described by the evangelist Matthew—who can be seen taking notes in the painting's lower left.)

The nine remaining apostles try in vain to heal a boy possessed by demons. Jesus is gone, but "Lady Faith" in the center exhorts them to carry on.

Raphael died in 1520, leaving this final work to be finished by his pupils. The last thing Raphael painted was the beatific face of Jesus, perhaps the most beautiful Christ in existence.
• *Heading back down the parallel corridor, stop in Room IX at the brown, unfinished work by Leonardo.*

Leonardo da Vinci—*St. Jerome* (c. 1482)

This unfinished work gives us a glimpse behind the scenes at Leonardo's technique. Even in the brown undercoating we see the psychological power of Leonardo's genius. The intense penitence and painful ecstasy of the saint come through loud and clear in the anguished body on the rocks and in Jerome's joyful eyes, which see divine forgiveness. Leonardo wrote that a good painter must paint two things: "man and the movements of his spirit." (The patchwork effect is due to Jerome's head having been cut out and used as the seat of a stool in a shoemaker's shop.)
• *Roll on through the sappy sweetness of the Mannerist rooms into the shocking, ultrarealistic world of Caravaggio (Room XII).*

Caravaggio—*Deposition*

Caravaggio was the first painter to intentionally shock his viewers. By exaggerating the contrast between light and dark, shining a brutal third-degree-interrogator-type light on his subjects, and using everyday models in sacred scenes, he takes a huge leap away from the Raphael-pretty past and into the "expressive realism" of the modern world.

A tangle of grief looms out of the darkness as Christ's heavy, dead body nearly pulls the whole group with him from the cross into the tomb.
• *Walk through the rest of the gallery's canvas history of art, enjoy one last view of the Vatican grounds and Michelangelo's dome, then follow the grand spiral staircase down. Go in peace.*

ST. PETER'S BASILICA
TOUR

rome

St. Peter's is the greatest church in Christendom. It represents
the power and splendor of Rome's 2,000-year domination of the
Western world. Built on the memory and grave of the first pope,
St. Peter, this is where the grandeur of ancient Rome became
the grandeur of Christianity.

Orientation

Cost: Free (€4.20 to climb dome).

Dress Code: The dress code is strictly enforced. No shorts or bare
shoulders (applies to men, women, and children), and no miniskirts.

Hours: Daily May through September 07:00 to 19:00, October
through April 07:00 to 18:00. Mass is held daily at 08:30, 09:00,
10:00, 11:00, 12:00, and 17:00 (Sun at 17:45). The lift to the dome
opens daily at 08:30 and closes one hour before the church closes.
The best time to visit the church is early or late.

Getting There: Subway to Ottaviano, then a 10-minute walk
south on Via Ottaviano. Several city buses go right to St. Peter's
Square (#64 is convenient for pickpockets). Taxis are reasonable.

Information: The TI on the left (south) side of the square is excellent (Mon–Sat 08:30–18:30, closed Sun, free Vatican and church
map, for tours see page 156, tel. 06-6988-1662). WCs are to the
right and left (near TI) of the church and on the roof. Drinking
fountains are at the obelisk and near WCs. The post office is
next to the TI.

Tour Length: One hour, plus another hour if you climb the
dome (elevator plus 300 steps one-way).

Checkroom: Free, usually mandatory bag check is outside at
right of entrance.

Starring: Michelangelo, Bernini, Bramante, St. Peter, a heavenly
host, and, occasionally, the pope.

Vatican City

This tiny independent country of just over 100 acres, contained entirely within Rome, has its own postal system, armed guards, helipad, mini–train station, and radio station (KPOP). Politically powerful, the Vatican is the religious capital of 800 million Roman Catholics. If you're not a Catholic, become one for your visit.

Small as it is, Vatican City has two huge sights: St. Peter's Basilica (with Michelangelo's *Pietà*) and the Vatican Museum (with the Sistine Chapel). A helpful TI is just to the left of St. Peter's Basilica (Mon–Sat 08:30–18:30, closed Sun, tel. 06-6988-1662; Vatican switchboard tel. 06-6982, www.vatican.va). The nearest Metro stops are still a 10-minute walk away from either sight: For St. Peter's, the closest stop is Ottaviano; for the Vatican Museum, it's Cipro-Musei Vaticani.

Post Office: The Vatican post, with offices on St. Peter's Square (next to TI) and in the Vatican Museum, is more reliable than Italy's mail service (Mon–Sat 08:30–18:30). The stamps are a collectible bonus (Vatican stamps good throughout Rome; Italian stamps not good at Vatican).

Tours: The Vatican TI conducts free 90-minute tours of St. Peter's (depart from TI at 15:00 Mon, Wed, and Fri, confirm schedule at TI, tel. 06-6988-1662). Tours are the only way to see the Vatican Gardens; book at least a day in advance by calling 06-6988-4466 (€9, Mon–Sat 10:00–12:00, tours start at museum tour desk and finish on St. Peter's Square). To tour the necropolis of St. Peter's and the saint's tomb, call the Excavations Office at 06-6988-5318 (€8, 2 hrs, office open Mon–Fri 09:00–17:00).

OLD ST. PETER'S

• *Find a shady spot where you like the view under the columns around St. Peter's oval-shaped "square." If the pigeons left a clean spot, sit on it.*

Nearly 2,000 years ago, this area was the site of Nero's Circus—a huge Roman chariot racecourse. The obelisk you see in the middle of the square stands where the chariots made their hairpin turns. The Romans had no marching bands, so for halftime entertainment they killed Christians. This persecuted minority was forced to fight wild animals and gladiators, or they were simply crucified. Some were tarred up, tied to posts, and burned—human torches to light up the evening races.

One of those killed here, around A.D. 65, was Peter, Jesus'

VATICAN CITY OVERVIEW

Seeing the Pope: Your best chances for a sighting are on Sunday and Wednesday. The pope usually gives a blessing at noon on Sunday from his apartment on St. Peter's Square (except Aug–Sept, when he speaks at his summer residence at Castel Gandolfo, 40 km from Rome; train

leaves Rome's Termini station at 08:35, returns after his talk). On Wednesday at 10:00, the pope blesses the crowds at St. Peter's from a balcony or canopied platform on the square (except in winter, when he speaks at 11:00 in the 7,000-seat Aula Paola VI Auditorium, next to St. Peter's Basilica). To find out the pope's schedule or to book a free spot for the Wednesday blessing (either for a seat on the square or in the auditorium), call 06-6988-3017. The weekly entertainment guide *Roma c'è* always has a "Seeing the Pope" section. If you don't want to see the pope, minimize crowd problems by avoiding these times.

right-hand man, who had come to Rome to spread the message of love. Peter was crucified on an upside-down cross at his own request because he felt unworthy to die as his master had. His remains were buried in a nearby cemetery where, for 250 years, they were quietly and secretly revered.

When Christianity was finally legalized in 313, the Christian emperor Constantine built a church on the site of the martyrdom of this first "pope," or bishop of Rome, from whom all later popes claimed their authority as head of the Church. "Old St. Peter's" lasted 1,200 years (A.D. 324–1500).

By the time of the Renaissance, old St. Peter's was falling apart and was considered unfit to be the center of the Western Church.

The new, larger church we see today was begun in 1506, and was actually built around the old one. As the project was completed 120 years later, after many changes of plans, old St. Peter's was dismantled and carried out the doors of the new one.

• *Ideally, you should head out to the obelisk to view the square and read this. But let me guess—it's 95 degrees, right? OK, read on in the shade of these stone sequoias.*

ST. PETER'S SQUARE

St. Peter's Square, with its ring of columns, symbolizes the arms of the church "maternally embracing Catholics, heretics, and the faithless." It was designed by the Baroque architect Bernini,

who also did much of the work we'll see inside. Numbers first: 284 columns, 17 meters high, in stern Doric style. Topping them are Bernini's 90 favorite saints, each three meters tall. The "square" itself is elliptical, 200 by 150 meters.

The obelisk in the center is 27 meters of solid granite weighing over 300 tons. Think for a second about how much history this monument has seen. Erected originally in Egypt over 2,000 years ago, it witnessed the fall of the pharoahs to the Greeks and then to the Romans. It was then moved to Imperial Rome, where it stood impassively watching the slaughter of Christians at the racecourse and the torture of Protestants by the Inquisition (in the yellow and rust building just outside the square, to the left of the church). Today, it watches over the church, a reminder that each civilization builds on the previous ones. The puny cross on top reminds us that our Christian culture is but a thin veneer over our pagan origins.

• *Now venture out across the burning desert to the obelisk, which provides a narrow sliver of shade.*

Face the church, then turn about-face and say "*Grazie, Benito.*" I don't make a habit of thanking fascist dictators, but in the 1930s, Benito Mussolini did open up this broad boulevard, finally letting people see the dome of St. Peter's, which had been hidden for centuries by the facade. From here at the obelisk, Michelangelo's magnificent dome can only peek its top over the bulky Baroque front entrance.

The gray building at two o'clock to the right (as you face the church), rising up behind Bernini's colonnade, is where the

ST. PETER'S SQUARE

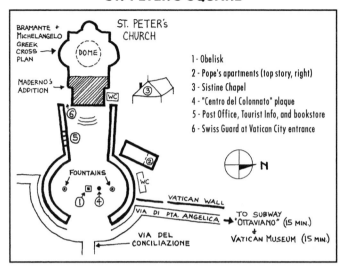

ST. PETER's CHURCH

BRAMANTE + MICHELANGELO GREEK CROSS PLAN →

(DOME)

MADERNO's ADDITION →

WC

③

⑥

⑤

FOUNTAINS

① ④

②

WC

1 - Obelisk
2 - Pope's apartments (top story, right)
3 - Sistine Chapel
4 - "Centro del Colonnato" plaque
5 - Post Office, Tourist Info, and bookstore
6 - Swiss Guard at Vatican City entrance

N

VATICAN WALL

VIA DI PTA. ANGELICA

VIA DEL CONCILIAZIONE

TO SUBWAY
→ "OTTAVIANO" (15 MIN.)
↓
VATICAN MUSEUM (15 MIN.)

pope lives. The last window on the right of the top floor is his bedroom. The window to the left of that is his study, where he appears occasionally to greet the masses. If you come to the square at night as a Poping Tom, you might see the light

on—the pope burns much midnight oil.

On more formal occasions (which you may have seen on TV), the pope appears from the church itself, on the small balcony above the central door.

The Sistine Chapel is just to the right of the facade—the small gray-brown building with the triangular roof-topped by an antenna. The tiny chimney (the pimple along the roofline midway up the left side) is where the famous smoke signals announce the election of each new pope. If the smoke is black, a 75 percent majority hasn't been reached. White smoke means a new pope has been selected.

Walk to the right, five pavement plaques from the obelisk, to one marked "Centro del Colonnato." From here, all of Bernini's columns on the right side line up. The curved Baroque square still pays its respects to Renaissance mathematical symmetry.

• *Climb the gradually sloping stairs past crowd barriers and the huge statues of St. Paul with his two-edged sword and St. Peter with his bushy hair and keys.*

You'll pass two of the entrances to Vatican City—one to the left of the facade, one to the right in the crook of Bernini's "arm." Guarding this small but powerful country's border crossing are the mercenary guards from Switzerland. You have to wonder if they really know how to use those pikes. Their colorful uniforms are said to have been designed by Michelangelo, though he was not known for his sense of humor.

• *Enter the atrium (entrance hall) of the church. You'll pass by the dress-code enforcers and a gaggle of ticked-off guys in shorts.*

THE BASILICA

The Atrium

The atrium is itself bigger than most churches. Facing us are the five famous bronze doors, leading into the main church. The central door, made from the melted-down bronze of the original door of old St. Peter's, is only opened on special occasions.

The far-right entrance is the Holy Door, opened only during Holy Years. On Christmas Eve every 25 years, the pope knocks three times with a silver hammer and the door opens, welcoming pilgrims to pass through. After opening the door on Christmas Eve, 1999, he bricked it up again with a ceremonial trowel a year later to await another 24 years. On the door, note Jesus' shiny knees, polished by pious pilgrims who touch them for a blessing.

The other doors are modern, reminding us that amid all this tradition, the Catholic Church has changed enormously even within our lifetimes. Door #2 (second from left) commemorates the kneeling pope, John (Giovanni) XXIII, who opened the landmark Vatican II Council in the early 1960s. This meeting of Church leaders brought the medieval Church into the modern age—they dropped outdated rituals, such as the use of Latin in the Mass—and made old doctrines "relevant" to modern times.

• *Now for one of Europe's great "wow" experiences. Enter the church. Gape for a while. But don't gape at Michelangelo's famous Pietà (on the right). That's this tour's finale. I'll wait for you at the round maroon pavement stone between the entrance and exit doors.*

The Church

While ancient Rome fell, its grandeur survived. Roman basilicas became churches, senators became bishops, and the Pontifex Maximus (Emperor)...remained the Pontifex Maximus (Pope). This church is appropriately huge.

ST. PETER'S BASILICA

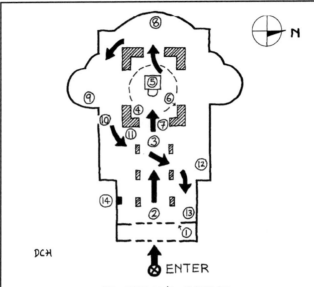

DCH

ST. PETER'S SQUARE

1 - Holy Door

2 - Site of Charlemagne's coronation, 800 AD

3 - Extent of the original "Greek Cross" church plan

4 - St. Andrew statue (view the dome from here)

5 - Main altar directly over Peter's tomb. BERNINI's 70-foot bronze canopy covers the altar

6 - Stairs down to the crypt : the foundation of old St. Peter's, chapels and tombs of popes
(the entrance moves around)

7 - Statue of St. Peter with irresistibly kissable toe

8 - BERNINI - Dove window and "St. Peter's Throne"

9 - Site of Peter's crucifixion

10 - Museum entrance

11 - RAPHAEL - "Transfiguration" mosaic

12 - Blessed Sacrament Chapel

13 - MICHELANGELO - Pieta

14 - Elevator to roof and dome-climb
(this entrance moves around - sometimes it is even outside)

Size before beauty: The golden window at the far end is two
football fields away. The dove in the window above the altar has
the wingspan of a 747 (OK, maybe not quite, but it is big). The
church covers six acres—if planted with wheat, it could feed a
small city. The babies at the base of the pillars along the main hall

(the nave) are adult size. The lettering in the gold band along the top of the pillars is two meters high. Really. The church has a capacity of 60,000 standing worshipers (that's more than 1,200 tour groups).

The church is huge and it feels huge, but everything is actually designed to make it seem smaller and more intimate than it really is. For example, the statue of St. Teresa near the bottom of the first pillar on the right is five meters tall. The statue above her near the top looks the same size, but is actually two meters taller, giving the impression that it's not as far away as it really is. Similarly, the fancy bronze canopy over the altar at the far end is as tall as a seven-story building. That makes the great height of the dome seem smaller.

Looking down the nave, we get a sense of the grandeur of ancient Rome that was carried on by the Catholic Church. The floor plan is based on the ancient Roman basilica, or law-court building, with a central aisle (nave) flanked by two side aisles.

The goal of this unprecedented building project was to "put the dome of the Pantheon atop the Forum's Basilica of Constantine." If you've seen these two Roman structures, you have an idea of this megavision. In fact, many of the stones used to build St. Peter's were scavenged from the ruined law courts of ancient Rome.

On the floor near the central doorway is a round slab of porphyry stone in the maroon color of ancient Roman officials. This is the spot where, on Christmas night in A.D. 800, the French King Charlemagne was crowned "Holy Roman Emperor." Even in the Dark Ages, when Rome was virtually abandoned and visitors reported that the city "had more thieves and wolves than decent people," its imperial legacy made it a fitting place to symbolically establish a briefly united Europe.

You're surrounded by marble, gold, stucco, mosaics, columns of stone, and pillars of light. This is Baroque, the decorative style popular at the height of the wars between Protestants and Catholics. It was intended to overwhelm and impress the masses with the authority of the Church. St. Peter's was very expensive to build and decorate. The popes financed it by selling "indulgences," allowing the rich to literally buy forgiveness from the Church. This kind of corruption inspired an obscure German monk named Martin Luther to rebel and start the Protestant Reformation. The Baroque interior by Bernini was part of the Church's "Counter"-Reformation, a time when the Church aggressively defended itself and art became a powerful propaganda tool. Here, we see a glorious golden vision of heaven available to anyone— who remained a good Catholic.

• *Now, walk straight up the center of the nave toward the altar.*

"Michelangelo's Church"—The Greek Cross

The plaques on the floor show where other, smaller churches of the world would end if they were placed inside St. Peter's: St. Paul's Cathedral in London (Londinense), the Florence Cathedral, and so on.

You'll also walk over circular golden grates. Stop at the second one (at the 3rd pillar from the entrance). Look back at the entrance and realize that if Michelangelo had had his way, this whole long section of the church wouldn't exist. The nave was extended after his death.

Michelangelo was 70 years old when the pope persuaded him to take over the church project and cap it with a dome. He agreed, intending to put the dome over Bramante's original "Greek Cross" floor plan (+), with four equal arms. In optimistic Renaissance times, this symmetrical arrangement symbolized perfection—the orderliness of the created world and the goodness of man (who was created in God's image). But Michelangelo was a Renaissance Man in Counter-Reformation times. The Church, struggling against Protestants and its own corruption, opted for a plan designed to impress the world with its grandeur—the Latin cross of the Crucifixion with its nave extended to accommodate the grand religious spectacles of the Baroque period.

• *Continue toward the altar, entering Michelangelo's Church. Park yourself in front of the statue of St. Andrew to the left of the altar, the guy holding an X-shaped cross. Like Andrew, gaze up into the dome. Gasp if you must—never stifle a gasp.*

The Dome

The dome soars higher than a football field on end, 130 meters to the top of the lantern. It glows with light from its windows, the blue and gold mosaics creating a cool, solemn atmosphere. In this majestic vision of heaven, we see (above the windows) Jesus, Mary, and a ring of saints, more rings of angels above them, and, way up in the ozone, God the Father (a blur of blue and red, without binoculars).

Listen to the hum of visitors echoing through St. Peter's. Churches are an early form of biofeedback where we can become aware of ourselves, hear our own human sounds, and reflect on our place in the cosmos. Half animal, half angel, stretched between heaven and earth, born to live only a short while, a bubble of foam on a great cresting wave of humanity.
• *But I digress.*

Peter

The base of the dome is ringed with a gold banner telling us in massive blue letters why this church is so important. According to Catholics, Peter was selected by Jesus to head the church. The banner in Latin quotes from the Bible where Jesus says to him, "You are Peter (*Tu es Petrus*) and upon this rock I will build my church" (Matthew 16:18). Peter was the first bishop of Rome, and his authority has supposedly passed in an unbroken chain to each succeeding bishop of Rome—that is, the 250-odd popes that followed.

Under the dome, under the bronze canopy, under the altar, some seven meters under the marble floor, rest the bones of St. Peter, the "rock" upon which this particular church was built. Go to the railing and look down into the small, lighted niche below the altar with a box containing bishops' shawls—a symbol of how

 Peter's authority spread to the other churches. Peter's tomb is just below this box.

Are they really the bones of Jesus' apostle? According to a papal pronouncement: definitely maybe. The traditional site of his tomb was sealed up when Old St. Peter's was built on it in A.D. 326, and it remained sealed until 1940, when it was opened for archaeological study. Bones were found, dated from the first century, of a robust man who died in old age. His body was wrapped in expensive cloth. Various inscriptions and graffiti in the tomb indicate that second- and third-century visitors thought this was Peter's tomb. Does that mean it's really Peter? Who am I to disagree with the pope? Definitely maybe.

If you line up the cross on the altar with the dove in the window, you'll notice that the niche below the cross is just off-center compared with the rest of the church. Why? Because Michelangelo built the church around the traditional location of the tomb, not the actual location discovered by modern archaeology.

Back in the nave sits a bronze statue of Peter under a canopy. This is one of a handful of pieces of art that was in the earlier church. In one hand he holds the keys, the symbol of the authority given him by Christ, while with the other he blesses us. He's wearing the toga of a Roman senator. It may be that the original statue was of a senator and the bushy head and keys were added later to make it Peter. His big right toe has been worn smooth by the lips of pilgrims. Stand in line and kiss it, or, to avoid hoof-and-mouth disease, touch your hand to your lips, then rub the toe. This is simply an act of reverence with no legend attached, though you can make one up if you like.

The Main Altar

The main altar beneath the dome and canopy (the white marble slab with cross and candlesticks) is used only when the pope himself says Mass. He often conducts the Sunday morning service when he's in town, a sight worth seeing. I must admit, though, it's a little strange being frisked at the door for weapons at the holiest place in Christendom.

The tiny altar would be lost in this enormous church if it weren't for Bernini's seven-story bronze canopy, which "extends" the altar upward and reduces the perceived distance between floor and ceiling.

Gian Lorenzo Bernini (1598–1680) is the man most responsible for the interior decoration of the church. The altar area was his masterpiece, a "theater" for holy spectacles. Bernini did: (1) the bronze canopy; (2) the dove window in the apse surrounded by bronzework and statues; (3) the statue of lance-bearing St. Longinus (which became the model for the other 3 statues); (4) the balconies above the four statues, incorporating the actual corkscrew columns looted from Solomon's Temple in Jerusalem; and (5) much of the marble floor decoration. Bernini, the father of Baroque, gave an impressive unity to an amazing variety of pillars, windows, statues, chapels, and aisles.

The bronze canopy is his crowning touch. The Baroque-looking corkscrew columns are enlarged copies of the ancient

Bernini Blitz

Nowhere is there such a conglomeration of works by the flamboyant genius who remade the church—and the city—in the Baroque style. Here's your scavenger-hunt list. You have 20 minutes. Go.

1. St. Peter's Square: design and statues
2. Constantine equestrian relief (right end of atrium)
3. Decoration (stucco, gold leaf, marble, etc.) of side aisles (flanking the nave)
4. Tabernacle (the templelike altarpiece) inside Blessed Sacrament Chapel
5. Much of the marble floor throughout church
6. Bronze canopy over the altar
7. St. Longinus statue (holding a lance) near altar
8. Balconies (above each of the four statues) with corkscrew, Solomonic columns
9. Dove window, bronze sunburst, angels, "Throne," and Church Fathers (in the apse)
10. Tomb of Pope Urban VIII (far end of the apse, right side)
11. Tomb of Pope Alexander VII (near the left transept, over a doorway, with the gold skeleton smothered in jasper poured like maple syrup).
    Bizarre . . . Baroque . . . Bernini.

columns from Solomon's Temple. The bronze used here was taken and melted down from the ancient Pantheon. On the marble base of the columns are three bees on a shield, the symbol of the Barberini family, who commissioned the work and ordered the raid on the Pantheon. As the saying went, "What the barbarians didn't do, the Barberini did."

Starting from the column to the left of the altar, walk clockwise around the canopy. Notice the female faces on the marble bases, about eye level above the bees. Someone in the Barberini family was pregnant during the making of the canopy, so Bernini put the various stages of childbirth on the bases. Continue clockwise to the last base to see how it came out.

• *Walk into the apse (it's the front area with the golden dove window) and take a seat.*

The Apse

Bernini's dove window shines above the smaller front altar used for everyday services. The Holy Spirit, in the form of a two-meter dove, pours sunlight onto the faithful through the alabaster windows, turning into artificial rays of gold and reflecting off swirling gold clouds, angels, and winged babies. This is the epitome of Baroque—a highly decorative, glorious, mixed-media work designed to overwhelm the viewer.

Beneath the dove is the centerpiece of this structure, the so-called "Throne of Peter," an oak chair built in medieval times for a king. Subsequently, it was encrusted with tradition and encased in bronze by Bernini as a symbol of papal authority. Statues of four early church fathers support the chair, a symbol of how bishops should support the pope in troubled times— times like the Counter-Reformation. Bernini's Baroque was great propaganda for the power of the Catholic Church.

This is a good place to remember that St. Peter's is a church, not a museum. In the apse, Mass is said daily (Mon–Sat at 17:00, Sun at 17:45) for pilgrims, tourists, and Roman citizens alike. Wooden confessional booths are available for Catholics to tell their sins to a listening ear and receive forgiveness and peace of mind. The faithful renew their faith and the faithless gain inspiration. Sit here, look at the light streaming through the windows, turn and gaze up into the dome, and quietly contemplate your god.

Or...

Contemplate this: the mystery of empty space. The bench you're sitting on and the marble at your feet, solid as they may seem, consist overwhelmingly of open space—99.9999 percent open space. The atoms that form these "solid" benches are themselves mostly open space. If the nucleus of your average atom were as large as the period at the end of this sentence, its electrons would be specks of dust orbiting around it—at the top of Michelangelo's dome. Empty space. Perhaps matter is only an aberration in an empty universe.

• *Like, wow.*

Now head to the left of the main altar into the south transept. At the far end, look left at the dark painting of St. Peter crucified upside down.

Left Transept

The painting is at the exact spot (according to tradition) where Peter was killed 1,900 years ago.

The Romans were actually quite tolerant of other religions. All they required of their conquered peoples was allegiance to the empire by worshiping the emperor as a god. For most religions, this was no problem, but monotheistic Christians were children of a jealous God who would not allow worship of any others. They refused to worship the emperor and valiantly stuck by their faith even when burned alive, crucified, or thrown to the lions. Their bravery, optimism in suffering, and message of love struck a chord among slaves and members of the lower classes. The religion started by a poor carpenter grew, despite occasional pogroms (surprise attacks) by fanatical emperors. In three short centuries, Christianity went from a small Jewish sect in Jerusalem to the official religion of the world's greatest empire.

While this is a true painting, nearly all the other "paintings" in the church are actually mosaic copies made from thousands of colored chips the size of your little fingernail. Smoke and humidity would damage real paintings. Around the corner on the right (heading back toward the central nave), pause at the copy of Raphael's huge "painting" (mosaic) of *The Transfiguration*, especially if you won't be seeing the original in the Vatican Museum.

• *Back near the entrance to the church, in the far corner, behind bullet-proof glass is . . .*

The *Pietà*

Michelangelo was 24 years old when he completed this *Pietà* (pee-ay-TAH) of Mary with the dead body of Christ taken from the cross.

Michelangelo, with his total mastery of the real world, captures the sadness of the moment. Mary cradles her crucified son in her lap. Christ's lifeless right arm drooping down lets us know how heavy this corpse is. His smooth skin is accented by the rough folds of Mary's robe. Mary tilts her head downward, looking at her dead son with sad tenderness. Her left hand is upturned as if asking, "How could they do this to you?"

Michelangelo didn't think of sculpting as creating a figure, but as simply freeing the God-made figure from the prison of marble around it. He'd attack a project like this with an inspired passion, chipping away to reveal what God put inside.

Realistic as this work is, its true power lies in the subtle "unreal" features. Look how small and childlike Christ is compared with the massive Mary. Unnoticed at first, this accentuates the subconscious impression of Mary enfolding Jesus in her maternal

love. Notice how young Mary is. She's the mother of a 33-year-old man, but here she's portrayed as a teenage girl. Michelangelo did it to show how Mary was the eternally youthful "handmaiden" of the Lord, always serving Him, even at this moment of supreme sacrifice. She accepts God's will, even if it means giving up her own son.

The statue is a solid pyramid of maternal tenderness. Yet within this, Christ's body tilts diagonally down to the right and Mary's hem flows with it. Subconsciously, we feel the weight of this dead God sliding from her lap to the ground.

On Christmas morning, 1972, a madman with a hammer entered St. Peter's and began hacking away at the *Pietà*. The damage was repaired, but that's why there's a shield of bullet-proof glass today.

This is Michelangelo's only signed work. The story goes that he overheard some pilgrims praising his finished *Pietà*, but attributing it to a second-rate sculptor from a lesser city. He was so enraged he grabbed his chisel and chipped "Michelangelo Buonarotti of Florence did this" in the ribbon running down Mary's chest.

On your right is the inside of the Holy Door. It won't be opened until Christmas Eve, 2024, the dawn of the next Jubilee Year. If there's a prayer inside you, ask that when it's next opened, St. Peter's will no longer need security checks or bulletproof glass.

Up to the Dome (Cupola)

A good way to finish a visit to St. Peter's is to go up to the dome for the best view of Rome anywhere.

There are two levels, the rooftop of the church and the very top of the dome. An elevator (€4.20) takes you to the first level, on the church roof just above the facade. Even from there, you have a commanding view of St. Peter's Square, the statues on the colonnade, Rome across the Tiber in front of you, and the dome itself—almost terrifying in its nearness—looming behind you.

From here, you can also go inside to the gallery ringing the interior of the dome, where you can look down inside the church. Notice the dusty top of Bernini's seven-story-tall canopy far below. Study the mosaics up close—and those huge letters! It's worth the elevator ride for this view alone.

From this level, if you're energetic, continue all the way up to the top of the dome. The staircase (free at this point) actually winds between the outer shell and the inner one. It's a long, sweaty, stuffy, claustrophobic, 15-minute climb, but worth it. The view from the summit is great, the fresh air even better. Find the big, white Victor Emmanuel Monument with the two statues on top and the Pantheon with its large, light, shallow dome. The large rectangular building to the left of the obelisk is the Vatican Museum, stuffed with art. Survey the Vatican grounds, with its mini–train system and lush gardens. Look down into the square on the tiny pilgrims buzzing like electrons around the nucleus of Catholicism.

The dome opens daily at 08:30 and closes at 18:00 May through September and at 17:00 October through April. Allow one hour for the full trip up and down, a half hour to go only to the roof and gallery. The entry to the elevator is just outside the basilica, on the porch, on the north side of St. Peter's. Look for signs to the *cupola*.

THE REST OF THE CHURCH

The Crypt: You can go down to the foundations of old St. Peter's, containing tombs of popes and memorial chapels. But you won't see St. Peter's tomb unless you take a tour (€8, call Excavations Office at 06-6988-5318). The staircase entrance varies, but it's usually inside the church near St. Andrew or one of his three fellow statues. Seeing the crypt is free, but the visit takes you back outside the church, a 15-minute detour. (Do it when you're ready to leave.)

The Museum (Museo-Tesoro): If you like old jewels and papal robes, you'll find the treasures and splendors of Roman Christianity a marked contrast to the poverty of early Christians. It's located near (but not in) the left transept, through a gray portal.

Blessed Sacrament Chapel: You're welcome to step through the metalwork gates into this oasis of peace reserved for prayer and meditation. It's located on the right-hand side of the church, about midway to the altar.

PILGRIM'S ROME

Pilgrims to Rome try to visit four great basilicas: St. Peter's (of course), Santa Maria Maggiore, San Giovanni in Laterano, and San Paolo Fuori Le Mura. For your sightseeing pleasure, we've replaced inconvenient San Paolo (daily 07:00–18:00, Metro: San Paolo) with the fascinating and more handy San Clemente.

The pilgrim industry helped shape Rome. Ancient Rome's population peaked at about 1.2 million. When Rome fell in 476, barbarians cut off the water supply by breaking the aqueducts, Romans fled the city, and the Tiber silted up. During the Dark Ages, mosquitoes ruled over a pathetic village of 50,000 . . . bad news for pilgrims, bad news for the Vatican. Back then, the Catholic Church was the Christian Church. Because popes needed a place fit for pilgrimages, the Church revitalized the city. Hotel- and restaurant-owners cheered.

In 1587, Pope Sixtus V reconnected aqueducts and established boulevards connecting the great churches and pilgrimage sites. To make his Renaissance capital easy to navigate, he built long, straight streets for pilgrims. Obelisks served as markers. As you explore the city, think like a pilgrim. Look down long roads and you'll see either a grand church or an obelisk (from which you'll see a grand church). For example, Via XX Settembre is a montage of pilgrimage churches connecting the Catacombs of St. Agnese (to the east) with the pope's home on the Quirinal (to the west).

SAN GIOVANNI IN LATERANO

Imagine the jubilation when this church—the first Christian church in the city of Rome—was opened around A.D. 318. Christians could finally "come out" and worship openly without fear of reprisal. After that glorious beginning, the church has served as the center of Catholicism and the home of the popes

PILGRIM'S ROME

up until the Renaissance renovation of St. Peter's. Until 1870, all popes were "crowned" here. Even today, it's the home church of the Bishop of Rome—the pope. (Free, Mon–Sat 06:15–12:00, 15:00–18:15, Sun 06:15–12:00, 15:30–18:45, on Piazza San Giovanni in Laterano, Metro: San Giovanni.)

Exterior

The massive facade is 18th-century, with Christ triumphant on the top. The blocky adjacent building on the right is the Lateran Palace, standing on the site of the old Papal Palace—residence of popes until about 1300. Across the street to your right are the pope's private chapel and the Holy Stairs (Scala Santa), popular with pilgrims. Behind you, through the gate in a well-preserved chunk of the ancient Roman wall, is the San Giovanni Metro stop.

1. Statue of Constantine
(inside the portico, far left end)

It's October 28, A.D. 312, and Constantine—sword tucked under his arm and leaning confidently on a (missing) spear—has conquered Maxentius and liberated Rome. Constantine marched to this spot where his enemy's personal bodyguards lived, trashed their pagan idols, and dedicated the place to the god who gave him his victory—Christ. The holes in Constantine's head once held a golden, halolike crown for the emperor who legalized Christianity.

2. Central Doorway
(in the portico)

These bronze doors, with their floral designs and acorn studs, are the original doors from ancient Rome's Senate House (Curia) in the Forum. The Church moved these here in the 1650s to remind people that from the 13th century, the Church was Europe's lawmaker. The star borders were added to make these big doors bigger.

3. Giotto Fresco
(inside church, 2nd pillar in right aisle)

Pope Boniface VIII proclaims the first (modern) Jubilee Year in 1300, in this fading fresco attributed to the first "modern" painter, Giotto. A servant holds the pope's cue cards.

4. Basilica Floor Plan

San Giovanni was the first public church in Rome and the model for all later churches, including St. Peter's. The floor plan—a large central hall (nave) flanked by two side aisles—was based on the ancient Roman basilica (law courts) floor plan. These buildings were big enough to accommodate the large Christian congregations.

5. Baldacchino
(canopy over altar)

In the upper cage are two silver statues of saints Peter (with keys) and Paul (sword), containing their . . . heads.

6. Golden Columns from Temple of Jupiter
(left transept)

Tradition says that these gilded bronze columns once stood in pagan Rome's holiest spot—the Temple of Jupiter, the King of all Gods, on the summit of Capitol Hill (c. 50 B.C.). Now they support a pediment topped by a bearded, Jupiter-like God the Father.

SAN GIOVANNI IN LATERANO

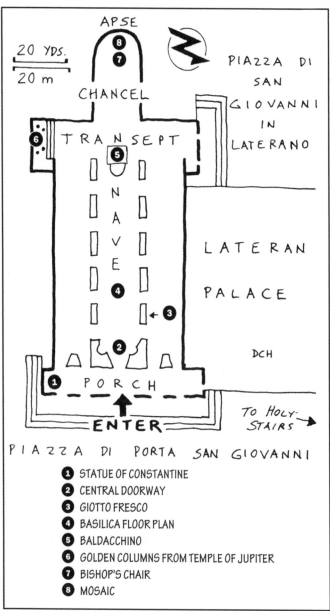

20 YDS.
20 m

APSE

❽
❼

CHANCEL

PIAZZA DI SAN GIOVANNI IN LATERANO

❻ T R A N S E P T

❺

N A V E

❹

← ❸

LATERAN

PALACE

❷

DCH

❶ P O R C H

ENTER

TO HOLY-STAIRS →

PIAZZA DI PORTA SAN GIOVANNI

❶ STATUE OF CONSTANTINE
❷ CENTRAL DOORWAY
❸ GIOTTO FRESCO
❹ BASILICA FLOOR PLAN
❺ BALDACCHINO
❻ GOLDEN COLUMNS FROM TEMPLE OF JUPITER
❼ BISHOP'S CHAIR
❽ MOSAIC

7. Bishop's Chair (in apse)

The chair (or "cathedra") reminds visitors that this is the cathedral of Rome...and the pope himself is the bishop that sits here.

8. Mosaic

(in semicircular dome of apse)
The original design dates from about 450. (The mosaic was remodeled with the addition of saints in the 13th century.) Pop in a coin for light. You'll see a cross, animals, plants, and the River Jordan running along the base.

Mosaic, of course, was an ancient Roman specialty adapted by medieval Christians. The figure of Christ (above the cross) must have been a glorious sight to early worshipers. It was one of the first legal images of Christ ever seen in formerly pagan Rome.

Holy Stairs (Scala Santa)

The stairs are outside the church and across the street.

In 326, Emperor Constantine's mother (St. Helena) brought home the 28 marble steps of Pilate's residence. Jesus climbed these steps on the day he was sentenced to death. Each day, hundreds of "penitent faithful" climb these steps on their

knees (reciting a litany of prayers, available at the desk to the right of the entry). The steps—covered with walnut wood with small glass-covered holes showing stains from Jesus' blood—lead to the "Holy of Holies" (Sancta Sanctorum), the private chapel of the popes in the Middle Ages. With its world-class

relics, this chapel was considered the holiest place on earth. While the relics are now in the Vatican and the chapel is locked up, you can look through the grated windows in the doors atop the staircase.

On September 20, 1870, as nationalist forces unifying Italy took Rome and ended the pope's temporal power, Pope Pius IX left his Quirinal Palace home for the last time. He stopped here to climb the steps, pray in his chapel, and bless his supporters from the top of the steps. Then he fled to the Vatican, where he spent the rest of his days.

SANTA MARIA MAGGIORE

The basilica of Santa Maria celebrates Holy Mary, the mother of Jesus. One of Rome's oldest and best-preserved churches, it sports fifth-century mosaics, which give it the feel of the early Christian community. (It's on Piazza Santa Maria Maggiore, Metro: Vittorio.)

Exterior

Mary's column originally stood in the Forum's Basilica of Constantine. The fifth-century church built in her honor proclaims she was indeed the Mother of God—a fact disputed by hair-splitting theologians of the day. When you step inside the church, you'll be exiting Italy and entering the Vatican—the "Maggiore" indicates this church, a Vatican possession, was much more important than other churches dedicated to the Virgin Mary.

Interior

Despite the Renaissance ceiling and Baroque crusting, you still feel like you're walking into an early Christian church. The stately rows of columns, the simple layout, the cheery colors, the spacious nave—it's easy to imagine worshipers finding an oasis of peace here as the Roman Empire crashed around them.

1. Manger Fragments (under altar in lighted niche)

A kneeling pope prays before a glass case with an urn that contains several pieces of wood, bound by iron and said to be from Jesus' crib. The church was built around these relics of Mary's motherhood. Are they the real thing? Look into the eyes of pilgrims who visit.

2. Mosaics in Chancel Arch

(the ceiling arch that "frames" the altar's purple canopy)
Colorful panels tell Mary's story in fifth-century Roman terms. Mary (in panel just left of center) sits on a throne in royal purple like an empress, surrounded by haloed senator-saints in white togas. The angel Gabriel swoops down to announce to Mary that she'll conceive Jesus, and the Dove of the Holy Spirit follows. Below (bottom left panel) are sheep, representing the apostles, entering the city of Jerusalem ("Hiervsalem").

3. Apse Mosaic (in semicircular dome of apse)

This 13th-century mosaic shows Mary being crowned by Jesus. By the Middle Ages, her cult status was secure.

4. Nave Mosaics (right side of nave, starting near altar)

The church contains some of the world's oldest and best-preserved mosaics from Christian Rome. Those with good eyesight or

SANTA MARIA MAGGIORE

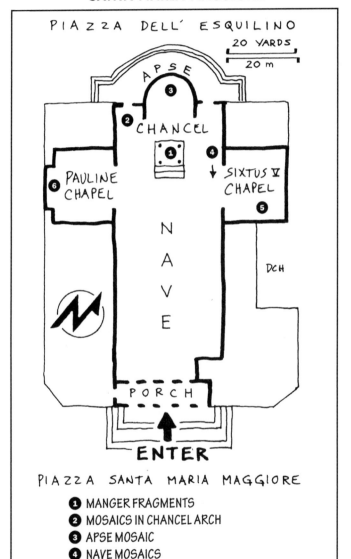

PIAZZA DELL' ESQUILINO

20 YARDS

20 m

APSE

❸

❷ CHANCEL

❶

PAULINE
❻ CHAPEL

❹ ↓ SIXTUS V
CHAPEL

❺

N
A
V
E

DCH

PORCH

ENTER

PIAZZA SANTA MARIA MAGGIORE

❶ MANGER FRAGMENTS
❷ MOSAICS IN CHANCEL ARCH
❸ APSE MOSAIC
❹ NAVE MOSAICS
❺ TOMB OF SIXTUS V
❻ MADONNA PAINTING AND MIRACLE RELIEF

binoculars will enjoy watching the story of Moses unfold in a series of surprisingly colorful and realistic scenes—more sophisticated than anything that would be seen for a thousand years.

The small, square mosaic panels are above the columns, on the right-hand side of the nave. Start at the altar and work back toward the entry.

1. It's a later painting, skip it.
2. Pharaoh's daughter (upper left) and her maids take baby Moses from the Nile.
3. Moses (lower half of panel) sees a burning bush that reconnects him with his Hebrew origins.
4. The Israelites (left side) flee Egypt through a path in the Red Sea, while Pharaoh's troops drown.
5. Moses leads them across the Sinai desert (upper half), and God provides for them with a flock of quail (lower half).
6. Moses (upper half) sticks his magic rod in a river to desalinate it.
7. The Israelites battle their enemies while Moses commands from a hillside.
8. Moses (upper left) brings the Ten Commandments, then goes with Joshua (upper right) to die.
9. Joshua crosses the (rather puny) Jordan River...
10. ...attacks Jericho...
11. ...and the walls come a-tumblin' down.

5. Tomb of Sixtus V
(right transept, the praying pope on right-hand wall)

The Rome we see today is due largely to Pope Sixtus V (or was it Fiftus VI)? This energetic pope (1585–1590) leveled shoddy medieval Rome and erected grand churches connected by long, broad boulevards spiked with obelisks as focal points. (The city of Rome has 13 Egyptian obelisks—all of Egypt has only 5.) The relief panels (upper right) show some of the obelisks and buildings he commissioned.

6. Madonna Painting and Miracle Relief
(left transept, over altar)

The altar, a geologist's delight, is adorned with jasper, agate, amethyst, lapis lazuli, and gold angels. Amid it all is a simple, iconic version of the lady this church is dedicated to: Mary.

Above the painting is a bronze relief panel showing a pope, with amazed bystanders shoveling snow. In 352 Mary appeared to Pope Liberius in a dream, telling him: "Build me a church where the snow falls." The next morning, they discovered a small patch of snow here on the Esquiline Hill—on August 5—and this church, dedicated to Santa Maria, was begun.

SAN CLEMENTE

Here, like nowhere else, you'll enjoy the layers of Rome—a 12th-century basilica sits atop a fourth-century Christian basilica, which sits atop a second-century Mithraic Temple and some even earlier Roman buildings. (€2.60, Mon–Sat 09:00–12:30, 15:00–18:00, opens Sun at 10:00, on Via di San Giovanni in Laterano, Metro: Colosseo.)

Upper Church—12th Century

The church (at today's ground level) is dedicated to the fourth pope, Clement, who was martyred by drowning around A.D. 100—tied to an anchor by angry Romans and tossed overboard. You'll see his symbol, the anchor around the church. While today's entry is on the side, the original entry was through the courtyard in back.

Start your visit in this courtyard—a kind of defensive atrium common in medieval times. Entering the church from here, notice (on the left) the reconstructions of some ancient frescoes. You'll see the faded originals in the lower church, but note the splendid detail of these first.

The chapel in the corner is dedicated to St. Catherine of Alexandria, a noblewoman martyred for her defense of persecuted Christians. This chapel was frescoed, at least in part, by the proto-Renaissance master Masaccio in the early 15th century. Working from left to right, follow the story: Catherine protests in defense of the Christians to Emperor Maxentius; her famously brilliant defense of Christianity against 50 philosophers; Catherine convert-ing the empress during a prison visit; Maxentius beheads his empress and condemns Catherine to be broken between two spiked wheels; an angel rescues Catherine, then she's beheaded; and finally two angels carry her to the top of Mount Sinai. Also notice the delight-ful Annunciation above the chapel on the arch and the big St. Christopher (patron saint of travelers, on the right—with 500-year-old graffiti from pilgrims still visible).

The carved marble choir enclosure in the middle of the church (Schola Cantorum) was where the cantors sat. About 1,200 years ago, it stood in the old church beneath us.

In the apse, study the fine 12th-century mosaics. The deli-cate Crucifixion—with Christ

sharing the cross with a dozen apostles as doves—is engulfed
by a richly inhabited Tree of Life. Above it all, a triumphant Christ,
one hand on the Bible, blesses the congregation.

Lower Church—Fourth Century

Buy a ticket in the bookshop and descend 800 years to the time
when Christians were razzed on their way to church by pagan
neighbors. The first room you enter was the original atrium
(entry hall)—the nave extends to the right.

Pagan Inscription (in atrium)

This two-sided, marble, recycled burial slab—one side for a
Christian, the other for a pagan (you can turn it)—shows how
the two Romes lived side by side in the fourth century.

Fresco of St. Clement and Sisinnius
(in nave near altar, on left wall)

Clement (center) holds a secret Mass for early Christians back
when it was a capital crime. Theodora, a prominent Roman (in
yellow, to the right), is one of the undercover faithful. Her pagan
husband, Sisinnius, has come to retrieve and punish her when—
zap!—he's struck blind and has to be led away (right side).

But Sisinnius is still unconvinced. When Clement cures his
blindness, Sisinnius (lower panel, far right) orders two servants
to drag Clement off to the authorities. But the package they carry
is not really Clement, who lives to die another day—notice the
anchor carved into the church's altar nearby.

Presumed Burial Place of St. Cyril
(near the top of the staircase leading down)

Cyril, who died in A.D. 869 (see the iconlike mosaic of him), was
an inveterate traveler who spread Christianity to the Slavic lands
and Russia—today's Russian Orthodox faithful. Along the way, he
introduced the Cyrillic alphabet used by Russians and Slavs.

Temple of Mithras (Mithreum)—Second Century

Now descend farther to the Mithraic Temple (Mithreum). Nowhere
in Rome is there a better place to experience this weird cult.

Worship Hall (the barred room to the left)

Worshipers of Mithras—men only—sat on the benches on either
side of the room. At the far end is a small statue of the god
Mithras. In the center sits an altar carved with a relief showing
Mithras fighting with a bull that contains all life. A scorpion,
a dog, and a snake try to stop Mithras, but he wins, running

his sword through the bull. The blood spills out, bringing life to the world.

Mithras' fans gathered here, in this tiny microcosm of the universe (the ceiling was decorated with stars), to celebrate the victory with a ritual meal. Every spring, Mithras brings new life again, and so they ritually kept track of the seasons—the four square shafts in the ceiling represent the seasons, the seven round ones were the great constellations. Initiates went through hazing rituals representing the darkness of this world, then emerged into the light-filled world brought by Mithras.

The religion, stressing loyalty and based on the tenuousness of life, was popular among soldiers. It dates back to the time of Alexander the Great, who brought it from Persia. By Imperial times, it was one of several mystery cults from the East (like Christianity) that filtered into Rome. When Christians gained power, they banished it.

Facing the barred room are two Corinthian pilasters supporting three arches of the temple's entryway, decorated with a fine stucco, coffered ceiling. At the far end of the hallway, another barred door marks the equivalent of a Mithraic Sunday School room. Exit signs direct you down several steps into a vast Roman public area. Look down at the stream—part of the aqueduct system that brought fresh drinking water to first-century Rome. Now climb 2,000 years back to today's street level.

DAYTRIPS
FROM ROME

Tivoli • Ostia Antica • Naples and Pompeii

While the eternal city can keep you busy for ages, here are a few excuses to leave Rome for a day. Tivoli (with a villa of Roman ruins and a villa of Baroque fountains) is famous, but a pain to get to. Its tired fountains have a certain nostalgic charm, and the ruins are impressive. But for ruins, those at Ostia Antica—Rome's ancient port—are better, and it's easier to visit. While Ostia rivals Pompeii for a look at the ruins of a Roman town, Pompeii is the ultimate. A trip south to Naples and Pompeii is the most demanding of the daytrips listed (6 hrs of train travel), but also the most rewarding, with a chance to wander Rome's most evocative ruins and go on an urban safari in what is perhaps Europe's most intense city.

Note that Villa d'Este (at Tivoli) and Ostia Antica are closed Monday, and Naples' Archeological Museum is closed Tuesday. Hadrian's Villa (at Tivioli) and Pompeii are open daily.

TIVOLI

At the edge of the Sabine Hills, 30 kilometers east of Rome, sits the medieval hill town of Tivoli, a popular retreat since ancient times. Today, it's famous for two very different attractions: Hadrian's Villa, an emperor's hot and dusty retirement villa, and Villa D'Este, the lush and watery villa of a cardinal in exile.

The town of Tivoli, with Villa d'Este in its center, is about four kilometers from Hadrian's Villa (Villa Adriana in Italian). The **TI** is on Largo Garibaldi near the garden entry (closed Mon, tel. 0774-334-522).

To get from Rome to Tivoli, take a Metro/bus combination. Ride Metro line B to Ponte Mammolo, then take the local LILA/Cotral bus (3/hr, direction: Tivoli) and get off at Via Tiburtina for Hadrian's Villa (500 meters away from the stop). The same bus continues to the town of Tivoli and Villa d'Este (end of the line).

Villa d'Este—Ippolito d'Este's grandfather was the pope ...
probably the only reason Ippolito became a cardinal. Ippolito's
claim to fame: his pleasure palace at Tivoli. In the 1550s, Ippolito
destroyed a Benedictine monastery to build this fanciful, late-
Renaissance palace. Like Hadrian's Villa, it's a large residential
villa. But this one features hundreds of fountains, all gravity-
powered. The Aniene River, frazzled into countless threads,
weaves its way entertainingly through the villa. At the bottom
of the garden, the exhausted little streams once again team up to
make a sizable river.

The cardinal had a political falling-out with Rome and was
exiled. With this watery wonderland on a cool hill with fine views,
he made sure Romans would come to visit. It's symbolic of the
luxury and secular interests of the cardinal. Senior travelers—the
least able to handle its many stairs—like it best (€6.20, Tue–Sun
from 08:30–18:30, last entry 1 hour before closing, closed Mon,
tel. 077-431-2070).

▲**Hadrian's Villa**—Built at the peak of the Empire by Hadrian
(ruled A.D. 125–134), this was the emperor's retreat from the political
complexity of court life in Rome. The Spanish-born Hadrian—an
architect, lover of Greek culture (nicknamed "the Little Greek"),
and great traveler—created a microcosm of cosmopolitan Rome.
In the spirit of Legoland, Disneyworld, and Las Vegas, he re-created
famous structures from around the world, making the largest and
richest Roman villa anywhere. Today, the ruins of Hadrian's retreat/
retirement home sprawl over 300 evocative acres.

Start your visit at the plastic model. Find the Egyptian Cano-
pus (Sanctuary of the god Serapis, a canal lined with statues), the
Greek Pecile (from Athens), and the Teatro Marittimo (a circular
palace, favorite retreat on an island where Hadrian did his serious
thinking). This "Versailles of ancient Rome" was plundered by
barbarians. The marble was burned to make lime for cement.
The art was scavenged and wound up in museums throughout
Europe (€6.20, daily from 09:00 until 1 hr before sunset, last entry
1 hr before closing, audioguide-€3.60). Getting there is complicated and time-consuming, and the site is hot and comes with
lots of unavoidable walking.

OSTIA ANTICA

Rome's ancient seaport, less than an hour from downtown Rome,
is the next best thing to Pompeii. Ostia had 80,000 people at the
time of Christ, later became a ghost town, and is now excavated.
Start at the 2,000-year-old theater, buy a map, explore the town,
and finish with its fine little museum (note that museum closes at
14:00). To get there, take the Metro's B Line to the Piramide stop

(consider popping out to see ancient Roman pyramid tomb). From the Piramide stop, catch the Lido train to Ostia Antica (2/hr). Then follow the signs to (or ask for) "*scavi* Ostia Antica" (€4.20, Tue–Sun 08:30–18:00 in summer, 09:00–16:00 in winter, closed Mon, museum closes for lunch, tel. 06-5635-8099). Just beyond is Rome's filthy beach (*lido*).

NAPLES AND POMPEII

If you like Italy as far south as Rome, go farther south. It gets better. If Italy is getting on your nerves, don't go farther. Italy intensifies as you plunge deeper. Naples is Italy in the extreme— its best (birthplace of pizza and Sophia Loren) and its worst (home of the Camorra, Naples' "family" of organized crime).

Italy's third-largest city—with more than 2 million people— has almost no open spaces or parks, which makes its position as Europe's most densely populated city plenty evident. Watching the police try to enforce traffic sanity is almost comical in Italy's grittiest, most polluted, and most crime-ridden city. But Naples surprises the observant traveler with its impressive knack for living, eating, and raising children in the streets with good humor and decency. Overcome your fear of being run down or ripped off long enough to talk with people—enjoy a few smiles and jokes with the man running the neighborhood tripe shop or the woman taking her daycare class on a walk through the traffic. (Ask a local about the New Year's Eve tradition of tossing chipped dinner plates off of balconies into the streets.)

Twenty-five hundred years ago, Neapolis ("new city") was a thriving Greek commercial center. It remains southern Italy's leading city, offering a fascinating collection of museums, churches, and eclectic architecture.

The pulse of Italy throbs in Naples. Like Cairo or Bombay, it's appalling and captivating at the same time, the closest thing to "reality travel" you'll find in Western Europe. But this tangled mess still somehow manages to breathe, laugh, and sing—with a captivating Italian accent.

For those with a week in Rome who are interested in maxi-mum travel thrills, spend a day visiting Naples and Pompeii.

Planning Your Time

Breakfast on the early Rome–Naples express (07:10–9:00). From Naples, get to Pompeii by either catching a taxi or the Circum-vesuviana (commuter train from the central train station base-ment), tour the excavation (11:00–13:00), then take a taxi or the same train back to Naples. Visit the Archaeological Museum, do the Naples urban jungle walk, have pizza in its birthplace, and ride

NAPLES

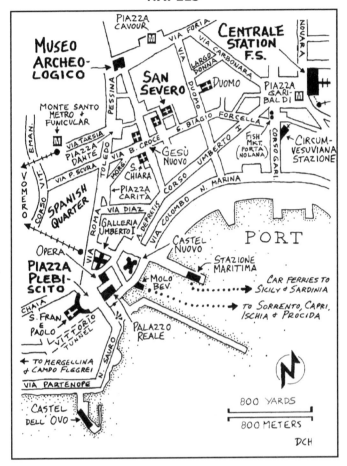

the late evening train (2 hrs) back to Rome. In the afternoon, Naples' street life slows and many sights close as the temperature soars. The city comes back to life in the early evening. Note that Naples' Archaeological Museum, one of the main reasons for visiting the city, is closed on Tuesday.

Arrival in Naples

There are several Naples stations. You want Naples Centrale (facing Piazza Garibaldi), which has a Circumvesuviana stop for commuter trains to Pompeii, baggage check, and a TI (Mon–Sat

09:00–20:00, Sun 09:00–13:00, with your back to the tracks, TI is in the lobby to your left; then, within the lobby, TI is to your right, tel. 081-268-779). As Centrale is a dead-end station, through trains often stop at Piazza Garibaldi (actually a subway station just down-stairs from Centrale), Campi Flegrei, or Napoli Mergellina across town. The stations of Campi Flegrei and Mergellina (which also has a TI) are connected to Centrale by a direct subway route; a railpass or train ticket to Napoli Centrale covers the ride (subway trains depart about every 10 min, less often on Sun). While on the train to Naples, ask the conductor which Naples stations your train stops at. Get off at Mergellina or Campi Flegrei only if your train does not stop at Centrale or Garibaldi.

Continuing to Pompeii: For about €50, you can ride a **taxi** from Naples to Pompeii; agree on a fixed price without the meter and pay upon arrival.

Naples and Pompeii are on the **commuter train**, the Ferrovia Circumvesuviana, handy for tourists, commuters, and pickpockets (see "Theft Alert," below). Catch it in the basement of Naples' central train station; look for the ticket windows marked Circum-vesuviana. Schedules are posted on the wall. When you buy your ticket, ask which track your train will depart from (*"Che binario?"*— kay bee-NAH-ree-oh). Don't go through the turnstiles opposite the ticket windows. Instead, continue down the corridor and jog right when it does, down another long corridor that has turnstiles at the end (insert your ticket). The platforms are just beyond. Two trains per hour, marked "Sorrento," get you to Pompeii in 40 minutes (€2.50 one-way, not covered by railpasses; check schedule carefully or confirm with a local before boarding to make sure the train is going to Pompeii). The faster express trains are marked "DD" on the schedule (12/day). When returning to Naples Centrale station on the Circumvesuviana, get off at the second-to-last station, the Collegamento FS or Garibaldi stop (Centrale station is just up the escalator).

Theft Alert: Lately Naples, under a new activist mayor, has been occupied by an army of police and feels much safer. Still, err on the side of caution. Don't venture into neighborhoods that make you uncomfortable. Walk with confidence, as if you know where you're going and what you're doing. Assume able-bodied beggars are thieves. Tighten your moneybelt and keep it completely hidden. Any jostle or commotion is probably a thief-team smokescreen.

Perhaps your biggest risk of theft is catching or riding the Circumvesuviana commuter train. If you're connecting from a major train, you'll be stepping from a relatively secure compart-ment into a crowded Naples subway, filled with thieves hunting disoriented American tourists with luggage. While I ride the Circumvesuviana comfortably and safely, each year I hear of many who get ripped off on this ride. You won't be mugged— just conned or pickpocketed. Con artists may say you need to "transfer" by taxi to catch the Circumvesuviana; you don't. There are no porters at the Centrale station or in the basement where the Circumvesuviana station is located; anyone offering to help you with your bags is likely a thief. Wear your moneybelt, hang on to your bag, and don't display any valuables.

Getting around Naples

Naples' subway, the Servizio Metropolitano, runs from the Centrale station through the center of town (direction: Pozzouli), stopping at Piazza Cavour (Archaeological Museum). Tickets, which cost €0.75, are good for 90 minutes. If you can afford a taxi, don't mess with the buses. A short taxi ride costs €3 to €5 (insist on the meter; supplement charged on Sun).

Getting to the Museum: Take a taxi or the metro. From the Centrale train station, follow signs to "Metropolitano" (downstairs, buy tickets from window on right, ask which track—"*Binario*?" to Piazza Cavour; it's usually track 4, "*quattro*"; go through a *solo metropolitano* turnstile and ride the subway 1 stop). As you leave the Metro, take the exit to the right. Walk through the park. At the end of cluttered Piazza Cavour, you'll see several pink buildings. The museum is the pink building on the right side of the street.

Sights—Naples

▲▲▲**Museo Archeologico**—For lovers of antiquity, this museum alone makes Naples a worthwhile stop. It offers the only possible peek into the artistic jewelry boxes of Pompeii and Herculaneum. The actual sights are impressive but barren; the best art and all the artifacts ended up here.

Hours, Cost, and Information: €6.20, Wednesday through Monday 09:00 to 20:00, summer Saturday until 23:00, closed Tuesday. Tours in English are offered weekdays at 11:30 and 15:30 (except on Tue when museum is closed) and on Saturday and Sunday at 10:00, 11:00, 12:00, and 15:30 (€3, 1.5 hrs, depart from entry, confirm tour times by calling 081-440-166). Audio-guides cost €3.75 (at bookshop, rentable for 3 hrs). Photos are allowed without a flash. The shop sells a worthwhile green guide-book, *National Archeological Museum of Naples* (€7.75).

Orientation: At the desk next to the ticket booth, you can sign up for a free 20-minute tour of the Secret Room (containing erotic art from Pompeii and Herculaneum). You'll be given a tour time; meet at the Secret Room (*Gabinetto Segreto*) on the mezzanine near the *Battle of Alexander* mosaic. These short tours, generally offered at the top and bottom of every hour, are usually given in Italian, but English tours are possible—ask.

After passing through the turnstile, orient yourself this way: Face the grand staircase. For the Farnese Collection of marble statues, turn right just before the staircase (and walk way back). The Pompeii mosaics and the Secret Room are on the small mezzanine level (up the grand staircase and on your left). The huge first floor (top of the grand staircase) contains bronze statues from Herculaneum, frescoes from Pompeii, and vases from Paestum. Stairs behind the grand staircase lead to the basement WCs.

Statues, Frescoes, and Artifacts (top floor): Climb the stairs to the top floor. Before you enter the great hall, look right to locate the entrance to the bronze statues of Herculaneum. This large collection—including a dozen bronze statues, plus busts and marble statues—came from Villa Papiri (Papyrus) in Herculaneum. Look into the lifelike blue eyes of the two intense *atleta* (athletes); they are bent on doing their best.

Step inside the great hall. When your back is to the entrance, the rooms on your left feature the Pompeii frescoes, paintings, artifacts, and an interesting model of the town of Pompeii (called *plastico di Pompeii*; near the glass objects). The rooms on your right feature ancient Greek art: a model of Paestum and ancient vases discovered on-site. (Paestum, a temple complex south of Naples, was part of a once-thriving region known as Greater Greece; for more info, see "Paestum," below.) If you contrast all of this ancient art with the darkness of medieval Europe, it becomes clear that classical art hugely inspired and enlightened the Renaissance greats.

Mosaics (mezzanine): On the mezzanine floor below (directly under the bronze statues from Herculaneum), you'll find a small, exquisite collection of Pompeian mosaics and the sexy Secret Room. Most of these mosaics were taken from the House of the Faun, which you'll see at Pompeii. Don't miss the house's delightful centerpiece: a small bronze statue of the *Dancing Faun* on a pedestal. A highlight of the mosaics is the grand *Battle of Alexander* (a 1st-century-B.C. copy of a 4th-century-B.C. Greek original). It decorated a floor in the House of the Faun.

The **Secret Room**, to the left of the *Battle of Alexander* mosaic, contains a small assortment of frescoes, pottery, and statues that once decorated bedrooms, brothels, and even shops at Pompeii and Herculaneum (enter only with a guide, see "Orientation," above). If you didn't bother with making an appointment, you can still peek through the iron gate.

When this earthy art was unearthed in the mid-18th

century, people were upset to find their view of the Romans as wise administrators and lawmakers upended. Actually, the meaning of an erect penis was more complex back then than today—dealing with abundance and good luck, as well as good sex.

Farnese Collection (ground floor): This floor has enough Egyptian, Greek, Roman, and Etruscan art to put any museum on the map. Its highlight is the Farnese Collection, a giant hall of huge, bright, and wonderfully restored statues excavated from Rome's Baths of Caracalla. The Toro Farnese—a tangled group with a woman being tied to a bull—is the largest intact statue from antiquity. Actually a third-century copy of a Hellenistic original, it was carved out of one piece of marble and restored by Michelangelo and others.

Once upon an ancient Greek time, King Lykos was bewitched by Dirce and abandoned his pregnant wife (standing regally in the background). The single mom gave birth to twin boys (shown here) who grew up to kill their deadbeat dad and tie Dirce to the horns of a bull to be bashed against a mountain.

You can almost hear the bull snorting. Read the worthwhile descriptions on the walls. At the far end of the hall (opposite the Toro, behind Hercules), a small room contains the sumptuous Farnese Cup, a large ancient cameo made of agates (well-described).

▲▲▲**The Slice-of-Neapolitan-Life Walk**—Walk from the museum through the heart of town and back to the station (allow at least 2 hrs plus lunch and sightseeing stops). Sights are listed in the order you'll see them on this walk.

Naples, a living medieval city, is its own best sight. Couples artfully make love on Vespas, surrounded by more fights and smiles per cobble here than anywhere else in Italy. Rather than seeing Naples as a list of sights, see the one great museum and then capture its essence by taking this walk through the core of the city. Should you become overwhelmed or lost, step into a store and ask for help: "*Dov'è la stazione centrale?*" (DOH-vay lah staht-zee-OH-nay chen-TRAH-lay?) Or point to the next sight in this book.

Via Toledo and the Spanish Quarter (city walk, first half): Leaving the Archaeological Museum at the top of Piazza Cavour (Metro: Piazza Cavour), cross the street and walk through the ornate *galleria* (the grand, arched gallery) on your way to Via Pessina. The first part of the walk is a straight 1.5-kilometer ramble down this boulevard to Galleria Umberto I near the Royal Palace.

Busy Via Pessina leads downhill to Piazza Dante, which is marked by a statue of Dante. Originally, a statue of a Spanish Bourbon king stood here. The grand red and gray building is typical of the Bourbon buildings from that period. In 1861,

NAPLES WALK

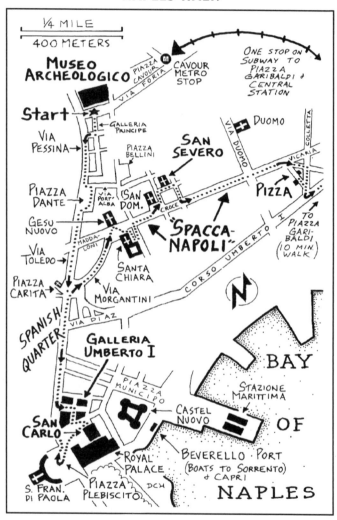

with the unification of Italy, the king, symbolic of Italy's colonial subjugation, was replaced by Dante, considered the father of the Italian language and a strong symbol of Italian nationalism.

Poor old Dante looks out over the urban chaos with a hopeless gesture. Unknowingly, he points the way to the Alba Gate (part of Naple's old wall and the entrance to a small street often lined with streetside book vendors). Via Pessina, the long, straight road we're walking, originated as a military road built by Spain around 1600. It skirted the old town wall to connect the Spanish military headquarters (now the museum) with the royal palace (down by the bay).

A new subway station has recently been built here on Piazza Dante. Construction was slowed by the city's rich underground history: four meters down—Roman ruins, seven meters down—Greek ruins.

Continue walking downhill, remembering that here in Naples, red lights are considered "decorations." The people here are survivors; a long history of corrupt and greedy colonial overlords has taught Neapolitans to deal with authority creatively. Many credit this aspect of Naples' past for the advent of organized crime here.

Via Pessina becomes Via Toledo, Naples' principal shopping street. In 1860, from the white marble balcony (on the neoclassical building) overlooking Piazza Sette Settembre, the famous revolutionary Garibaldi declared Italy united and Victor Emanuel its first king. A year later, the dream of Italian unity was actually realized.

Continue straight on Via Toledo (even though the arterial jogs left). About five blocks below Piazza Dante, at Via Maddaloni, you cross the long, straight street called **Spaccanapoli** (literally, "split Naples"). Look left. Look right. Since ancient times, this thin street (which changes names several times) has bisected the city. (We'll be coming back to this point later. If you want to abbreviate this walk, turn left here and skip down to the Spaccanapoli section.)

Via Toledo runs through Piazza Carita (also known by its new name, Piazza Salvo D'Acquisto), with fascist architecture (from 1938, sternly straight and obedient lines) overlooking the square. Wander down Via Toledo a few blocks, past more fascist architecture—the two banks on the left. Try robbing the second one (Banco di Napoli, Via Toledo 178).

Up the hill to your right is the **Spanish Quarter**, Naples at its rawest, poorest, and most historic. Thrill-seekers (or someone in need of a prostitute) can take a stroll up one of these streets and loop back to Via Toledo.

The only predictable things about this Neapolitan tidepool are the ancient grid plan of its streets (which survives from Greek times), the friendliness of its shopkeepers, and the boldness of its mopeds. Concerned locals will tug on their lower eyelids, warning you to be wary. Pop into a grocery shop and ask the man to make you his best ham and mozzarella sandwich. Trust him on the price—it should be around €3.

Continue down Via Toledo to Piazza Plebiscito. From here, you'll see the Church of San Francesco di Paola, with its

Pantheon-inspired dome and broad, arcing colonnades. Opposite is the **Royal Palace**, which has housed Spanish, French, and even Italian royalty. The lavish interior is open for tours (€4, Thu–Tue 09:00–20:00, Sat until 23:00, closed Wed, shorter hours off-season; a TI is inside the Royal Palace). Next door, peek inside the neo-classical Teatro San Carlo, Italy's second-most-respected opera house (after Milan's La Scala). The huge castle on the harbor front, just beyond the palace, houses government bureaucrats and is closed to tourists.

Under the Victorian iron and glass of the 100-year-old **Galleria Umberto I**, enjoy a coffee break or sample a unique Neapolitan treat called *sfogliatella* (crispy, scallop shell–shaped pastry filled with sweet ricotta cheese). Go through the tall yellow arch at the end of Via Toledo or across from the opera house. Gawk up.

Spaccanapoli back to the station (city walk, 2nd half): To continue your walk, double back up Via Toledo past Piazza Carita to Via Maddaloni. (Consider going via the backstreets.) You're back at the straight-as-a-Greek-arrow Spaccanapoli. Formerly the main thoroughfare of the Greek city of Neapolis, it starts up the hill near the Montesanto funicular.

The rest of this walk is basically a straight line down a series of streets locals nicknamed Spaccanapoli. Turn right off Via Toledo and walk down Via Maddaloni to two bulky old churches on Piazza Gesu Nuovo. The square is marked by a towering monument to the Counter-Reformation (Baroque, early 18th century). With their Spanish heritage, Jesuits were powerful in Naples. But locals never attacked Protestants with the full fury of the Spanish Inquisition.

Check out the austere, fortress-like church of **Gesu Nuovo**. The unique pyramid grill facade was from a fortress (1470) that pre-dated the church (1600s). Step inside for a brilliant Baroque interior. The second chapel on the right features a much-kissed statue of Giuseppe Moscati, a Christian doctor famous for helping the poor. Moscati was made a saint in 1987. Continue to the third chapel and enter the Sale Moscati for a huge room filled with Ex Voto—tiny red and silver plaques of thanksgiving for miracles attributed to Saint Moscati. Each has a relief symbolic of the ailment cured. Naples' practice of "Ex Voto," while incorporated into its Catholic rituals, goes back to its pagan Greek roots. A glass case displays possessions and photos of the great doctor. As you leave, notice the big bomb casing hanging in the corner. It fell through the church's dome in 1943, but never exploded . . . yet another miracle.

Across the street, the simpler Gothic church of **Santa Chiara** dates from a period of French Angevin rule (14th century). Notice the stark Gothic/Baroque contrast between this church and the

Gesu Nuovo. The faded Trinity (from the school of Giotto, left of entry) is an example of the fine frescoes that once covered the walls (most removed during Baroque times). The altar is adorned with the finely carved Gothic tomb of an Angevin king (free, Mon–Sat 08:30–13:00, 15:30–18:30, Sun 08:30–13:00).

Continue straight down traffic-free Via B. Croce. Since this is a university district, you'll see lots of students and bookstores. This neighborhood is also extremely superstitious. You may see incense-burning women with carts of good-luck charms for sale. At Via Santa Chiara, a detour left leads to shops of antique musical instruments.

The next square is Piazza S. Domenico Maggiore—marked by an ornate 17th-century plague monument. The venerable **Scaturchio Pasticceria** is another good place to try Naples' *sfogliatella* pastry (€1 to go, costs double at a table in the square).

From this square, detour left (along the right side of the castle-like church, then follow yellow signs and take 1st right) to **Cappella Sansevero** (€4, Mon and Wed–Sat 10:00–18:20, Sun 10:00–13:30, closed Tue, Via de Sanctis 19). No photos are allowed in the chapel (postcards available in gift shop).

This small chapel is a Baroque explosion mourning the body of Christ, who lies on a soft pillow under an incredibly realistic veil. It's also the personal chapel of Raimondo de Sangro, an eccentric Freemason and inventor (he's credited with a crude 18th-century version of Gore-Tex). The monuments to his relatives have a second purpose: to share the Freemason philosophy of freedom through enlightenment. For example, the statue of *Despair* struggling with a marble rope net (carved out of a single piece of marble) shows how knowledge—in the guise of an angel—frees the human mind.

Study the incredible *Veiled Christ* in the center. It's all carved out of marble and is like no other statue I've seen (by Giuseppe "howdee-doodat" Sammartino, 1753). The Christian message (Jesus died for our salvation) is accompanied by a Freemason message. (The veil represents how the body and ego are obstacles to real spiritual free-dom.) As you walk from Christ's feet to his head, notice how the expression of Jesus' face goes from suffering to peace. When you stand directly behind Him the veil over the face and knees disappears.

To the right of *Despair* and the net, an inlaid, Escher-esque maze on the floor leads to de Sangro's tomb. The maze is another Freemason reminder of the importance of how the quest for know-ledge gets you out of the maze of life. Your Sansevero finale is downstairs: two mysterious...skeletons. Perhaps another of the inventor's fancies: injecting a corpse with a fluid to fossilize the veins so they'll survive the body's decomposition.

Return to Via B. Croce, then turn left and continue your

Spaccanapoli cultural scavenger hunt. At the intersection of Via Nilo, find the statue of *The Body of Naples*, with the abundant cornucopia symbolizing the abundance of Naples. (I asked a Neapolitan man to describe the local women, who are famous for their beauty. He replied simply, "Abundant.") This intersection is considered the center of old Naples.

At Via San Gregorio Armeno, a left leads you into a very colorful district (kitschy Baroque church on left with a Vesuvius lava shrine in its portico, lots of shops selling tiny components of fantastic manger scenes).

As Via B. Croce becomes Via S. Biagio dei Librai, notice the gold and silver shops. Some say stolen jewelry ends up here, is melted down immediately, and appears in a saleable form as soon as it cools. The wonderful Sr. Grassi runs the Ospedale delle Bambole (doll hospital) at #81.

Cross busy Via Duomo. The street and side-street scenes along Via Vicaria intensify. Paint a picture with these thoughts: Naples has the most intact street plan of any ancient Roman city. Imagine this city then (like Pompeii), with streetside shopfronts that close up after dark to form private homes. Today, it's just one more page in a 2,000-year-old story of a city: all kinds of meetings, beatings, and cheatings; kisses, near misses, and little-boy pisses.

You name it, it occurs right on the streets today, as it has since ancient times. People ooze from crusty corners. Black-and-white death announcements add to the clutter on the walls. Widows sell cigarettes from buckets. For a peek behind the scenes in the shade of wet laundry, venture down a few side streets. Buy two carrots as a gift for the woman on the fifth floor if she'll lower her bucket to pick them up. The neighborhood action seems best around 18:00.

At the tiny, fenced-in, triangular park, veer right onto Via Forcella. Turning right on busy Via Pietro Colletta, walk 50 meters and step into the North Pole. Reward yourself for surviving this safari with a stop at the **Polo Nord Gelateria** (Via Pietro Colletta 41, sample their *bacio* or "kiss" flavor before ordering). Via Pietro Colletta leads past Napoli's two most competitive **pizzerias** (see "Pizza in Naples" sidebar on page 195) to Corso Umberto.

Turn left on the grand-boulevardian Corso Umberto. From here to the station, it's a 10-minute walk (if you're tired, hop on a bus; they all go to the station). To finish the walk, continue on Corso Umberto—past a gauntlet of purse/CD/sunglasses salesmen and shady characters hawking stolen camcorders—to the vast, ugly Piazza Garibaldi. On the far side is the Centrale station.

Markets—Naples' **fish market** is fun for photos, with sawed–off swordfish, wriggly eels in pans, and mussels taking a shower. It's at Piazza Nolana, a few blocks southwest of the train station (at the

Pizza in Naples

Drop by one of the two most traditional pizzerias. Naples, baking just the right combination of fresh dough, mozzarella, and tomatoes in traditional wood-burning ovens, is the birthplace of pizza. **Antica Pizzeria da Michele**, a few blocks from the train station, is for purists (Mon–Sat 11:00–23:00, closed Sun, cheap, filled with locals, 50 meters off Corso Umberto on Via Cesare Sersale, look for the vertical red "Antica Pizzeria" sign, tel. 081-553-9204). It serves two kinds: *margherita* (tomato sauce and mozzarella) or *marinara* (tomato sauce, oregano, and garlic, no cheese). A pizza with beer costs €5. Some locals prefer **Pizzeria Trianon** across the street. Da Michele's archrival offers more choices, higher prices, air-conditioning, and a cozier atmosphere (daily 10:00–15:30, 18:30–23:00, Via Pietro Colletta 42, tel. 081-553-9426).

piazza, follow your nose and go through the old gate; market spills down small street, Vico Sopramuro). A bigger **general market** starts at the far corner of Piazza Capuana (several blocks northwest of the train station), filling the street Via Sant' Antonio Abate with a mix of clothes, olives, bags of gnocchi, hanging hams, shoes, produce, umbrellas, and shoppers on foot or on Vespas. These colorful markets are both open daily from early in the morning until about 16:00 Monday through Saturday, 13:00 on Sunday.

POMPEII

Stopped in its tracks by the eruption of Mount Vesuvius in A.D. 79, Pompeii offers the best look anywhere at what life in Rome must have been like 2,000 years ago. An entire city of well-preserved ruins is yours to explore. Once a thriving commercial port of 20,000, Pompeii grew from Greek and Etruscan roots to become an important Roman city. Then it was buried under nine meters (30 feet) of hot mud and volcanic ash. For archaeologists, this was a shake-and-bake windfall, teaching them almost all they know about daily Roman life. Rediscovered in the 1600s, the first excavations began in 1748.

Cost, Hours, Information: €8.25, €13.50 combo ticket includes Herculaneum and three lesser sites—valid three days, April through October daily 08:30 to 19:30, November through March daily 08:30 to 17:00. The ticket office closes 90 minutes before closing time. A good map is included with admission (for more information, check www.pompeiisites.org). A free baggage check is near the ticket window.

POMPEII

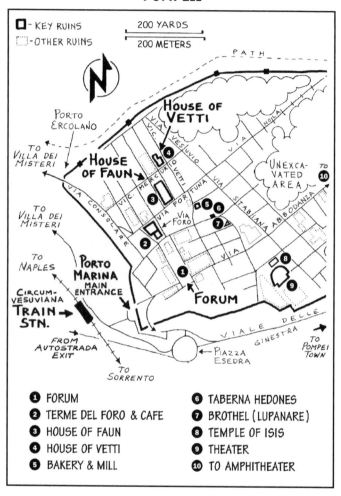

□ - KEY RUINS
▢ - OTHER RUINS

200 YARDS
200 METERS

❶ FORUM
❷ TERME DEL FORO & CAFE
❸ HOUSE OF FAUN
❹ HOUSE OF VETTI
❺ BAKERY & MILL

❻ TABERNA HEDONES
❼ BROTHEL (LUPANARE)
❽ TEMPLE OF ISIS
❾ THEATER
❿ TO AMPHITHEATER

Stop by the bookshop. A guidebook on Pompeii makes this site more meaningful. (Books are also on sale in Sorrento.) The small Pompeii and Herculaneum *Past and Present* book has a helpful text and allows you to re-create the ruins with plastic overlays—with the "present" actually being 1964 (available for €9.50 in bookstore unless they're "finished"; if you buy from a street vendor, pay no more than €9.50). Audioguides may be available—ask. Live guides cluster near the ticket booth. If you gather

10 people and split the price, it's reasonable (around €10 apiece, total cost about €100, 2 hrs). For a local guide, consider Gaetano Manfredi (tel. 081-863-9816, cellular 33-033-7567).

Background: Pompeii was a booming Roman trading city. Most streets would have been lined with stalls and jammed with customers from sunup to sundown. Chariots vied with shoppers for street space, and many streets were off-limits to chariots during shopping hours (you'll still see street signs with pictures of men carrying vases—this meant pedestrians only).

Fountains overflowed into the streets, flushing the gutters into the sea (thereby cleaning the streets). The stones you see at intersections allowed pedestrians to cross the constantly gushing streets. A single stone designated a one-way street (just enough room for one chariot, stone straddled by its two oxen), and two stones meant a two-way chariot street. There were no posh neighborhoods. Rich and poor mixed it up, as elegant homes existed side by side with simple homes throughout Pompeii. While nearby Herculaneum would be a classier place to live (traffic-free streets, more elegant homes, far better drainage), Pompeii was the place for action and shopping. It served its estimated 20,000 residents with more than 40 bakeries; 30 brothels; and 130 bars, restaurants, and hotels. Rome controlled the entire Mediterranean 2,000 years ago—making it a kind of free-trade zone—and Pompeii was a central and booming port town. With most of its buildings covered by brilliant white ground-marble stucco, Pompeii in A.D. 79 was an impressive town. Remember, Pompeii's best art is in the Naples Archaeological Museum, described above.

Tour of Pompeii: Allow at least three hours to tour the site. Consider the following route, starting at the Porta Marina (town gate) after the ticket booth. Before Vesuvius blew, the sea came nearly to this gate. As you approach the Porta Marina, notice the two openings—big for chariots, small for pedestrians.

From the Porta Marina, Via Marina leads straight to Pompeii's main square, the Forum.

The **Forum** (*Foro*), Pompeii's commercial, religious, and political center, stands at the intersection of the city's two main streets. While the most ruined part of Pompeii, it's grand nonetheless—with temples, lots of pedestals which once sported statues (now in the museum in Naples), and the basilica (Pompeii's largest building, the ancient equivalent of law courts and stock market—on the right as you enter). The Curia (home of the government) stands at the end of the Forum. It's built of brick and mortar—a Roman invention. While brick now, it was once faced with marble. Note that while Pompeii was destroyed by the eruption of A.D. 79, it was also devastated by an earthquake in A.D. 62.

It's safe to assume any brick you see dates from between A.D. 62 and A.D. 79—restoration work done by Pompeians after the quake.

Walk (away from the Curia) along the fenced, roofed area that runs alongside the Forum. Behind the iron fence are piles of pottery and, at the end, some eerie casts of volcano victims. With the unification of Italy in the 1860s, national spirit fueled efforts to excavate Pompeii. During this period, archaeologists made these molds (detecting hollows underfoot—left by decomposed bodies—as they dug, they'd pour liquid plaster into them, let 'em dry, and dig 'em up).

Such a busy square needed a public toilet. Just past the warehouse, turn left into an ancient public WC. Notice the ditch which led to the sewer (marked by an arch in the corner). The stone supports once held wooden benches with the appropriate holes. Even back then, this area had pay toilets.

Continue on, leaving the Forum through the gate at the end. Take an immediate right, then a left. You're on Via del Foro, passing a convenient 21st-century cafeteria (decent value, gelato, books, WCs upstairs; a fancier restaurant in a more elegant, ancient-gymnasium setting is adjacent).

Head down Via del Foro and enter the impressive baths, **Terme del Foro** (on the left, past the cafeteria). You'll enter through the gymnasium. After working out, clients would find four rooms: a waiting room; warm bath (*tepidarium*); hot bath (*caldarium*); and cold-plunge bath (*frigidarium*).

The *tepidarium* is ringed by mini-statues or telamones (male caryatids, figures used as supporting pillars), which divided clients' lockers. They'd undress and warm up here, perhaps stretching out on one of the benches near the bronze heater for a massage. Notice the ceiling: half crushed by the eruption, and half surviving with its fine blue-and-white stuccowork.

Next, in the *caldarium*, you'd get hot. Notice the engineering. The double floor was heated from below—so nice with bare feet (look into the grate to see the brick support towers). The double walls with brown terracotta tiles held the heat. Romans soaked in the big tub, which was filled with hot water. To keep condensation from dripping annoyingly from the ceiling, the fluting (ribbing) was added to carry the drips down the walls.

Next came the cold plunge in the *frigidarium*—a circular marble basin with the spout spewing frigid water, opposite the entry.

Exit the baths. Notice the oxcart wheel grooves and stepping stones in the street. During ancient rainstorms, streets would turn into filthy rivers. Do as the ancient Romans did. Keep your feet dry by using the stepping stones to cross the street. Directly in front of you is an ancient fast-food stand (notice the holes in the counters for pots). To your left, a few doors down, is the **House of the Tragic Poet** (*Casa de Poeta Tragico*), with its famous "Beware of Dog" (*Cave Canum*) mosaic in the entryway. On either side, grooves in the doorway indicate a shop with sliding doors.

Face the House of the Tragic Poet, then walk to your right two blocks to the House of the Faun (Casa del Fauno, Danzante). Notice the holes drilled into the curbs—to hitch your animal or perhaps to support an awning from your storefront.

Pompeii's largest home (with 40 rooms), the **House of the Faun**, provided Naples' Archaeological Museum with many of its top treasures, including the original dancing faun (you'll see a copy here) and the famous mosaic of the Battle of Alexander. Wander past the welcome mosaic (*HAVE* or "hail to you") and through its courtyards. The back courtyard leads to the exit. It's lined by pillars rebuilt after the quake. Take a close look at the brick, mortar, and fake-marble-stucco veneer.

Back on the street, turn right and look for the exposed 2,000-year-old lead pipes in the wire cage (ahead and down on the ground to your right). The lead was imported from Roman Britannia. A huge water tank—fed by an aqueduct—stood at the high end of town. Three independent pipe systems supplied water to the city from here: One each for baths, private homes, and public water fountains. In the case of a water shortage, supply could be limited. Democratic priorities prevailed: First the baths were cut, then the private homes. The last water to be cut was that which fed the public fountains (where the people got their water for drinking and cooking).

Take your first left on Vicolo dei Vetti. Enter Pompeii's best-preserved home, the House of the Vetti (*Casa dei Vetti*).

The **House of the Vetti**, which has retained its mosaics and frescoes, was the bachelor pad of two wealthy merchant brothers. In the entryway, see if you can spot the erection. This is not pornography. There's a meaning here: The penis and the sack of money balance each other on the goldsmith scale above a fine bowl of fruit. The meaning: Only with a balance of fertility and money can you have abundance.

Step into the atrium, with its open sky to collect light and rain-water. The pool, while decorative, was a functional water-supply tank. It's flanked by large money boxes anchored to the floor. They were certainly successful merchants, and possibly money-lenders, too.

Exit on the right, passing the tight servant quarters, and go into the kitchen with its bronze cooking pots (and a touchable lead pipe on the back wall). The passage dead-ends in the little Venus Room, with its erotic frescoes behind glass.

Return to the atrium and pass into the big colonnaded garden. It was planted according to the plan indicated by traces of roots excavated in the volcanic ash. This courtyard is ringed by richly frescoed entertainment rooms. Circle counterclockwise. The dining room is finely decorated in "Pompeiian red" (from iron rust) and black. Study the detail. Notice the lead humidity seal between the wall and the floor designed to keep the wet-sensitive frescoes dry. (Had Leonardo taken this clever step, his *Last Supper* in Milan might be in better shape today.) Continuing around, notice the square white stones inlaid in the floor. Imagine them reflecting like cat eyes as the brothers and their friends wandered around by oil lamp late at night. Frescoes in the Yellow Room (near the exit) show off the ancient mastery of perspective, which was not matched in Europe for nearly 1,500 years.

Leaving the House of the Vetti, go left past the pipes again. Then turn right following Vicolo dei Vetti to Via della Fortuna, where you'll see a public fountain. Intersections like this were busy neighborhood centers, where the rent was highest and people gathered.

Turn left on Via della Fortuna and take a quick right on Vicolo Storto, which leads down a curving street to the **bakery and mill** (*forno e mulini*). The ovens look like a modern-day pizza oven. And the stubby stone towers are flour grinders: After grain was poured into the top, donkeys pushed wooden bars that turned the stones, and eventually powdered grain dropped out the bottom as flour—flavored with tiny bits of rock.

Take the first left after the bakery onto Via degli Augustali and check out the mosaics on the left at the Taberna Hedones. This must be the tavern of hedonism—see the cute welcome mosaic reading *HAVE* ("hail to you"), with the bear licking his wounds.

Next turn right, over the street dam, and follow the signs to the **brothel** (*lupanare*), at #18. Prostitutes were nicknamed *lupas* (she-wolves). Wander into the brothel, a simple place with stone beds and pillows. The ancient graffiti includes stroke tallies and exotic names of the girls, indicating they came from all corners of the Mediterranean. The faded frescoes above the cells may have served as a kind of menu for services offered. Note the idealized portrayal of women (white, considered beautiful) and man (dark, considered horny). Outside at #17 is a laundry—likely to boil the sheets (thought to guard against venereal disease).

Leaving the brothel, go down the hill to Pompeii's main drag, Via Abbondanza. The Forum (and exit) is to the right. (The huge amphitheater—which you can skip—is 10 min to your left.) Go straight down Via dei Teatri, then left before the columns, down-hill to the **Temple of Isis** (on the right). This Egyptian temple served Pompeii's Egyptian community. The little shrine with the plastic roof housed holy water from the Nile. Pompeii must have had a synagogue, but it's yet to be excavated.

Immediately upon leaving, follow the lane at #17 to our last stop, the **Theater**. Originally a Greek theater (Greeks built theirs with the help of a hillside), this marks the birthplace of the Greek port here in 470 B.C. During Roman times, it sat 5,000 in three price ranges: the five marble terraces up close (filled with romantic, wooden seats for 2), the main section, and the cheap nosebleed section (surviving only on the right). The square stones above the cheap seats used to supported a canvas rooftop. Notice the high-profile boxes, flanking the stage, for guests of honor. From this perch you can see the gladiator barracks—the colonnaded courtyard beyond the theater. They lived in tiny rooms, trained in the court-yard, and fought in the nearby amphitheater.

There's much more to see; 75 percent of Pompeii's 164 acres has been excavated. But this tour's over. *Ciao!*

Getting to Pompeii: Pompeii is 40 minutes from Naples by direct Circumvesuviana train (2/hr). Get off at the "Pompei Scavi, Villa dei Misteri" stop. Note: You want "Pompei Scavi" on the Naples–Sorrento train line. A different line, which does *not* go to Sorrento, has a Pompeii stop that leaves you far from the excava-tion-site entrance. Check your bag at the train station (at the bar) for €0.75, or, better yet, near the Pompeii ticket desk for free. From the train station, turn right and walk down the road about a block to the entrance (first left turn). The TI is farther down the street, but not a necessary stop for your visit.

SLEEPING
IN ROME

The absolute cheapest beds (dorms or some cramped doubles) in
Rome are €18 in small, backpacker-filled hostels. A nicer hotel
(around €130 with a bathroom and air-conditioning) provides an
oasis and refuge, making it easier to enjoy this intense and grind-
ing city. If you're going door to door, prices are soft—so bargain.
Built into a hotel's official price list is a kickback for a room-
finding service or agency; if you're coming direct, they pay no
kickback and may lower the price for you. Many hotels have high-
season (mid-March–June, Sept–Oct) and low-season prices.
If traveling outside of peak times, ask about a discount. Room
rates are lowest in sweltering August. Easter, September, and
Christmas are most crowded and expensive. On Easter, April 25,
and May 1, the entire city gets booked up.

English works in all but the cheapest places. Traffic in Rome
roars. My challenge: To find friendly places on quiet streets. With
the recent arrival of double-paned windows and air-conditioning,
night noise is not the problem it was. Even so, light sleepers should
always ask for a *tranquillo* room. Many prices here are promised
only to people who show this book and reserve directly, without
using a room-finding service. And many places prefer hard cash.

Bed-and-breakfasts are booming in Rome, offering comfy
doubles in the old center for around €80. The Beehive hostel is
a good contact for booking B&Bs in Rome (www.cross-pollinate
.com, see "Sleeping in Hostels and Dorms," below).

Your hotel can point you to the nearest **Laundromat** (usually
open daily 08:00–22:00, about €6 to wash and dry a 15-pound
load). The Bolle Blu chain comes with Internet access (€4.25/hr,
near train station at Via Milazzo 20, Via Palestro 59, and Via
Principe Amedeo 116, tel. 06-446-5804).

Most hotels are eager to connect you with a shuttle service

Sleep Code

S = Single, **D** = Double/Twin, **T** = Triple, **Q** = Quad, **b** = bathroom, **s** = shower only, **CC** = Credit Cards accepted, **no CC** = Credit Cards not accepted, **SE** = Speaks English, **NSE** = No English. Breakfast is included in all but the cheapest places.

Exchange rate: €1.10 = about $1
Country phone code: 39

to the airport. It's reasonable and easy for leaving, but upon arrival, I think it's easiest to simply catch a cab or the shuttle train.

Almost no hotels have parking, but nearly all have a line on spots in a nearby garage (about €21/day).

Sleeping on Via Firenze (zip code: 00184)

I generally stay on Via Firenze because it's safe, handy, central, and relatively quiet. It's a 10-minute walk from the central train station and airport shuttle, and two blocks beyond Piazza della Repubblica and the TI. The Defense Ministry is nearby, and you've got heavily armed guards watching over you all night. Virtually all the orange buses that rumble down Via Nazionale (#64, #70, #115, #640) take you to Piazza Venezia (Forum) and Largo Argentina (Pantheon). From Largo Argentina, electric trolley #8 goes to Trastevere (1st stop after crossing the river) and #64 (jammed with people and thieves) continues to St. Peter's. Farmacia Piram is the neighborhood 24-hour pharmacy (Via Nazionale 228, tel. 06-488-4437).

Hotel Oceania is a peaceful slice of air-conditioned heaven. This 16-room, manor house–type hotel is spacious and quiet, with newly renovated and spotless rooms, run by a pleasant father-and-son team (Sb-€105, Db-€135, Tb-€165, Qb-€192, these prices through 2002 with this book only, additional 25 percent off in Aug and winter, phones, CC, Via Firenze 38, 3rd floor, tel. 06-482-4696, fax 06-488-5586, www.hoteloceania.it, e-mail: hoceania @tin.it, son Stefano SE, dad Armando serves world-famous coffee).

Hotel Aberdeen, while a more formal place, offers the same great value, with mini-bars, phones, and showers in its 36 modern, air-conditioned, and smoke-free rooms. It's warmly run by Annamaria, with support from her cousins Sabrina and Cinzia, and trusty Massimo riding shotgun after dark (Sb-€92, Db-€129, Tb-€154, Qb-€180, prices through 2002 with this book only, €30 less per room in Aug and winter, CC, free Internet access, nearby parking— €21/day, Via Firenze 48, tel. 06-482-3920, fax 06-482-1092, check

HOTELS NEAR THE TRAIN STATION

① HOTEL OCEANIA & NARDIZZI
② HOTEL ABERDEEN
③ RESIDENCE ADLER
   & RESIDENZA CELLINI
④ HOTEL REX
⑤ HOTEL BRITANNIA
⑥ HOTEL SONYA
⑦ HOTEL PENSIONE ITALIA
⑧ HOTEL CORTINA
   & CAFFETTERIA NAZIONALE
⑨ YWCA CASA STUDENTESSE
⑩ SUORE SANTA ELISABETTA

⑪ HOTEL MONTREAL
⑫ HOTEL FENICIA & MAGIC
⑬ ALBERGO SILEO
⑭ HOTEL DUCA D'ALBA
⑮ HOTEL GRIFO
⑯ SUORE DI SANT ANNA
⑰ SNACK BAR GASTRONOMIA
⑱ PASTICCERIA DAGNINO
⑲ HOSTARIA ROMANA
⑳ RISTORANTE GIOVANNI
㉑ PHARMACY

㉒ RIST. CINESE INT'L.
㉓ BEEHIVE HOSTEL
   & MONTE D.O.C. VINERIA
㉔ CASA OLMATA HOSTEL
㉕ PENSIONE PELLIGRINI
㉖ CLARIN HOTEL
㉗ TO HOTEL CASA KOLBE
㉘ HOTEL LANCELOT
㉙ HOTEL PABA
㉚ GULLIVER'S HOUSE ROME
㉛ REST. NERONE

for deals on the Web, and visit www.travel.it/roma/aberdeen, e-mail: hotel.aberdeen@travel.it, SE).

Residence Adler, with its wide halls, breakfast on a garden patio, and eight quiet, elegant, and air-conditioned rooms in a great locale, is another good deal. It's run the old-fashioned way by a charming family (Db-€103, Tb-€145, Qb-€176, prices through 2002 with this book only, CC, additional 5 percent off with cash, elevator, Via Modena 5, 2nd floor, tel. 06-484-466, fax 06-488-0940, gracious Sr. Brando Massini NSE but tries).

Residenza Cellini is a gorgeous new place with six rooms. It offers "ortho/anti-allergy beds" and four-star comforts and service on a small scale (Db-€155, larger Db-€181, €26 discount in off season—Nov–March plus Aug, these prices with this book and payment in cash through 2002, elevator, air-con, Via Modena 5, tel. 06-4782-5204, fax 06-4788-1806, www.residenzacellini.it, e-mail: residenzacellini@tin.it, SE).

Hotel Nardizzi Americana, with 18 simple, pleasant, air-conditioned rooms and a delightful rooftop terrace, is loosely run (Sb-€83, Db-€109, Tb-€129, Qb-€140, prices through 2002 with this book only, discounts for off-season and long stays, CC, additional 10 percent off with cash, elevator, Via Firenze 38, 4th floor, tel. 06-488-0368, fax 06-488-0035, SE).

Hotel Seiler is a quiet, serviceable place with 33 decent rooms (Sb-€83, Db-€119, Tb-€145, Qb-€165, these discounted prices good only with this book, CC, fans, elevator, Via Firenze 48, tel. 06-485-550, fax 06-488-0688, e-mail: acropoli@rdn.it, Silvio and Alessia SE).

Hotel Texas Seven Hills, a stark, institutional throwback to the 1960s, rents 18 dreary rooms (D-€83, Db-€93, often soft prices, CC, single-paned windows, Via Firenze 47, 1st elevator on the right to 3rd floor, tel. 06-481-4082, fax 06-481-4079, e-mail: reserva@texas7hills.com, NSE). Note: This place may go three stars in 2002.

Sleeping between Via Nazionale and Basilica Santa Maria Maggiore
(zip code: 00184 unless otherwise noted)

Hotel Pensione Italia, in a busy, interesting, and handy locale, is placed safely on a quiet street next to the Ministry of the Interior. Thoughtfully run by Andrea, Lena, and Alberico, it has 31 comfortable, airy, clean, and bright rooms (Sb-€67, Db-€93, Tb-€124, Qb-€145, air-con for €8 extra, prices through 2002 with this book and cash only, all rooms 20 percent off mid-July–Aug and winter, elevator, Via Venezia 18, just off Via Nazionale, tel. 06-482-8355, fax 06-474-5550, www.hotelitaliaroma.com, e-mail: hitalia@pronet.it, SE). Most rooms have a fan. Their fine singles are all on the quiet courtyard and the eight annex rooms across the street are a cut above the rest.

Clarin Hotel, a plain and worn slumbermill with 21 rooms, is quiet, safe, and run with a smile (Db-€88, Tb-€109, Qb-€129, prices good with this book and cash, 3 percent extra with CC, Via Palermo 36, tel. 06-4782-5170, fax 06-4788-1393, e-mail: clarin-hotel@hotmail.com, Renaldo, Franco and Marco SE).

Hotel Sonya is a small, family-run, but impersonal place with 20 comfortable, well-equipped rooms, a great location, and decent prices (Db-€119, Tb-€134, Qb-€155, Quint/b-€170, CC, air-con, elevator, facing the Opera at Via Viminale 58, tel. 06-481-9911, fax 06-488-5678, e-mail: hotelsonyaroma@katamail .com, Francesca SE).

Hotel Cortina rents 14 modern, air-conditioned rooms on a busy street. Ask for a quieter room on the courtyard or side street (Db-€129 in 2002 with this book, CC, Via Nazionale 18, tel. 06-481-9794, fax 06-481-9220, www.travel.it/roma/hotelcortina, e-mail: hotelcortina@pronet.it, John Carlo and Angelo SE).

Hotel Montreal, run with care, is a bright, solid, business-class place on a big street a block southeast of Santa Maria Maggiore (Db-usually €103 but €88 July–Aug and €78 in winter, CC; 21 of its 27 rooms have air-con; elevator, good security, 1 block from Metro: Vittorio, 3 blocks west of train station, Via Carlo Alberto 4, 00185 Roma, tel. 06-445-7797, fax 06-446-5522, www.hotelmontrealroma.com).

Splurges: **Hotel Britannia** stands like a marble fruitcake, offering all the comforts in tight quarters. Lushly renovated with over-the-top classical motifs, its 32 air-conditioned rooms are small but comfortable with bright, modern bathrooms (Db-€233 May–June and Sept–Oct, Db-€152 Aug, Db-€207 rest of the year, extra bed-€52, CC, free parking, Via Napoli 64, tel. 06-488-3153, fax 06-488-2343, www.hotelbritannia.it, e-mail: info@hotelbritannia.it).

Hotel Rex is a business-class, Art Deco fortress—a quiet, plain, and stately four-star place with 50 rooms and all the comforts (Sb-€201, Db-€253, Tb-€294, CC, elevator, air-con, Via Torino 149, tel. 06-482-4828, fax 06-488-2743, e-mail: hotel.rex@alfanet.it, SE).

YWCA and Convents: **YWCA Casa Per Studentesse** accepts men and women. It's an institutional place, filled with white-uniformed maids, colorful Third-World travelers, and 75 single beds (€26 per person in 3- and 4-bed rooms, S-€36, Sb-€46, D-€62, Db-€73, includes breakfast except on Sun, elevator, Via C. Albo 4, tel. 06-488-0460, fax 06-487-1028). The YWCA faces a great little street market.

Suore di Santa Elisabetta is a heavenly Polish-run convent. While often booked long in advance and a challenge in communication, it's an incredible value (S-€27, Sb-€34, D-€48, Db-€63, Tb-€80, Qb-€98, CC, elevator, fine view roof terrace, a block southwest of Basilica Santa Maria Maggiore at Via dell' Omata 9, tel. 06-488-8271, fax 06-488-4066).

Pensione Per Pelligrini is another nun-run place with 39 big, simple rooms and lots of twin beds. There's a language barrier, but the price is right (S-€34, Sb-€41, D-€67, Db-€78, Tb-€89, breakfast-€4.25, closed Aug, peaceful garden, elevator, just off Piazza Vittorio Emmanuel II, Istituto Buon Salvatore, Via Leopardi 17, from station take bus #714, #649, or #360 or Metro: Vittorio Emmanuel, tel. 06-446-7147 or 06-446-7225, fax 06-446-1382, Sister Anna Maria SE).

Sleeping Cheap, Northeast of the Train Station (zip code: 00185)

The cheapest hotels in town are northeast of the station. Some travelers feel this area is weird and spooky after dark, but these hotels feel plenty safe. With your back to the train tracks, turn right and walk two blocks out of the station. The first two hotels are located in the same building.

Hotel Fenicia rents 11 comfortable, well-equipped rooms at a fine price. The bigger rooms upstairs are quieter, but there's no elevator (Sb-€47, Db-€73, Tb-€98, bigger and fancier Db-€83, prices through 2002 with this book only, air-con-€10.50/day, breakfast-€5.25; they say they take CC, but they don't; Via Milazzo 20, tel. & fax 06-490-342, www.fenicia.web-page.net, e-mail: fenicia @tiscalinet.it, Georgio and Anna SE).

Hotel Magic, a clean, marbled, family-run place with 10 rooms, is high enough off the road to escape the traffic noise (Sb-€52, Db-€73, Tb-€103, Qb-€114, air con-€10.50/day, breakfast-€3.75, prices through 2002 with this book only, cheaper in Aug and winter, CC, thin walls, midnight curfew, Via Milazzo 20, 3rd floor, tel. & fax 06-495-9880, little English spoken).

Albergo Sileo is a shiny-chandeliered, 10-room place with an elegant touch. It has a contract to house train conductors who work the night shift, so most of the simple, pleasant rooms are rented from 19:00 to 09:00 only. If you can handle this, it's a great value. During the day, they store your luggage, and though you won't have access to a room, you're welcome to hang out in their lobby or bar (D-€39, Db-€47, Tb-€62, Db for 24 hours-€62—a steal, elevator, Via Magenta 39, tel. & fax 06-445-0246, friendly Alessandro and Maria Savioli NSE).

Sleeping near the Colosseum (zip code: 00184)

These places are buried in a Roman world of exhaust-stained, medieval ambience. Take the subway one stop from the train station to the Cavour Metro stop. The *electrico* bus line #117 (San Giovanni in Laterano, Colosseo, Trevi Fountain, Piazza di Spagna, and Piazza del Popolo) connects you with the sights.

Hotel Paba is a little six-room place, chocolate box–tidy and lovingly cared for by Alberta and Pasquale Castelli. While overlooking busy Via Cavour just two blocks from the Colosseum, it's quiet enough (Db-€124, extra bed-€21, show this book for 5 percent discount, CC, breakfast served in room, air-con, elevator, Via Cavour 266, tel. 06-4782-4902, fax 06-4788-1225, www .hotelpaba.com, e-mail: info@hotelpaba.com).

Hotel Duca d'Alba, a tight and modern pastel-marble-hardwood place, is more professional than homey (Sb-€134, Db-€201, much cheaper July–Aug and winter, extra bed-€21, CC, air con, safes, phones, TV, elevator, Via Leonina 14, tel. 06-484-471, fax 06-488-4840, check Web site for deals, www .hotelducadalba.com, SE).

Hotel Grifo has a homey, tangled floor plan with 20 modern rooms and a roof terrace. The double-paned windows almost keep out the Vespa noise (Db-€119, €109 July–Aug, CC, elevator, air con, some rooms have terraces, 2 blocks off Via Cavour at Via del Boschetto 144, tel. 06-487-1395, fax 06-474-2323, e-mail: alez@dds.nl, SE).

Suore di Sant Anna was built for Ukrainian pilgrims. The sisters are sweet. It's difficult (little English plus 23:00 curfew), but once you're in, you've got a comfortable home in a classic Roman-village locale (Sb-€41, Db-€67, Tb-€101, consider dinner for €15, off corner of Via dei Serpenti and Via Baccina at Piazza Madonna dei Monti 3, tel. 06-485-778, fax 06-487-1064, e-mail: santasofia@tiscalinet.it).

Behind the Colosseum: **Hotel Lancelot**, a favorite among United Nations workers, is a big, 60-room place with a shady courtyard, rooftop terrace, bar, and restaurant. It's quiet, safe, well-run by Faris and Lubna Khan, and popular with returning guests (Sb-€88–103, Db-€139, Tb-€163, Qb-€178, add €11 for balcony, CC, air-con, no elevator, parking-€11/day, behind Colosseum near San Clemente Church at Via Capo D'Africa 47, tel. 06-7045-0615, fax 06-7045-0640, www.venere.com/roma /lancelot/lancelot.html, e-mail: lancelot@italyhotel.com).

Near the Palatine: The **Hotel Casa Kolbe**, located in a former monastery, rents out 63 monkish, spartan rooms with no fans or air-conditioning. With vast public spaces and a peaceful garden, it's popular with groups. But the location is great: on the river side of the Palatine ruins, on a quiet side street about a block from a little-used entrance to the Forum (Sb-€62, Db-€78, Tb-€98, Qb-€109, breakfast-€5.25, CC, elevator, garden, courtyard, not handy to public transit so taxi from the station, Via S. Teodoro 44, tel. 06-679-4974 or 06-679-8866, fax 06-6994-1550, Maurizio and Antonio SE).

Sleeping near Campo de' Fiori (zip code: 00186)

You pay a premium to stay in the old center, but each of these places is romantically set deep in the tangled back streets near the idyllic Campo de' Fiori and, for many, worth the extra money.

Casa di Santa Brigida overlooks the elegant Piazza Farnese. With soft-spoken sisters gliding down polished hallways, and pearly gates instead of doors, this lavish 23-room convent makes exhaust-stained Roman tourists feel like they've died and gone to heaven. If you're unsure of your destiny (and don't need a double bed), this is worth the splurge (Sb-€78, Db-€134, 3 percent extra with CC, great €16 dinners, roof garden, plush library, air-con, physical address: Monserrato 54, mailing address: Piazza Farnese 96, 00186 Roma, tel. 06-6889-2596, fax 06-6889-1573, www .brigidine.org/case/italy/welcome.html, e-mail: hesselblad @tiscalinet.it, many of the sisters are from India and speak English). If you get no response to your fax or e-mail within three days, consider that a "no." Groups are very welcome here.

Hotel Smeraldo, while well-run, clean, and air-conditioned, is noisy at night, and its 50 rooms can be somewhat smoky (Sb-€73, D-€73, Db-€103, Tb-€124, CC, Civolo dei Chiodaroli 9, midway between Campo de' Fiori and Largo Argentina, tel. 06-687-5929, fax 06-6880-5495, www.hotelsmeraldoroma.com, e-mail: albergosmeraldoroma@tin.it).

Hotel Arenula, the only hotel in Rome's old Jewish quarter or ghetto, is a fine place in the thick of old Rome with 50 comfy rooms (Sb-€88, Db-€114, Tb-€134; €26 less in July, Aug, and winter; air conditioning-€10.50/day, CC, just off Via Arenula at Via Santa Maria de' Calderari 47, tel. 06-687-9454, fax 06-689-6188, www.hotelarenula.com, e-mail: hotel.arenula@flashnet.it).

Sleeping near the Pantheon (zip code: 00186)

These four places are buried in the pedestrian-friendly heart of ancient Rome, each within a four-minute walk of the Pantheon. You'll pay more here—but save time and money by being exactly where you want to be for your early and late wandering.

Hotel Due Torri hides out on a tiny, quiet street. It feels professional yet homey, with an accommodating staff, generous public spaces, and 26 comfortable-if-small rooms—four with

SLEEPING IN THE HEART OF ROME

1. CASA DI SANTA BRIGIDA
2. HOTEL SMERALDO
3. TO HOTEL ARENULA
4. HOTEL DUE TORRI
5. HOTEL NAVONA
6. RESIDENZA ZANARDELLI
7. HOTEL NAZIONALE
8. TAVERNA REST., VINERIA REST. & LA CARBONARA REST.
9. OSTARIA DA GIOVANNI AR GALLETTO
10. OSTERIA ENOTECA AL BRIC
11. FILETTI DE BACCALA & TRATTORIA DER PALLARO
12. RIST. GROTTE DEL TEATRO DI POMPEO
13. CUL DE SAC BAR & L'INSALATA RICCA REST.
14. BREK REST.
15. IL DELFINO REST.
16. OSTERIA DA MARIO REST.
17. REST. MYOSOTIS DI MARSILI
18. ENOTECA SPIRITI
19. TO RIST. ALLA RAMPA
20. RIST. LA TAVERNA DEGLI AMICI
21. RIST. PIZZERIA SACRO & PROFANO
22. GIOLITTI GELATERIA
23. GELATERIA DELLA PALMA

balconies (Sb-€98, Db-€165, family apartment-€222 for 3 and €248 for 4, CC, air-con, Vicolo del Leonetto 23, a block off Via della Scrofa, tel. 06-6880-6956, fax 06-686-5442, www .hotelduetorriroma.com, e-mail: hotelduetorri@interfree.it).

Piazza Navona: Hotel Navona, while pretty ramshackle, is a fine value, offering 35 basic rooms in an ancient building (with a perfect locale) a block off Piazza Navona. Top-floor rooms come with wood-beamed character and more stairs (D-€98, Db-€109, air-con €16/day, family rooms, no CC, Via dei Sediari 8, tel. 06-686-4203, fax 06-6880-3802, www.hotelnavona.com, e-mail: info@hotelnavona.com; run by a friendly Australian named Corry, his Italian wife Patricia, and her dad Pino).

Residenza Zanardelli is a sumptuous little place with six classy and quiet rooms. Also owned by Corry, it's two blocks north of Piazza Navona (Db-€134, air-con €10.50/day, no CC; on busy street; but double-paned windows minimize noise; Via G. Zanardelli 7, tiny name next to doorbell, tel. 06-6821-1392 or 06-6880-9760, fax 06-6880-3802).

Hotel Nazionale, a four-star landmark, is a 16th-century palace sharing a well-policed square with the national Parliament. Its 90 rooms are served by lush public spaces, fancy bars, and a uniformed staff. It's a big hotel with a revolving front door, but it's a worthy splurge if you want security, comfort, and the heart of old Rome at your doorstep (Sb-€186, Db-€289, extra person-€62, suite-€439, less in Aug and winter, CC, air-con, elevator, free loaner motorbikes, Piazza Montecitorio 131, tel. 06-695-001, fax 06-678-6677, www.nazionaleroma.it, e-mail: hotel@nazionaleroma.it, SE). See their Web site for weekend and summer discounts of about 25 percent.

Sleeping in Trastevere (zip code: 00153)

To locate hotel, see map on page 46.

Hotel Santa Maria sits like a lazy hacienda in the midst of Trastevere. Surrounded by a medieval skyline, you'll feel as if you're on some romantic stage set. Its 18 small but well-equipped rooms—former cells in a cloister—are all ground-floor, circling a gravelly courtyard of orange trees and stay-awhile patio furniture. Because this is the only hotel in Trastevere, you'll pay about 25 percent more—but for poets, it's a deal (Db-€155, Tb-€191, Qb-€217, for this special price it's cash only, prices good with this book through 2002, 3-night minimum, air conditioning, a block north of Piazza Maria Trastevere at Vicolo del Piede 2, tel. 06-589-4626, fax 06-589-4815, www.htlsantamaria.com, e-mail: hotelsantamaria@libero.it, Stefano SE).

Sleeping "Three Stars" near the Vatican Museum
(zip code: 00192)

To locate hotels, see map on page 44.

Hotel Alimandi is a good value, run by the friendly and entrepreneurial Alimandi brothers—Paolo, Enrico, and Luigi—and the next generation, Marta and Germano. Their 35 rooms are air-conditioned, modern, and marbled in white (Sb-€85, Db-€145, Tb-€168, 5 percent discount with this book and cash, CC, elevator, grand buffet breakfast served in great roof garden, self-service laundry, Internet access, pool table, piano lounge, free parking, down stairs directly in front of Vatican Museum, Via Tunisi 8, near Metro: Cipro-Musei Vaticani, reserve by phone, no reply to fax means they are full, tel. 06-3972-6300, toll-free in Italy tel. 800-122-121, fax 06-3972-3943, www.alimandi.org, e-mail: alimandi@tin.it, SE). They offer free airport pickup and drop-off, though you must reserve when you book your room and wait for a scheduled shuttle (every 2 hrs, see their Web site). Maria Alimandi rents out three rooms in her apartment, a 20-minute bus ride from the Vatican (Db-€78, see www.alimandi.org).

Hotel Spring House, with a hotelesque feel, offers 51 attractive rooms—some with balconies or terraces (Db-€129, Tb-€155, mention this book, 15 percent discount July–Aug and winter plus additional 5 percent discount for cash payment, CC, Internet access, air conditioning, elevator, free loaner bikes, Metro: Cipro-Musei Vaticani, Via Mocenigo 7, 2 blocks from Vatican Museum, tel. 06-3972-0948, fax 06-3972-1047, www.hotelspringhouse.com, Stefano Gabbani SE).

Hotel Gerber is sleek, modern, and air-conditioned, with 27 businesslike rooms, set in a quiet residential area (S-€62, Sb-€98, Db-€129, Tb-€150, Qb-€170, 10 percent discount with this book, CC, air-con, Via degli Scipioni 241, a block from Metro: Lepanto, at intersection with Ezio, tel. 06-321-6485, fax 06-321-7048, www.hotelgerber.it, Peter and Simonetta SE).

Hotel Sant' Anna is pricier than the rest, located on a charming-for-Rome pedestrian street that fills up with restaurant tables at dinnertime. Its 20 rooms are overly decorated with classical themes, but the furnishings are comfy (Sb-€145, Db-€181, Db-€145 July–Aug and winter, CC, air-con, elevator, courtyard, Borgo Pio 133, near intersection with Mascherino, a couple blocks from entrance to St. Peter's, tel. 06-6880-1602, fax 06-6830-8717, www.travel.it/roma/santanna, SE).

Hotel Bramante sits like a grand medieval lodge in the shadow of the fortified escape wall that runs from the Vatican to Castel San Angelo. The public spaces and the 16 rooms are generously-sized, with rough wood beams and high ceilings

(Sb-€129, Db-€181, Tb-€217, Qb-€253, 8 percent discount with this book, CC, air-con, no elevator, Vicolo delle Palline 24, tel. 06-6880-6426, fax 06-687-9881, www.hotelbramante.com, e-mail: bramante@excalhq.it, Loredana SE).

Sleeping in Hostels and Dorms (zip code: 00184)

For easy communication with young, friendly entrepreneurs, cheap dorm beds, and the very cheapest doubles in town—within a 10-minute hike of the train station—consider the following places:

Casa Olmata is a laid-back backpackers' place midway between the Termini train station and Colosseum (dorm beds €16–18, S-€34, bunkbed D-€36, one queen-size D-€55, lots of stairs, laundry service, free Internet access, video rentals, games, roof-top terrace with views, communal kitchen, dinners twice weekly, a block southwest of Basilica Santa Maria Maggiore, Via dell' Omata 36, 3rd floor, tel. 06-483-019, fax 06-474-2854, www.casaolmata.com, e-mail: casaolmata30@hotmail.com, Mirella and Marco).

The Beehive is especially good for older vagabonds. This tidy little place has two six-bed dorms (€16 beds) and a guests' kitchen on the main floor. Upstairs are five hotel-type rooms that are a great value (Sb-€39, D-€52, T-€78, Q-€103). It's thoughtfully run by a friendly young American couple, Steve and Linda (CC, dorms closed 13:00–16:00, 2 blocks south of Basilica Santa Maria Maggiore at Via Giovanni Lanza 99, tel. 06-474-0719, www.the-beehive.com). They also run a B&B booking service (fine private rooms in the old center, offering comparable quality for €65–95—about half the cost of a hotel, www.cross-pollinate.com).

Gulliver's House Rome is a fun little hostel in a very safe and handy locale, run by Simon and Sara. Its 24 beds in cramped quarters work fine for backpackers (€18 per bunkbed in 8-bed dorm, D-€57, no CC, closed 12:00–16:00, Via Palermo 36, tel. 06-481-7680, www.gullivershouse.com, e-mail: info@gullivershouse.com).

EATING
IN ROME

Romans spend their evenings eating, rather than drinking, and the preferred activity is to simply enjoy a fine, slow meal buried deep in the old city. Rome's a fun and cheap place to eat, with countless little eateries serving memorable $20 meals.

Although I've listed a number of restaurants, I recommend that you just head for a scenic area and explore. Piazza Navona, the Pantheon area, Campo de' Fiori, and Trastevere are neighborhoods packed with characteristic eateries. Sitting with tourists on a famous square enjoying the scene works fine. But for places more out of the way, consider my recommendations.

For Rome's best gelato, see "Eating near the Pantheon," below.

Eating in Trastevere

Colorful Trastevere is also now pretty touristy. Still, Romans join the tourists to eat on the rustic side of the Tiber River. Start at the central square (Piazza Santa Maria in Trastevere). Then choose: Eat with tourists enjoying the ambience of the famous square, or wander the back streets in search of a mom-and-pop place with barely a menu. Consider these places before making a choice (all are in the tangle of lanes between Ponte Sisto and the Piazza Santa Maria in Trastevere—see map on page 46):

At **Taverna del Moro da Tony**, Tony scrambles—with a great antipasti table—to keep his happy eaters (mostly tourists) well-fed and returning. Until we start telling him to "hold the mayo," his bruschetta will come buried in it (Tue–Sun 12:00–24:00, closed Mon, off Via del Moro at Vicolo del Cinque 36, tel. 06-580-9165).

For good home-cooking Roman-style, consider these two fun little places (within a block of each other): **Trattoria da Lucia** (closed Mon, indoor or outdoor seating, Vicolo del Mattonato 2, tel. 06-580-3601) and the homey **Trattoria de Olindo** (closed Sun, Vicolo della Scala 8, tel. 06-581-8835).

Osteria Ponte Sisto, a rough-and-tumble little place, specializes in traditional Roman cuisine. Since it's just outside of the tourist zone, it offers the best value and caters mostly to Romans. It's also easiest to find: As you approach Trastevere, crossing Ponte Sisto (pedestrian bridge), continue across the little square (Piazza Trilussa) and you'll find it on the right (open daily, Via Ponte Sisto 80, tel. 06-588-3411).

Panificio Arnese could be the most respected traditional bakery in town (daily 09:00–21:00, Via del Politeama 27). Pop in and eat something fresh out of the oven. The fine little *gelateria* (across from the church on Piazza della Scala) dishes up oh-wow pistachio.

Eating on and near Campo de' Fiori

While it is touristy, Campo de' Fiori offers a classic and romantic square setting. And, since it is so close to the collective heart of Rome, it remains popular with locals. For greater atmosphere than food value, circle the square, considering each place. Bars and pizzerias seem to overwhelm the square. The **Taverna** and **Vineria** at numbers 16 and 15 offer good perches from which to people-watch and nurse a glass of wine. The only real restaurant is **La Carbonara**. While not the birthplace of pasta carbonara, it does serve good food (closed Tue, Campo de' Fiori 23, tel. 06-686-4783). Meals on small nearby streets are a better value, but lack that Campo de' Fiori magic.

Nearby, on the more elegant and peaceful Piazza Farnese, **Ostaria Da Giovanni Ar Galletto** has a dressier local crowd; great outdoor seating; and moderate prices. Giovanni and his son Angelo serve fine food, but sometimes they turn single diners away (closed Sun, tucked in corner of Piazza Farnese at #102, tel. 06-686-1714). Of all my listings, Giovanni offers perhaps the best al fresco dining experience.

Osteria Enoteca al Bric is a mod Italian/French bistro-type place run by a man who loves to cook and serves good wine. Wine-case lids decorate the wall like happy memories. With candlelit elegance and no tourists, it's perfect for the wine snob in the mood for pasta and fine cheese. Choose your bottle (or half bottle) from the huge selection lining the walls as you enter (open from 19:30, closed Mon, CC, 100 meters off Campo de' Fiori at Via del Pellegrino 51, tel. 06-687-9533).

Filetti de Baccala is a tradition for many Romans. Basically a fish bar with paper tablecloths and cheap prices, it has grease-stained, hurried waiters, who serve old-time favorites—fried cod fillets, a

strange bitter *puntarelle* salad, and delightful anchovies with butter—
to nostalgic locals (Mon–Sat 17:30–23:00, closed Sun, a block east of
Campo de' Fiori tumbling onto a tiny and atmospheric square, Largo
dei Librari 88, tel. 06-686-4018).

Trattoria der Pallaro has no menu but plenty of return
eaters. Paola Fazi—with a towel wrapped around her head turban-
style—and her family serve up a five-course festival of typically
Roman food for €17.50, including wine, coffee, and a wonderful
mandarin liqueur. Their slogan: "Here, you'll eat what we want
to feed you." Make like Oliver Twist asking for more soup and get
seconds on the mandarin liqueur (Tue–Sun 12:00–15:30, 19:30–
24:00, closed Mon, indoor/outdoor seating on quiet square, a block
south of Corso Vittorio Emmanuele, down Largo del Chiavari to
Largo del Pallaro 15, tel. 06-6880-1488).

Ristorante Grotte del Teatro di Pompeo, sitting atop an
ancient theater, serves good food at fair prices with a smile (closed
Mon, Via del Biscione 73, tel. 06-6880-3686). This is great if you
want to dine on a characteristic street busy with strolling people.

Between Campo de Fiori and Piazza Navona: For interesting
bar munchies, try **Cul de Sac** on Piazza Pasquino (often crowded,
daily 12:00–18:00, 19:00–24:00, a block southwest of Piazza
Navona). **L'Insalata Ricca**, next door, is a popular chain that specializes in hearty and healthy salads (daily 12:00–15:45, 18:45-
22:00, Piazza Pasquino 72, tel. 06-6830-7881). Another branch is
nearby with more-spacious outdoor seating (just off Corso Vittorio
Emmanuele on Largo del Chiavari).

Eating near the Pantheon

You'll find a mix of cafeterias, groceries, restaurants, wine bars,
and gelato shops.

Cafeterias: **Brek**, on Largo Argentina just south of the
Pantheon, is an appealing, self-service restaurant with modern,
efficient atmosphere and really cheap prices (daily 12:00–15:30,
18:30–23:00, skip the sandwiches and pizza slices downstairs and
go to the "free flow" cafeteria upstairs, northwest corner of square,
Largo Argentina 1, tel. 06-6821-0353).

Il Delfino, also on Largo Argentina, is a tired but handy self-
service cafeteria that serves throughout the day (daily 07:00–21:00,
not cheap but fast). Across the side street, **Frullati di Frutta** sells
refreshing fruity frappés.

Grocery: The *alimentari* on the Pantheon square will make
you a sandwich for a temple-porch picnic. Sit at the base of a
column in the shade and munch lunch.

Restaurants: **Osteria da Mario**, a great little mom-and-pop
joint with a no-stress menu, serves delicious traditional favorites.

You'll feel right at home with locals who know a good value. The pop (Mario), who passed away—you'll see his photo on the wall—would be happy with the way his wife and kids are carrying on (Mon–Sat 13:00–15:00, 19:30–23:00, closed Sun, 2 blocks in front of Pantheon and to the left at Piazza delle Coppelle 51, tel. 06-6880-6349).

Ristorante Myosotis di Marsili, a dressy place with black-tie waiters and a coat check, is popular with local politicians and diners classy enough to look into the fish locker and make a knowledge-able choice. It has a traditional-yet-imaginative menu with a good wine list (Mon–Sat 12:30–15:30, 19:30–23:30, closed Sun, reservations smart, near Osteria da Mario, 2 blocks in front of Pantheon at Vicolo Della Vaccarella 3, tel. 06-686-5554).

Wine Bar: **Enoteca Spiriti**, a wine bar two blocks from the Pantheon, is run by Raffaele, son Matteo, and daughter Daria. They serve great wine ("*corposo*" means full-bodied) by the glass and light meals with integrity. Raffaele and I have designed a treat for travelers with this book: "A Taste of Italy for Two" includes two glasses of fine Amarone wine (or the equivalent in value), fresh bread, and a plate decorated with a tasty variety of Italian cheeses and meats for a total of €16. Choose: cool jazz interior or classic Roman sidewalk exterior (open at 12:30, very busy with local office workers at 13:30, dinner from 19:30, facing Pantheon walk around to the right and take 2 rights to Via S. Eustachio 5).

Gelato: Two of Rome's top ice-cream joints are a minute's walk in front of the Pantheon. The venerable **Giolitti's** (just off Piazza Colonna and Piazza Monte Citorio on Via Uffici del Vicario) is good, with cheap take-away prices and elegant old-world seating. But **Gelateria della Palma** is the new king of gelato—fresher, tastier, and with more options, including sugar-free and frozen-yogurt varieties (100 flavors, 2 blocks in front of Pantheon at Via della Maddalena 20, tel. 06-6880-6752).

Eating near the Spanish Steps

Ristorante Alla Rampa is a classic old restaurant tucked away just around the corner from the touristy crush of the Spanish Steps. You'll get quality Roman cooking here, with great indoor/outdoor ambience, for a moderate price. They take no reservations, so arrive by 19:30 or be prepared to wait (closed Sun, 100 meters east of Spanish Steps at Piazza Mignanelli 18, tel. 06-678-2621).

Eating near Piazza Venezia

Ristorante La Taverna degli Amici is a dressy yet friendly, candlelit place draped in ivy and tucked away on a sleepy square two blocks toward the Pantheon from the Victor Emmanuel Monument. This is a great and peaceful spot for a break before or after your Capital Hill sightseeing. The waiters are friendly and the clientele is local and upscale (reserve for dinner to avoid the basement, Tue–Sun 12:30–15:00, 19:30–24:00, closed Mon, Piazza Margana 36, tel. 06-6920-0493).

Eating near the Trevi Fountain

Ristorante Pizzeria Sacro e Profano is a bright and trendy place energetically filling an old church with spicy south Italian (Calabrian) cuisine and great pizzas. Run by friendly and helpful Pasquale and friends, this is just far enough away from the Trevi mobs (a block off Via del Tritone at Via dei Maroniti 29, tel. 06-6791-836).

Eating between the Colosseum and St. Peter-in-Chains Church

You'll find good views but poor value in the restaurants directly behind the Colosseum. To get your money's worth, eat a block away from the Colosseum. There are two handy eateries at the top of Terme Di Tito, a block uphill from the Colosseum, near St. Peter-in-Chains church (of Michelangelo's Moses fame).

For a real restaurant meal, try **Ostaria da Nerone**. The Santis family serves traditional Roman cuisine in a homey indoor or outdoor setting (Mon–Sat 12:00–15:00, 19:00–23:00, closed Sun, Via delle Terme di Titi 96, tel. 06-481-7952). Next door at **Caffè dello Studente**, Pina and Mauro serve typical "bar gastronomia" fare (pizza, toasted sandwiches, various drinks); stand up at the crowded bar, take away, or enjoy the outdoor tables (Mon–Sat 07:30–21:30, closed Sun, tel. 06-488-3240).

Eating near Via Firenze and Via Nazionale Hotels

Snack Bar Gastronomia is a great local hole-in-the-wall for lunch or dinner (daily 07:00–24:00; fresh meat or veggie sandwiches, fresh squeezed juices, and Greek-style yogurt—yummy with fruit; ask the price first; Via Firenze 34). There's a classic old-fashioned *alimentari* (grocery) across the street (7:00–19:30).

Pasticceria Dagnino—popular for its top-quality Sicilian specialties, especially pastries and ice cream—is frequented by people who work at my recommended hotels (daily 07:00–22:00, in Galleria Esedra off Via Torino, tel. 06-481-8660). Their *arancino*—a rice, cheese, and ham ball—is a greasy Sicilian favorite, and their cannoli is sweet. Direct the construction of your meal at the bar, pay for your trayful at the cashier, and climb upstairs, where you'll find the dancing Sicilian girls (free).

Hostaria Romana is a great place for traditional Roman cuisine. For an air-conditioned, classy, local favorite run by a jolly group of men who enjoy their work, eat here (closed Sun, midway between Trevi fountain and Piazza Barberini, Via del Boccaccio 1, at intersection with Via Rasella, no reservations needed before 20:00, tel. 06-474-5284). Go ahead and visit the antipasto bar in person to assemble your plate. They're happy to serve an *antipasti misto della casa* and pasta dinner. Take a hard look at their *Specialita Romane* list.

Ristorante da Giovanni is a serviceable, hardworking place feeding locals and tired travelers now for 50 years (tired €12 menu, Mon–Sat 12:00–15:00, 19:00–22:30, closed Sun, CC, just off Via XX Settembre at Via Antonio Salandra 1, tel. 06-485-950).

Cafeteria Nazionale, with woody elegance, offers light lunches—including salads—at reasonable prices (Mon–Sat 07:00–20:00, closed Sun, CC, Via Nazionale 26-27, at intersection with Via Agostino de Pretis, tel. 06-4899-1716). Their lunch buffet is a delight (€7.50, 12:30–15:00).

Ristorante Cinese Internazionale is your best neighborhood bet for Chinese (daily 12:00–15:00, 18:00–23:00, inexpensive, no pasta, just off Via Nazionale behind Hotel Luxor at Via Agostino de Pretis 98, tel. 06-474-4064).

Restaurant Target is a soulless, modern, but handy place serving decent pizza and pasta near recommended hotels (open daily, indoor and outdoor seating, don't expect great service, Via Torino 33, tel. 06-474-0066).

The **McDonald's** restaurants on Piazza della Repubblica (free piazza seating outside), Piazza Barberini, and Via Firenze offer air-conditioned interiors and salad bars.

Flann O'Brien Irish Pub is an entertaining place for a quick light meal (of pasta or something *other* than pasta, served early or late when other places are closed), fine Irish beer, live sporting events on TV, and perhaps the most Italian crowd of all (daily 07:30–01:00, Via Nazionale 17, at intersection with Via Napoli, tel. 06-488-0418).

Eating near Santa Maria Maggiore

For a classy taste of Tuscany in a woody wine bar filled with local office workers, drop by **Monti D.O.C. Vineria Wine Bar** for lunch (chalkboard shows daily specials, daily 10:00–24:00, 2 blocks from basilica next to recommended Beehive hostel at Via Giovanni Lanza 93, tel. 06-487-2696).

Eating near the Vatican Museum and St. Peter's

Avoid the restaurant pushers handing out fliers near the Vatican: bad food, expensive menu tricks. Try any of these instead.

Antonio's Hostaria dei Bastioni is tasty and friendly. It's conveniently located midway on your hike from St. Peters' to the Vatican Museum, with noisy streetside seating and a quiet interior (Mon–Sat 12:00–15:00, 19:00–23:30, closed Sun, €5.25–6.25 pastas, €7.75 *secondi*, no cover charge, at corner of Vatican wall, Via Leone IV 29, tel. 06-3972-3034). Antonio is your gracious host.

La Rustichella serves a sprawling antipasti buffet (€7.75 for a meal-sized plate). Arrive when they open at 19:30 to avoid a line and have the pristine buffet to yourself (Tue–Sun 12:30–15:00, 19:30–23:00, closed Mon, near Metro: Cipro-Musei Vaticani stop, opposite church at end of Via Candia, Via Angelo Emo 1, tel. 06-3972-0649). Consider the fun and fruity **Gelateria Millennium** next door.

Viale Giulio Cesare is lined with cheap **Pizza Rustica** shops and fun eateries, such as **Cipriani Self-Service Rosticcería** (closed Mon, pleasant outdoor seating, near Ottaviano subway stop, Viale Guilio Cesare 195). Restaurants like **Tre Pupazzi**, which line the pedestrian-only Borgo Pio—a block from Piazza San Pietro—are worth a look.

Turn your nose loose in the wonderful **Via Andrea Doria** open-air market, three blocks north of the Vatican Museum (Mon–Sat roughly 07:00–13:30, until 16:30 Tue and Fri except summer, between Via Tunisi and Via Andrea Doria). If the market is closed, try the nearby **IN's supermarket** (Mon–Sat 08:30–13:30 and 16:00–20:00, closed Thu eve, a half block straight out from Via Tunisi entrance of open-air market, Via Francesco 18).

ROME WITH
CHILDREN

Sorry, but Rome is not a great place for little kids. Parks are rare. Kid-friendly parks are more rare. The low-tech museums lack hands-on fun.

The good news for kids? Pizza and *gelato*. Any person under a meter (39 inches) tall travels free on the public transit. And Italians are openly fond of kids, so you'll probably get lots of friendly attention from locals.

Here are some tips:

- Take advantage of local information. *Roma c'è*, the periodical entertainment guide, has a children's section in English. Ask at Rome's TIs about kid-friendly activities. TIs often have a helpful "kid's pack."

- Don't overdo it. Tackle only one or two key sights a day (Vatican Museum, or Colosseum and Forum) and mix with a healthy dose of fun activities.

- Rome's hotels often give price breaks for kids. (Air-conditioning can be worth the splurge.)

- Eat dinner early (around 19:00) and you'll miss the romantic crowd. Skip the famous places. Look instead for self-serve cafeterias, bars (kids are welcome), or even fast-food restaurants where kids can move around without bothering others. Picnic lunches and dinners work well. For ready-made picnics, try the *rosticcerie* (delis) and Pizza Rustica shops (cheap take-out pizza; *diavola* is the closest thing on the menu to kid-friendly pepperoni).

- Public WCs are hard to find: Try museums, bars, gelato shops, and fast-food restaurants.

- Follow this book's crowd-beating tips to a tee. Kids don't like standing in a long line for a museum (which they might not even want to see).

Sights to Consider

Rome's many squares are traffic-free, with plenty of space to run and pigeons to feed while Mom and Dad enjoy a coffee at an outdoor table.

When visiting the ancient sites, have some fun with *Ancient Rome—Then and Now*, a fun book for kids, with plastic overlays showing how the ruins used to look. It's available at stalls near the entrance of ancient sites.

The Vatican Museum comes with mummies and fun statues of animals. There's an entire hall of statues with their penises broken off that my kids found entertaining.

Villa Borghese is Rome's sprawling central park. The best kids' zone is near Porta Pinciana where you'll find rental bikes, pony rides, and other amusements.

The ghoulish Cappucin Crypt (decorated with skeletons) and the Catacombs tunnels are goblin pleasers. (For Crypt, see page 42; for Catacombs, page 50.)

The Church of St. Ignazio, with its false dome, fascinates kids and adults (see page 94).

Bocca di Verità, the legendary Mouth of Truth, draws a young crowd. Stick your hand in the mouth of the gaping stone face on the wall. As the legend goes, if you're a liar, your hand will be gobbled up. (The Mouth is free and always open, on the porch of the Church of Santa Maria in Cosmedin, on Piazza Bocca della Verità, near the north end of Circus Maximus.)

Your children can go to Egypt (without the diarrhea) by visiting Rome's funky little pyramid (always viewable, Metro: Piramide).

Rome feels safe at night, and you can easily take your kids on the walks suggested in this book such as the Dolce Vita Stroll on page 226. ✪ On the Night Walk Across Rome (page 54), children enjoy slurping up chocolatey *tartufo* at the Tre Scalini café (Piazza Navona) and tossing coins in the Trevi Fountain.

The Luna Park at E.U.R. is a tired, old amusement park (Metro to Magliana, then bus to Via delle Tre Fontana, tel. 06-592-5933). Rome also has a big water park—Hydromania (€11.50, daily 09:30–18:30, Vicolo Casal Lumbroso 200, tel. 06-6618-3183).

SHOPPING
IN ROME

Shops are open from 09:00 to 13:00 and from 16:00 to 19:00. They're often closed on summer Saturday afternoons and winter Monday mornings.

If all you need are souvenirs, a surgical strike at any souvenir shop will do. Otherwise, try . . .

Department Stores

Large department stores offer relatively painless one-stop shopping. A good upscale department store is **La Rinascente**. Its main branch is on Piazza Fiume, and there's a smaller store on Piazza Colonna. **COIN**, near Piazza Fiume, is also fashionable (like an Italian Bon Marché). **UPIM** is the Roman Kmart (many branches, including Via Nazionale 111, Piazza Santa Maria Maggiore, and Via del Tritone 172). **Cinecitta Due** is the nearest shopping mall (Via P. Togliatti 2, Metro: Subaugusta, tel. 06-722-0902).

Boutiques

For top fashion, stroll the streets around the Spanish Steps, including **Via Condotti**, **Via Borgognona** (for the big-name shops), and **Via del Babuino** (trendy design shops and galleries). For antiques, stroll **Via de Coronari** (between Piazza Navona and the bend in the river), **Via Giulia** (between Campo de' Fiori and the river), or **Via Margutta** (classier, with art galleries too, from Spanish Steps to Piazza del Popolo).

Open-Air Produce Markets

Rome's outdoor markets provide a fun and colorful dimension of the city that even the most avid museum-goer should not miss. Wander through the easygoing neighborhood produce markets, which clog certain streets and squares every morning except Sunday. Consider the huge **Mercato Andrea Doria** (3 blocks in front of Vatican Museum at Via Andrea Doria). Smaller but equally charming slices of everyday Roman life are at markets on these streets and squares: **Piazza delle Coppelle** (near the Pantheon), **Via Balbo** (near recommended hotels off Via Nazionale near Termini station), **Piazza Vittorio** (near Termini train station), and **Via della Pace** (near Piazza Navona). The covered **Mercato di Testaccio** is mostly produce and a hit with photographers and people-watchers (Piazza Testaccio, near Metro: Piramide). And **Campo de' Fiori**, while newly renovated to fit European Union standards, is still a fun scene. These produce markets are generally open from 07:00 to 13:00 and closed Sunday.

Flea Market

For antiques and fleas, the granddaddy of markets is the **Porta Portese** *mercato delle pulci*—flea market (6:30–13:00 Sun only, Via Portuense and Via Ippolito Nievo, bus #75 from train station or tram #8 from Largo Argentina). Or consider **Via Sannio**, stuffed with clothing and some handicrafts, a couple of blocks south of the Basilica of San Giovanni in Laterano (Mon–Sat 08:00–13:00, Metro: San Giovanni). Wear your money belt; markets are magnets for pickpockets.

Airport Souvenirs

Leonardo da Vinci Airport ("Fiumicino") sells Italian specialty foods vacuum-packed to clear U.S. customs. Most shops are near the departure gates (after you check your bags and pass through security). Try Parmigiano-Reggiano cheese, dried porcini mushrooms or peppers, and better olive oil than you can buy at home.

NIGHTLIFE
IN ROME

Romans get dressed up and eat out in casual surroundings for their evening entertainment. For most visitors, the best after-dark entertainment is simply to stroll the medieval lanes that connect the romantic, floodlit squares and fountains. Head for Piazza Navona, the Pantheon, Campo de' Fiori, Trevi Fountain, Spanish Steps, Via del Corso, Trastevere, or Monte Testaccio. (★ See "Night Walk Across Rome," page 54 and "Dolce Vita Stroll," below.)

Get copy of either of the entertainment guides, *Roma c'è* (sold at newsstands, €1) or *L'Evento* (free at TI). Look at the current listings of concerts, operas (the opera house is at Via Firenze 72, near recommended Via Nazionale hotels, tel. 06-481-601), dance, and films. Posters around town also proclaim upcoming events.

At **Pasquino**, Rome's English movie theater, you'll find movies in English daily (3 screens, in Trastevere at Piazza S. Egidio 9, catch tram #8 from Largo Argentina, tel. 06-580-3622). **Warner Village Moderno** shows some films in English (usually Wed–Thu, Piazza Repubblica, near train station and recommended hotels, tel. 06-477-791). Some theaters around town run movies in their original language (look for "V.O."—*versione originale*).

An interesting place for club-hopping is **Monte Testaccio**. After 21:00, ride the Metro to Piramide and follow the noise. Monte Testaccio, once an ancient trash heap, is now a small hill whose cool caves house funky restaurants and trendy clubs. Students enjoy the **pub crawls** offered by Walks of Rome (see "Tours of Rome," page 30).

Some **museums** have late opening hours (especially on Sat in summer), offering a good chance to see art in a cooler, less crowded environment. Ask at any TI which museums are currently open late on Saturdays (possibly Castel Sant' Angelo, Capitol Hill Museum, and Borghese Gallery—reservations required only for Borghese).

The Dolce Vita Stroll down Via del Corso

This is the city's chic stroll, from Piazza del Popolo (Metro: Flaminio) down a wonderfully traffic-free section of Via del Corso, and up Via Condotti to the Spanish Steps each evening around 18:00 (Sat and Sun are best). Shoppers, people-watchers, and flirts on the prowl fill this neighborhood of Rome's most fashionable stores (open after siesta 16:30–19:30).

Throughout Italy, early evening is time to stroll. While elsewhere in Italy this is called the *passeggiata*, in Rome it's a cruder, big-city version called the *struscio*. (*Struscio* means "to rub.") Unemployment among Italy's youth is very high; many stay with their parents even into their 30s. They spend a lot of time being trendy and hanging out. Hardcore cruisers from the suburbs, which lack pleasant public spaces, congregate on Via del Corso to make the scene. The hot *vroom vroom* motorscooter is their symbol; haircuts and fashion are follow-the-leader. They are the *coatto*. In a more genteel small town, the *passeggiata* comes with sweet whispers of *"bella"* and *"bello"* ("pretty" and "handsome"). In Rome, the admiration is stronger, oriented toward consumption— they say *"buona"* and *"buono"*—meaning "good" (terms used to describe food). Despite how lusty this all sounds, you'll see as many chunky, middle-aged Italians on this walk as sexy youth on the prowl.

Start on **Piazza Popolo**. The delightfully car-free square is marked by an obelisk that was brought to Rome by Augustus after he conquered Egypt. (It used to stand in the Circus Maximus.) In medieval times, this area was just inside Rome's main entry.

The Baroque Church of **Santa Maria del Popolo**, on the square, contains Raphael's Chigi Chapel (kee-gee, third chapel on left) and two Caravaggio paintings (the side paintings in chapel left of altar). The church is open daily (Mon–Sat 07:00–12:00, 16:00–19:00; Sun 08:00–13:30, 16:30–19:30, next to the gate in the old wall, on the far side of Piazza del Popolo, to the right as you face the gate).

From Piazza del Popolo, shop your way down **Via del Corso**. If you need a rest, join the locals sitting on the steps of various churches along the street.

At Via Pontefici, historians turn right and walk a block to see the massive, rotting, round-brick **Mausoleum of Augustus**, topped with overgrown cypress trees. Beyond it, next to the river, is Augustus' Ara Pacis, or Altar of Peace (which will reopen in 2005 after renovation).

From the mausoleum, return to Via del Corso and the 21st century, continuing straight until **Via Condotti**. Shoppers should take a left to join the parade to the **Spanish Steps**. The streets that parallel Via Condotti to the south (Borgognona and Frattini) are just as popular. You can catch a taxi home at the taxi stand a block south of the Spanish Steps (at Piazza Mignonelli, near American Express and McDonald's).

Historians: Ignore Via Condotti. Continue a kilometer down Via del Corso—straight since Roman times—to the Victor Emmanuel monument. Climb Michelangelo's stairway to his glorious (especially when floodlit) square atop Capitol Hill. From the balconies at either side of the mayor's palace, catch the lovely views of the Forum as the horizon reddens and cats prowl the unclaimed rubble of ancient Rome.

TRANSPORTATION
CONNECTIONS

ROME'S TRAIN STATIONS

Rome's main train station, **Termini**, is a minefield of tourist services: a TI (daily 08:00–21:00, off-season 09:00–20:00), train info office (daily 07:00–21:45), ATMs, late-hours banks, 24-hour thievery, luggage lockers (near track 24), the main city-bus hub (in front of train station), a subway stop, and the handy, cheery Chef Express Self-Service Ristorante (daily 11:00–22:30, WC at entrance, near east end of station; although there are several Chef Express bars scattered throughout the station, the most comfortable is this sit-down Ristorante). In the modern mall downstairs, under the station, you'll find a grocery (oddly named "Drug Store," daily 07:00–24:00, downstairs), pharmacy (daily 07:30–22:00), public showers (downstairs), and Internet access at Thenetgate (daily 06:00–23:30, near Dunkin Donuts, cheapest to buy a €5.25 60-minute card, can return or use at branches at Trevi Fountain or Vatican). The station has some sleazy sharks with official-looking cards. In general, avoid anybody selling anything at the station if you can.

Long-distance buses (e.g., from Siena and Assisi) arrive at Rome's small **Tiburtina** station, which is on Metro line B, with easy connections to the main train station (a straight shot 4 stops away) and the entire Metro system.

Most of my hotel listings are easily accessible by foot (those near the Termini train station) or by Metro (those in the Colosseum and Vatican neighborhoods). The train station has its own Metro stop (Termini).

Types of Trains

You'll encounter several types of trains in Italy. Along with the various milk-run trains, there are the slow IR (Interregional) and *directo* trains, the medium *expresso*, the fast IC (Intercity), and the

ITALY'S PUBLIC TRANSPORTATION

KEY: — RAIL ---BUS ···· SHIP
NOT TO SCALE ● GOOD OVERNIGHT STOPS

bullet-train T.A.V.—Treno Alta Velocita (supplement costs
€16 even with train pass). Fast trains, even with supplements, are
affordable (e.g., a 2nd-class Rome–Venice ticket costs about
$50 with an express supplement). Buying supplements on the train
comes with a nasty penalty. Buying them at the station can be a

time-waster. Try to buy them at travel agencies (CIT or AmEx) in towns. The cost is the same, the lines and language barrier are smaller, and you'll save time.

Schedules

Newsstands sell up-to-date regional and all-Italy timetables (€3.75, ask for the *orario ferroviaro*). There is now a single all-Italy telephone number for train information—848-888088 (daily 07:00–21:00, automated Italian recording, have an Italian-speaker listen for you). On the Web, check www.reiseauskunft .bahn.de/bin/query.exe/en, www.fs-on-line.com, or www.itwg .com/trains.

Strikes are common. Strikes generally last a day, and train employees will simply say "*sciopero*" (strike). Still, sporadic trains—following no particular schedule—lumber down the tracks during most strikes.

By train from Rome to: Venice (6/day, 5–8 hrs), **Florence** (12/day, 2 hrs, most stop at Orvieto en route), **Pisa** (8/day, 3–4 hrs), **Genova** (7/day, 6 hrs, overnight possible), **Milan** (12/day, 5 hrs, overnight possible), **Naples** (6/day, 2 hrs), **Brindisi** (2/day, 9 hrs), **Amsterdam** (2/day, 20 hrs), **Bern** (5/day, 10 hrs), **Frankfurt** (4/day, 14 hrs), **Munich** (5/day, 12 hrs), **Nice** (2/day, 10 hrs), **Paris** (5/day, 16 hrs), **Vienna** (3/day, 13–15 hrs).

ROME'S AIRPORTS

Rome's two airports—Fiumicino (a.k.a. Leonardo da Vinci) and the small Ciampino—share the same Web site (www.adr.it).

Fiumicino Airport: Rome's major airport has a TI (Mon–Sat 08:00–19:00, closed Sun, tel. 06-6595-4471), ATMs, banks, luggage storage, shops, and bars.

A slick, direct train connects the airport and Rome's central Termini train station in 30 minutes. Trains run twice hourly in both directions from roughly 07:30 to 22:00. From the airport, trains depart at :07 and :37 past the hour (from airport's arrival gate, follow signs to "Stazione/Railway Station"; buy ticket from a machine or the Biglietteria office; €9, CC). From the Termini train station, trains depart at :21 and :51 past the hour, usually from track 25; look for signs that say "Fiumicino" and confirm with an official or a local on the platform that the train is indeed going to the airport (€9, buy ticket from any *tabacchi* shop in station or at Alitalia desk near entrance to track 25; to reach track 25, walk along track 24 midway through the station, then follow signs that take you inside—to Alitalia desk—and down the escalator). Read your ticket: If it requires validation, stamp it in a yellow machine near the platform before boarding.

Your hotel can arrange a taxi to the airport at any hour for about €40. To get from the airport into town cheaply by taxi, try teaming up with any tourist also just arriving (most are heading for hotels near yours in the center). Splitting a taxi and hopping out once downtown at a taxi stand to take another to your hotel will save you about €15. Avoid unmarked, unmetered taxis.

For airport information, call 06-65951. To inquire about flights, call 06-6595-3640 (Alitalia: tel. 06-65643, British Air: toll-free tel. 848-812-266, Delta: toll-free tel. 800-864-114, KLM/Northwest: tel. 06-6501-1441, Lufthansa: tel. 06-6568-4004, SAS: tel. 06-6501-0771, Swiss Air: tel. 06-847-0555, United: tel. 0266-7481).

Ciampino Airport: Rome's smaller airport (tel. 06-794-941) handles budget and charter flights. To get to downtown Rome from the airport, take the LILA/Cotral bus (2/hr) to the Anagnina Metro stop, where you can connect by Metro to the stop nearest your hotel.

DRIVING IN ROME

Greater Rome is circled by the Grande Raccordo Anulare. This ring road has spokes that lead you into the center. Entering from the north, leave the autostrada at the Settebagni exit. Following the ancient Via Salaria (and the black-and-white *"Centro"* signs), work your way doggedly into the Roman thick of things. This will take you along the Villa Borghese park and dump you right on Via Veneto (where there's an Avis office). Avoid rush hour and drive defensively: Roman cars stay in their lanes like rocks in an avalanche. Parking in Rome is dangerous. Park near a police station or get advice at your hotel. The Villa Borghese underground garage is handy (€18/day, Metro: Spagna).

Consider this: Your car is a worthless headache in Rome. Avoid a pile of stress and save money by parking at the huge, easy, and relatively safe lot behind the Orvieto station (follow "P" signs from autostrada) and catch the train to Rome (every 2 hrs, 75 min).

APPENDIX

ROMAN HISTORY—THREE MILLENNIA IN FIVE PAGES

History in a Hurry

Ancient Rome lasted a thousand years (500 B.C.–A.D. 500), half as an expanding republic, half as a dominating empire. When Rome fell to invaders, all Europe suffered a thousand years of poverty and ignorance (500–1500 A.D.), though Rome's influence could still be felt in the Catholic Church. Popes rebuilt Rome for pilgrims, in Renaissance then Baroque and neoclassical styles (1500–1800). As capital of a newly united Italy, Rome followed Fascist Mussolini into World War II (and lost) but rebounded in Italy's postwar economic boom.

Want more?

Legendary Birth (1200–500 B.C.)

Aeneas flees burning Troy (1200 B.C.), wanders like Odysseus, and finally finds a home along the Tiber. His descendants, 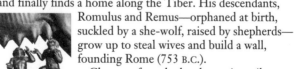 Romulus and Remus—orphaned at birth, suckled by a she-wolf, raised by shepherds— grow up to steal wives and build a wall, founding Rome (753 B.C.).

Closer to fact, the local agrarian tribes were dominated by more sophisticated neighbors to the north (Etruscans) and south (Greek colonists). Their convenient location on the Tiber was perfect for a future power.

Sights

- Romulus' "hut" and wall (Palatine Hill)
- She-wolf statue (Capitol Hill Museum)
- Frescoes of Aeneas and Romulus (National Museum of Rome)
- Bernini's Aeneas statue (Borghese Gallery)
- Etruscan wing (Vatican Museum)
- Etruscan Museum (in Villa Borghese gardens)
- Etruscan legacy (the original Circus Maximus, the drained Forum)

The Republic (509–27 B.C.)

The city expands throughout the Italian peninsula (500–300 B.C.), then defeats Hannibal's North African Carthaginians (the Punic Wars, 264–146 B.C.) and Greece (168 B.C.). Rome is master of the Mediterranean, and booty and captured slaves pour in. Romans bicker among themselves over their slice of the pie, pitting wealthy landowners (the ruling Senate) against the working class (plebes) and rebellious slaves (Spartacus' revolt, 73 B.C.). In the chaos, charismatic generals like Julius Caesar, who can provide wealth and security, become dictators. Change is necessary . . . and coming.

Sights

- Forum's Curia, Temple of Saturn, Temple of Castor and Pollux, Rostrum, Basilica Aemilia, Temple of Julius Caesar, and Basilica Julia (all rebuilt later)
- Appian Way built, lined with tombs
- Aqueducts, which carry water to a growing city
- Portrait busts of citizens (National Museum of Rome)
- The Republic's "S.P.Q.R." belief and motto, seen today on statues, buildings, and even manhole covers: the **S**enatus and **P**ublicus **Q** (which constitute) **R**omanus

The Empire—The "Roman Peace," or Pax Romana (A.D. 1–200)

After Julius Caesar was killed by disgruntled Republicans, his adopted son Augustus took undisputed control, ended the civil wars, declared himself emperor, and established his family to succeed him, setting the pattern of rule for the next 500 years.

Rome ruled an empire of 54 million people, stretching from Scotland to Africa, from Spain to Turkey. The city, with over a million inhabitants, was decorated with Greek-style statues and monumental structures faced with marble . . . it was the marvel of the known world. The empire prospered on a (false) economy of booty, slaves, and trade, surviving the often turbulent and naughty behavior of emperors like Caligula and Nero.

Sights
- Colosseum
- Forum
- Palatine Hill palaces
- Poems by Virgil, Catullus, Horace, and Ovid (from time of Augustus)
- Augustus' house (Casa di Livia) on Palatine Hill
- Pantheon
- Trajan's Column and Forum
- Greek and Greek-style statues and emperor's busts (National Museum of Rome, Vatican Museum, Capitol Hill Museum)
- Piazza Navona (former stadium)
- Hadrian's Villa (Tivoli) and tomb (now Castel Sant' Angelo)

Rome Falls (200–476)

Corruption, disease, and the constant pressure of barbarians pecking away at the borders slowly drained the unwieldy empire. Despite Diocletian's division of the empire and Constantine's legalizing Christianity (313), the city was sacked (410) and the last emperor checked out (476). Rome fell like a huge column, kicking up dust that would plunge Europe into a thousand years of darkness.

Sights
- Arch of Constantine
- The Forum's Basilica of Constantine
- Baths of Diocletian
- Old Roman Wall (gates at Via Veneto or Piramide)

Medieval Rome (500–1500)

The once-great city of a million people dwindled to a rough village of 10,000, with a corrupt pope, forgotten ruins, and malaria-carrying mosquitoes. Cows grazed in the ruined Forum and wolves prowled the Vatican at night. During the 1300s, even the popes left Rome to live in France. What little glory Rome retained was in the pomp, knowledge, and wealth of the Catholic Church.

Sights
* The damage done to ancient Roman monuments caused by disuse, barbarian looting, and pillaging for pre-cut stones
* Early Christian churches built before Rome fell (Santa Maria Maggiore, San Giovanni in Laterano, and San Clemente)
* Churches of Santa Maria sopra Minerva and Santa Maria in Trastevere
* Castel Sant' Angelo

Renaissance and Baroque Rome (1500–1800)

As Europe's economy recovered, energetic popes rebuilt Rome to attract pilgrims. The best artists decorated palaces and churches, carved statues, and built fountains. The city was not a great political force, but, as the  center of Catholicism during the struggle against Protestants (c.1520–1648), it was an influential religious and cultural capital.

Renaissance Sights
* Michelangelo's Sistine Chapel (Vatican Museum), dome of St. Peter's, *Pietà* (St. Peter's), Moses (St. Peter–in–Chains church), Christ statue (*Santa Maria sopra Minerva*), Capitol Hill Square, Santa Maria  degli Angeli church (in former Baths of Diocletian)
* Raphael's *School of Athens* and *Transfiguration* (Vatican Museum)
* Paintings by Raphael, Titian, and others (Borghese Gallery)

Baroque Sights
* St. Peter's Square and interior (largely by Bernini)
* Bernini statues (at Borghese Gallery; also *St. Teresa in Ecstasy* at Santa Maria della Vittoria church) and fountains (Piazza Navona, Piazza Barberini)
* Ancient obelisks erected in squares (Piazza del Popolo, Piazza Navona)
* Trevi Fountain and Spanish Steps
* Gesu and St. Ignazio churches
* Caravaggio's *Calling of St. Matthew* (San Luigi dei Francesi church) and other paintings (Borghese Gallery and Vatican Museum)
* Baroque paintings (Borghese Gallery)
* Borromini's facade of Santa Agnese church (Piazza Navona)

Modern Rome (1800–2000)

Rome becomes the capital of a newly reunited Italy (1870), is modernized by Fascist Mussolini, and survives the destruction of World War II. Italy's postwar "economic miracle" makes Rome a world-class city of cinema, banking, and tourism.

Sights

- Victor Emmanuel II Monument, which honors modern Italy's first (democratic) king
- Mussolini: The balcony he spoke from (at Palazzo Venezia, on Piazza Venezia), his planned city (E.U.R.), grand boulevards (Via dei Fori Imperiali, Via Conciliazione), and Olympic Stadium
- Cinecitta film studios and Via Veneto nightlife, which have faint echoes of Fellini's "La Dolce Vita" Rome
- Subway system, broad boulevards, smog

Rome Today

After surviving the government-a-year turbulence and Mafia-tainted corruption of the postwar years, Rome is stabilizing. Today, the average Roman makes more money than the average Englishman. The city is less polluted and more organized. A couple of years ago, in celebration of the millennium, this eternal city gave its monuments a facelift. Rome is ready for pilgrims, travelers, and you to come and make more history.

Let's Talk Telephones

Here's a primer on making phone calls in Europe. For information specific to Italy, see "Telephones" in the Introduction.

Making Calls within a European Country: About half of all European countries use area codes; the other half uses a direct-dial system without area codes.

To make calls within a country that uses a direct-dial system (Italy, Belgium, Denmark, France, Portugal, Norway, Spain, and Switzerland), you dial the same number whether you're calling across the country or across the street.

In countries that use area codes (such as Austria, Britain, the Czech Republic, Finland, Germany, Ireland, the Netherlands, and Sweden), you dial the local number when calling within a city, and you add the area code if calling long-distance within the country.

Making International Calls: You always start with the international access code (011 if you're calling from the U.S. or Canada, or 00 from Europe), then dial the country code of the country you're calling (see chart below).

What you dial next depends on the phone system of the

country you're calling. If the country uses area codes, drop the initial zero of the area code, then dial the rest of the number.

Countries that use direct-dial systems (no area codes) vary in how they're accessed internationally by phone. For instance, if you're making an international call to Italy, Denmark, Norway, Portugal, or Spain, simply dial the international access code, country code, and phone number. But if you're calling Belgium, France, or Switzerland, drop the initial zero of the phone number.

International Access Codes
When dialing direct, first dial the international access code (00 if calling from Europe, 011 if calling from the U.S. or Canada). Virtually all European countries—including Italy—use "00" as their international access code; the only exceptions are Finland (990) and Lithuania (810).

Country Codes
After you've dialed the international access code, dial the code of the country you're calling.

Austria—43	Greece—30
Belgium—32	Ireland—353
Britain—44	Italy—39
Canada—1	Morocco—212
Czech Rep.—420	Netherlands—31
Denmark—45	Norway—47
Estonia—372	Portugal—351
Finland—358	Spain—34
France—33	Sweden—46
Germany—49	Switzerland—41
Gibraltar—350	United States—1

Useful Italian Phone Numbers
Emergency (English-speaking police): 113
Emergency (military police): 112
Road Service: 116
Directory Assistance (for €0.50, an Italian-speaking robot gives the number twice, very clearly): 12
Telephone help (in English; free directory assistance): 170

Public Holidays and Festivals
Italy has more than its share of holidays. Each town has a local festival honoring its patron saint. Italy (including most major sights) closes down on these national holidays: January 1, January 6 (Epiphany), Easter Sunday and Monday, April 25 (Liberation Day), May 1 (Labor Day), May 20 (Ascension Day), August 15

(Assumption of Mary), November 1 (All Saints Day), December 8 (Immaculate Conception of Mary), and December 25 and 26. In addition, June 29 (Saints Peter and Paul Day) is a Roman holiday. This isn't a complete list. Holidays strike without warning.

Numbers and Stumblers

- Europeans write a few of their numbers differently than we do. 1 = 1 , 4 = 4 , 7 = 7 . Learn the difference or miss your train.
- In Europe, dates appear as day/month/year, so Christmas is 25/12/02.
- Commas are decimal points and decimals are commas. A dollar and a half is 1,50, and there are 5.280 feet in a mile.
- When pointing, use your whole hand, palm down.
- When counting with fingers, start with your thumb. If you hold up your first finger to request one item, you'll probably get two.
- What Americans call the second floor of a building is the first floor in Europe.
- Europeans keep the left "lane" open for passing on escalators and moving sidewalks. Keep to the right.

Metric Conversion (approximate)

1 inch = 25 millimeters
1 foot = 0.3 meter
1 yard = 0.9 meter
1 mile = 1.6 kilometers
1 centimeter = 0.4 inch
1 meter = 39.4 inches
1 kilometer = .62 mile

32 degrees F = 0 degrees C
82 degrees F = about 28 degrees C
1 ounce = 28 grams
1 kilogram = 2.2 pounds
1 quart = 0.95 liter
1 square yard = 0.8 square meter
1 acre = 0.4 hectare

Rome's Climate

First line—average daily low; second line—average daily high; third line—days of no rain.

J	F	M	A	M	J	J	A	S	O	N	D
40°	42°	45°	50°	56°	63°	67°	67°	62°	55°	49°	44°
52°	55°	59°	66°	74°	82°	87°	86°	79°	71°	61°	55°
13	19	23	24	26	26	30	29	25	23	19	21

Basic Italian Survival Phrases

Hello (good day).	**Buon giorno.**	bwohn **jor**-noh
Do you speak English?	**Parla inglese?**	**par**-lah een-**glay**-zay
Yes. / No.	**Si. / No.**	see / noh
I'm sorry.	**Mi dispiace.**	mee dee-spee**ah**-chay
Please.	**Per favore.**	pehr fah-**voh**-ray
Thank you.	**Grazie.**	**graht**-seeay
Goodbye!	**Arrivederci!**	ah-ree-vay-**dehr**-chee
Where is...?	**Dov'è...?**	doh-**veh**
...a hotel	**...un hotel**	oon oh-**tehl**
...a youth hostel	**...un ostello della gioventù**	oon oh-**stehl**-loh **day**-lah joh-vehn-**too**
...a restaurant	**...un ristorante**	oon ree-stoh-**rahn**-tay
...a supermarket	**...un supermercado**	oon soo-pehr-mehr-**kah**-doh
...the train station	**...la stazione**	lah staht-seeoh-nay
...tourist information	**...informazioni per turisti**	een-for-maht-seeoh-nee pehr too-**ree**-stee
...the toilet	**...la toilette**	lah twah-**leht**-tay
men	**uomini, signori**	**woh**-mee-nee, seen-**yoh**-ree
women	**donne, signore**	**don**-nay, seen-**yoh**-ray
How much is it?	**Quanto costa?**	**kwahn**-toh **kos**-tah
Cheap(er).	**(Più) economico.**	(pew) ay-koh-**noh**-mee-koh
Is it included?	**È incluso?**	eh een-**kloo**-zoh
I would like...	**Vorrei....**	vor-**rehee**
...a ticket.	**...un biglietto.**	oon beel-**yay**-toh
...a room.	**...una camera.**	**oo**-nah **kah**-may-rah
...the bill.	**...il conto.**	eel **kohn**-toh
one	**uno**	**oo**-noh
two	**due**	**doo**-ay
three	**tre**	tray
four	**quattro**	**kwah**-troh
five	**cinque**	**cheeng**-kway
six	**sei**	**se**hee
seven	**sette**	**seht**-tay
eight	**otto**	**ot**-toh
nine	**nove**	**nov**-ay
ten	**dieci**	dee**ay**-chee
hundred	**cento**	**chehn**-toh
thousand	**mille**	**mee**-lay
At what time?	**A che ora?**	ah kay **oh**-rah
now / soon / later	**adesso / presto / tardi**	ah-**dehs**-soh / **prehs**-toh / **tar**-dee
today / tomorrow	**oggi / domani**	**oh**-jee / doh-**mah**-nee

For more user-friendly Italian phrases, check out *Rick Steves' Italian Phrase Book and Dictionary* or *Rick Steves' French, Italian & German Phrase Book and Dictionary.*

Faxing Your Hotel Reservation

Use this handy form for your fax (or find it online at
www.ricksteves.com/reservation). Photocopy and fax away.

One-Page Fax

To: _____ @ _____
         hotel   *fax*

From: _____ @ _____
           name   *fax*

Today's date: ____ / ____ / ____
            day *month* *year*

Dear Hotel _____ ,

Please make this reservation for me:

Name: _____

Total # of people: _____ # of rooms: _____ # of nights: _____

Arriving: ____ / ____ / ____ My time of arrival (24-hr clock): _____
       day *month* *year* (I will telephone if I will be late)

Departing: ____ / ____ / ____
        day *month* *year*

Room(s):   Single___   Double___   Twin___   Triple___   Quad___

With: Toilet___   Shower___   Bath___   Sink only___

Special needs: View___   Quiet___   Cheap___   Ground Floor___

Credit card: Visa___   MasterCard___   American Express___

Card #: _____

Expiration date:_____

Name on card: _____

You may charge me for the first night as a deposit. Please fax, e-mail, or
mail me confirmation of my reservation, along with the type of room
reserved, the price, and whether the price includes breakfast. Please also
inform me of your cancellation policy. Thank you.

_____
Signature

_____
Name

_____
Address

_____
City   *State*   *Zip Code*   *Country*

_____
E-mail Address

Road Scholar Feedback for ROME 2002

We're all in the same travelers' school of hard knocks. Your feedback help us improve this guidebook for future travelers. Please fill this out (or use the online version at www.ricksteves.com/feedback), attach more info or any tips/favorite discoveries if you like, and send it to us. As thanks for your help, we'll send you our quarterly travel newsletter free for one year. Thanks! **Rick**

Of the recommended accommodations/restaurants used, which was:

Best _____

    Why? _____

Worst _____

    Why? _____

Of the sights/experiences/destinations recommended by this book, which was:

Most overrated _____

    Why? _____

Most underrated _____

    Why? _____

Best ways to improve this book:

_____

_____

I'd like a free newsletter subscription:

_____ Yes   _____ No   _____ Already on list

_____
Name

_____
Address

_____
City, State, Zip

_____
E-mail Address

Please send to: ETBD, Box 2009, Edmonds, WA 98020

INDEX

accommodations, 12–15, 202–213. *See also* Sleeping

airports, 230–231: souvenirs, 224

ancient Rome 23, 32–36, 67: map, 60

ancient sights, 233

Antaquario Palatino Museum, 80

Appian Way, 50–52

Ara Pacis, 42

Arch of Constantine, 35–36, 62–63

Arch of Titus, 66–67

ATM machines, 5–6

banking, 5–6

Baroque sights, 235

Basilica Aemilia, 70–71

Baths of Caracalla, 54–55

Basilica of Constantine, 72–73

Baths of Diocletian, 40, 95–100

Belvedere Torso, 135–136

Bernini, 166

Borghese Gallery, 41–42: tour 120–128

Boutiques, 223

bus transportation, 29–30

cafés, 18–19

Caligula's Palace, 71

Campo de' Fiori, 54–55

Capitol Hill 36–38: museums, 37, 114–119

Cappuccin Crypt, 42

Castel Sant' Angelo, 43–45

catacombs, 50–52

cell phones, 11–12

children, 221–222

Church of San Luigi dei Francesi, 38, 89

Church of Santa Maria degli Angeli, 40, 95–98

Church of Santa Maria Sopra Minerva, 93

Church of St. Ignazio, 38, 94

Ciampino Airport, 231

Circus Maximus, 79–80

climate, 4–5, 238

Colosseum, 32, 34–35: tour, 59–63

costs, trip, 3–4

Cryptoporticus Tunnel, 81

culture shock, 20

Curia, 69–70

daily reminder, 25

daytrips, from Rome, 182–201

department stores, 223

Dolce Vita Stroll, 226–227

dorms, sleeping in, 213

driving, 231

eating, 15–20, 214–220: alternatives to restaurants, 17–19; cafés and bars 18–19; in Naples, 195; picnics 20; restaurants, 17; Roman cuisine, 15–16. *See also* Eating by neighborhood

eating by neighborhood:
Campo de' Fiori 215–216;
Colosseum, 218; Pantheon,
216–217; Piazza Venezia,
217–218; Santa Maria
Maggiore, 219; Spanish
Steps, 217; Trevi Fountain,
218; Trastevere, 214–215;
Vatican Museum, 219–220;
Via Firenze and Via
Nazionale, 218–219
e-mail, 12
embassies, U.S., 27
emergency phone numbers,
27–28, 237
Etruscan Museum, 42
euro, 4
E.U.R., 52–53
Europe Through the Back
Door, 22
exchange rate, 4

Fall of Rome, 234
feedback, reader, 21, 241
festivals, 237–238
Fiumicino airport, 230–231
flea markets, 224
Forum, Roman, 36: tour 64–74
Four Rivers fountain, 56

Gesu Church, 38, 90
getting around Rome, 28–30
Giancicolo Hill Viewpoint, 47
guidebooks, 7–9:
Rick Steves', 7–9

Hadrian's Villa, 183
health, 28
hints, helpful, 27–28
history, Roman, 67, 232–236
holidays, 237–238
Holy Stairs, 175
hostels, sleeping in, 213
hotels, 12–15, 202–213:
making reservations, 14–15;

reservation form, 240
House of Livia and Augustus, 81
House of the Vestal Virgins,
71–72

Il Gesu Church, 90
Imperial Palace, 75–82
Internet access, 7, 12
Iron Age huts, 81–82
Italian survival phrases, 18, 239
itineraries, 23–26

Julius Caesar, Temple of, 68–69

Laöcoon, 134–135
Loggia Stati Mattei Museum, 79

mail, 12
making reservations, 14–15
Mammertine Prison, 36
maps, iv, 9, 24, 29, 39, 40, 44,
46, 49, 53, 55, 60, 65, 66, 76,
85, 96, 103, 107, 121, 130,
132, 139, 141, 146, 147, 153,
172, 174, 177, 185, 190, 196,
204, 210, 229
medieval sights, 235
metric conversions, 238
Metro (subway), 28–29
medical needs, 28
modern sights, 236
money, 5–6
Monte Testaccio, 49–50
Museo Archeologico, 187–189
Museum of the Bath, 41, 95,
99–100
museum pass, 34
Museum of Roman
Civilization, 53

Naples, 184–195: maps, 185, 190
National Museum of Rome,
39–40: tour 101–113
Nero's Golden House, 33–34
Night Walk across Rome,

54–58: map, 55
nightlife, 225–227
numbers and stumblers, 238

Octagonal Hall, 40–41, 95,
   98–99
open-air markets, 194–195,
   223–224
Old St. Peter's, 156–158
Ostia Antica, 183–184

Palace of the Civilization of
   Labor, 52–53
Palace of Tiberius and
   Caligula, 81
Palatine Hill, 36: tour 75–82
Palazzo dei Conservatori,
   117–119
Palazzo Nuovo, 115–117
Pantheon, 38, 57–58: tour,
   87–89; churches near, 89–94
Philosophy, Back Door, 22
Piazza Capranica, 57
Piazza Colonna, 57
Piazza di Spagna (Spanish
   Steps), 58
Piazza Navona, 55–56
Piazza Repubblica, 100
Piazza Venezia, 37–38
picnics, 20
Pinacoteca, 152–154
planning your time: in Naples
   and Pompeii, 184–185; in
   Rome, 23–26
Pietà, the, 168–169
Pilgrim's Rome, 171–181
Pompeii, 195–201: map, 196
Ponte Sant' Angelo, 45
Pope, seeing the, 157
Porta Ostiense, 48–49
Protestant Cemetery, 49
public holidays, 237–238
Pyramid of Gaius Cestius, 48

Raphael, 142–144

reader feedback, 21, 241
red tape, 5–6
Renaissance sights, 233
Republic sights, 233
reservations, hotel, 14–15:
   fax form, 240
restaurants, 17. *See also* Eating
   by neighborhood
Roman cuisine, 15–16
Roman Forum, 36: tour 64–74
Roman history, 232–236
Romulus and Remus, 81–82
Rostrum (Rostri), 70

Sacred Area, 38
San Clemente, 179–181
San Giovanni in Laterano, 171
Santa Maria degli Angeli, 40,
   95–98
Santa Maria della Vittoria, 41
Santa Maria in Trastevere, 46
Santa Maria Maggiore, 176–179
Santa Maria sopra Minerva,
   38, 93
Scala Santa (Holy Stairs), 175
shopping, 223–224
sightseeing, priorities, 23–26:
   tips, 34–35
Sistine Chapel, 144–152
sleep code, 13, 203
sleeping, 12–15, 202–213:
   cheap, 207; hotels, 12–15,
   202–213; hostels and dorms,
   213; making reservations,
   14–15; reservation form, 240.
   See also Sleeping by
   neighborhood.
sleeping by neighborhood:
   Campo de' Fiori and Piazza
   Navona, 209; Colosseum,
   208–209; near the Pantheon,
   209–211; train station, 207;
   Trastevere, 211; Vatican
   Museum, 212–213; Via
   Firenze, 203–205; Via

Nazionale and Basilica Santa
    Maria Maggiore, 205–207
Slice-of-Neapolitan-life Walk,
    189–195: map, 190
Spanish Steps, 58
St. Ignazio, church of, 38, 94
St. Peter-in-Chains Church
    (San Pietro in Vincoli), 33
St. Peter's, 43: tour, 155–170;
    Old St. Peter's, 156–158; St.
    Peter's Square, 158–160;
    Basilica, 43, 160–163

Tabularium, 117
Tavola Calda bars, 17–18
taxi, 30
telephones, 9–12, 236–237
Temple of Antoninus and
    Faustina, 72
Temple of Cybele (Temple of
    the Magna Mater), 82
Temple of Julius Caesar, 68–69
Temple of the Magna Mater, 82
Temple of Vesta, 71
Terme del Foro, Pompeii, 198
Termini train station, 228
Testaccio, 48–50
theft alerts, 27, 186–187
Tiburtina train station, 228
Tivoli, 182–183
tourist information: in U.S.A.,
    7; in Rome, 26
tours: of Pompeii, 197; of
    Rome, 9, 30–31
trains, 228–230
Trajan's Column, 36, 83–84
Trajan's Forum, 36, 84–85

Trajan's Market, 36, 85–86
transportation, 9, 28–30,
    228–231: airports, 230–231;
    bus, 29–30; driving, 231;
    subway (metro), 28–29; taxi,
    30; trains, 228–230
Trastevere, 23, 45–47: map, 46
travel smart, 6
Treno Alta Velocita (T.A.V.),
    228–230
Tre Scalini, 56
Trevi Fountain, 39, 58
trip costs, 3–4

U.S. Embassies, 27

Vatican City, 156–157, 231.
    See also Sistine Chapel, St.
    Peter's, Vatican Museum
Vatican Museum, 43: tour,
    129–154 (maps, 130, 132,
    139, 141)
Vestal Virgins, House of, 71–72
Via del Corso, 226–227
videos, Rick Steves', 7
View Cafe, 119
Victor Emmanuel Monument, 38
Villa Borghese, 41
Villa d'Este, 183

walking tours: of Naples,
    189–195 (map, 190); of
    Rome, 31, 54–58 (map, 55)
weather, 4–5, 238
Web sites on Rome and Italy, 7
when to go, 4–5

FREE-SPIRITED TOURS FROM
Rick Steves

Great Guides

Big Buses

Small Groups

No Grumps

Best of Europe ■ **Village Europe** ■ **Eastern Europe** ■ **Turkey** ■ **Italy** ■ **Britain**
Spain/Portugal ■ **Ireland** ■ **Heart of France** ■ **South of France** ■ **Village France**
Scandinavia ■ **Germany/Austria/Switzerland** ■ **London** ■ **Paris** ■ **Rome**

Looking for a one, two, or three-week tour that's run in the Rick Steves style? Check out Rick Steves' educational, experiential tours of Europe.

Rick's tours include much more in the "sticker price" than mainstream tours. Here's what you'll get with a Europe or regional Rick Steves tour...

- **Group size:** Your tour group will be no larger than 26.

- **Guides:** You'll have two guides traveling and dining with you on your fully guided Rick Steves tour.

- **Bus:** You'll travel in a full-size 48-to-52-seat bus, with plenty of empty seats for you to spread out and read, snooze, enjoy the passing scenery, get away from your spouse, or whatever.

- **Sightseeing:** Your tour price includes all group sightseeing. There are no hidden extra charges.

- **Hotels:** You'll stay in Rick's favorite small, characteristic, locally-run hotels in the center of each city, within walking distance of the sights you came to see.

- **Price and insurance:** Your tour price is guaranteed for 2002. Single travelers do *not* pay an extra supplement (we have them room with other singles). ETBD includes prorated tour cancellation/interruption protection coverage at no extra cost.

- **Tips and kickbacks:** All guide and driver tips are included in your tour price. Because your driver and guides are paid salaries by ETBD, they can focus on giving you the best European travel experience possible.

Interested? Call (425) 771-8303 or visit www.ricksteves.com for a free copy of Rick Steves' 2002 Tours booklet!

Rick Steves' Europe Through the Back Door

130 Fourth Avenue North, PO Box 2009, Edmonds, WA 98020 USA
Phone: (425) 771-8303 ■ Fax: (425) 771-0833 ■ www.ricksteves.com

FREE TRAVEL GOODIES FROM

Rick Steves

EUROPEAN TRAVEL NEWSLETTER

My *Europe Through the Back Door* travel company will help you travel better *because* you're on a budget—not in spite of it. To see how, ask for my 64-page *travel newsletter* packed full of savvy travel tips, readers' discoveries, and your best bets for railpasses, guidebooks, videos, travel accessories and free-spirited tours.

2002 GUIDE TO EUROPEAN RAILPASSES

With hundreds of railpasses to choose from in 2002, finding the right pass for your trip has never been more confusing. To cut through the complexity, ask for my 64-page *2002 Guide to European Railpasses.* Once you've narrowed down your choices, we give you unbeatable prices, including important extras with every Eurailpass, **free:** my 90-minute *Travel Skills Special* video or DVD; your choice of one of my 16 country guidebooks and phrasebooks; and answers to your "top five" travel questions.

RICK STEVES' 2002 TOURS

We offer 18 different one, two, and three-week tours (180 departures in 2002) for those who want to experience Europe in Rick Steves' Back Door style, but without the transportation and hotel hassles. If a tour with a small group, modest family-run hotels, lots of exercise, great guides, and no tips or hidden charges sounds like your idea of fun, ask for my 48-page 2002 Tours booklet.

YEAR-ROUND GUIDEBOOK UPDATES

Even though the information in my guidebooks is the freshest around, things do change in Europe between book printings. I've set aside a special section at my website (www.ricksteves.com/update) listing *up-to-the-minute changes* for every Rick Steves guidebook.

*Call, fax, or visit **www.ricksteves.com** to get your...*

- ☑ **FREE EUROPEAN TRAVEL NEWSLETTER**
- ☑ **FREE 2002 GUIDE TO EUROPEAN RAILPASSES**
- ☑ **FREE RICK STEVES' 2002 TOURS BOOKLET**

Rick Steves' Europe Through the Back Door

130 Fourth Avenue North, PO Box 2009, Edmonds, WA 98020 USA
Phone: (425) 771-8303 ■ Fax: (425) 771-0833 ■ www.ricksteves.com

Free, fresh travel tips, all year long.

Call (425) 771-8303 to get Rick's free
64-page newsletter, or visit
www.ricksteves.com for even more.

AVALON TRAVEL
p u b l i s h i n g

How far will our travel guides take you? As far as you want.

Discover a rhumba-fueled nightspot in Old Havana, explore prehistoric tombs in Ireland, hike beneath California's centuries-old redwoods, or embark on a classic road trip along Route 66. Our guidebooks deliver solidly researched, trip-tested information—minus any generic froth—to help globetrotters or weekend warriors create an adventure uniquely their own.

And we're not just about the printed page. Public television viewers are tuning in to Rick Steves' new travel series, *Rick Steves' Europe*. On the Web, readers can cruise the virtual black top with *Road Trip USA* author Jamie Jensen and learn travel industry secrets from Edward Hasbrouck of The *Practical Nomad*.

In print. On TV. On the Internet.

We supply the information. The rest is up to you.

Avalon Travel Publishing

Something for everyone

www.travelmatters.com

Avalon Travel Publishing guides are available at your favorite book or travel store.

FOGHORN OUTDOORS

guides are for campers, hikers, boaters, anglers,bikers, and golfers of all levels of daring and skill. Each guide focuses on a specific U.S. region and contains site descriptions and ratings, driving directions, facilities and fees information,and easy-to-read maps that leave only the task of deciding where to go.

"Foghorn Outdoors has established an ecological conservation standard unmatched by any other publisher." **~Sierra Club**

WWW.FOGHORN.COM

TRAVEL SMART

guidebooks are accessible, route-based driving guides focusing on regions throughout the United States and Canada. Special interest tours provide the most practical routes for family fun, outdoor activities, or regional history for a trip of anywhere from two to 22 days. Travel Smarts take the guesswork out of planning a trip by recommending only the most interesting places to eat, stay, and visit.

"One of the few travel series that rates sightseeing attractions. That's a handy feature. It helps to have some guidance so that every minute counts." **~San Diego Union-Tribune**

CiTY·SMaRT™

guides are written by local authors with hometown perspectives who have personally selected the best places to eat, shop, sightsee, and simply hang out. The honest, lively, and opinionated advice is perfect for business travelers looking to relax with the locals or for longtime residents looking for something new to do Saturday night.

Moon Handbooks

provide comprehensive coverage of a region's arts, history, land, people, and social issues in addition to detailed practical listings for accommodations, food, outdoor recreation, and entertainment. Moon Handbooks allow complete immersion in a region's culture—ideal for travelers who want to combine sight-seeing with insight for an extraordinary travel experience in destinations throughout North America, Hawaii, Latin America, the Caribbean, Asia, and the Pacific.

WWW.MOON.COM

Rick Steves shows you where to travel and how to travel—all while getting the most value for your dollar. His Back Door travel philosophy is about making friends, having fun, and avoiding tourist rip-offs.

Rick has been traveling to Europe for more than 25 years and is the author of 22 guidebooks, which have sold more than a million copies. He also hosts the award-winning public television series *Rick Steves' Europe.*

WWW.RICKSTEVES.COM

ROAD TRIP USA

Getting there is half the fun, and Road Trip USA guides are your ticket to driving adventure. Taking you off the interstates and onto less-traveled, two-lane highways, each guide is filled with fascinating trivia, historical information, photographs, facts about regional writers, and details on where to sleep and eat—all contributing to your exploration of the American road.

"[Books] so full of the pleasures of the American road, you can smell the upholstery."
~BBC radio

WWW.ROADTRIPUSA.COM